Underground Violence

Underground Violence

On the Nature of Terrorism

Luis De la Calle
and
Ignacio Sánchez-Cuenca

Great Clarendon Street, Oxford, OX2 6DP,
United Kingdom

Oxford University Press is a department of the University of Oxford.
It furthers the University's objective of excellence in research, scholarship,
and education by publishing worldwide. Oxford is a registered trade mark of
Oxford University Press in the UK and in certain other countries

© Luis De la Calle and Ignacio Sánchez-Cuenca 2024

The moral rights of the authors have been asserted

All rights reserved. No part of this publication may be reproduced, stored in
a retrieval system, or transmitted, in any form or by any means, without the
prior permission in writing of Oxford University Press, or as expressly permitted
by law, by licence or under terms agreed with the appropriate reprographics
rights organization. Enquiries concerning reproduction outside the scope of the
above should be sent to the Rights Department, Oxford University Press, at the
address above

You must not circulate this work in any other form
and you must impose this same condition on any acquirer

Published in the United States of America by Oxford University Press
198 Madison Avenue, New York, NY 10016, United States of America

British Library Cataloguing in Publication Data

Data available

Library of Congress Control Number: 2023949205

ISBN 9780198904816

DOI: 10.1093/oso/9780198904816.001.0001

Printed and bound by
CPI Group (UK) Ltd, Croydon, CR0 4YY

Links to third party websites are provided by Oxford in good faith and
for information only. Oxford disclaims any responsibility for the materials
contained in any third party website referenced in this work.

Preface

In the Natural Sciences, concepts are created by the scientists themselves: 'electron', 'gene', 'hydrogen', and 'gravity' are some well-known examples. The concepts are defined in a precise way, their meaning is relatively fixed, and the scientific discussion is not affected by what is said or thought beyond the walls of academia. In the Social Sciences, by contrast, many of the concepts that are studied, analysed, and discussed have a life of their own; they cannot be so easily moulded by the scholarly community. People use them in many different contexts, independently of what social scientists may prescribe. Think of how we routinely struggle in our public conversations to agree on the meaning of concepts such as 'populism', 'rights', 'legitimacy', 'social movements', or ... 'terrorism'.

The nature of terrorism is particularly elusive, as it generates deep disagreements both in public debate and in academic circles. Moreover, the term has evolved significantly. After Al Qaeda's attacks of 9/11, it underwent several mutations. On the one hand, most researchers and pundits abandoned the very idea of state terrorism, which used to be quite widespread; today, terrorism is commonly understood to be violence carried out by rebels, insurgents, criminals, or any other non-state actor. On the other, terrorist violence has spilled over into other types of violence that in the past were routinely described as insurgent or guerrilla violence, transforming terrorism into an umbrella term that covers all non-legitimate violence.

The literature on the Islamic State of Iraq and Syria (ISIS) attests to this confusion. Governments and state agencies classify ISIS as a terrorist group, and many scholars follow suit. However, there are a significant number of dissenting voices who consider that an armed group that constituted itself as a conventional army, with around 30,000 fighters at its peak, with territorial control over an area larger than Britain, and acting like a state under the form of a caliphate, cannot be regarded as a terrorist group, or at least not in the same sense in which we say that, for instance, the Italian Red Brigades acting in the late 1970s and early 1980s were a terrorist group. Further, others adopt a more nuanced position, arguing that ISIS is not a terrorist group, but an insurgency that commits terrorist attacks.[1]

---

[1] For ISIS as a terrorist group, see, for instance, Klausen (2022: 8). For the questioning of this thesis, see Cronin (2015). For a general review about ISIS in which the author claims that ISIS is an insurgency that commits terrorist attacks, see Beccaro (2018).

The example of ISIS well illustrates the problem at hand. It is not that the facts are contested or blurred. On the contrary, there are no disagreements about the fundamental characteristics of this armed group in terms of size, tactics, ruling over the local population, goals, structure, or technology of violence. The problem lies rather in our categories, which mean different things for different people.

The debate is not only terminological; it has profound implications both for counter-terrorist strategies and for the search of the determinants of political violence. The means used to combat the Red Brigades are most likely inadequate when it comes to fighting ISIS. And, likewise, the conditions under which a group such as the Red Brigades emerges are probably not the same as those associated with the formation of ISIS.

This book argues that despite all the conceptual fog, there is an underlying logic in the way in which we speak about terrorism. This logic is often buried under layers of ideology and confusion, but through a careful analysis of how the term has been used in the past, we can gain access to this logic.

In our view, we do not have to relinquish the term 'terrorism' and invent a new category from scratch; nor do we need to follow the post-9/11 trend that conflates terrorism and political violence more generally. Rather, in this book, we walk a thin line in seeking to uncover some deep truths in the ways in which we speak about terrorism, while filtering out some accidental or contingent traits that are sometimes associated with it.

What makes terrorism unique, or so we argue, is the underground nature of its violence. We are not the first to advance this thesis. In the following chapters we acknowledge other authors who claimed something similar before us. Our contribution is to explore all the implications of this idea and to build a conceptual framework in which the nature of terrorism is clearly distinguished from other types of political violence.

Unlike other forms of violence, underground political violence does not require any control of the territory in which the deed takes place. Because there is no dominion of the space, perpetrators must act secretly and their attacks cannot unfold in time (compared with the duration of battles or armed assaults). The quintessential underground attack is the activation of an improvised explosive device. The bomb is planted secretly in the enemy's terrain and is exploded from a distance (suicide bombers are but a variation of this theme). These types of explosive device fit particularly well the constraints under which underground organizations operate.

Understanding terrorism as underground political violence makes sense of many traits that are commonly associated with the term—for instance, that terrorism is the 'weapon of the weak', or that terrorism is an extreme form of asymmetric violence. When an actor cannot take control of a well-defended territory because it lacks the necessary military power, it may resort to underground tactics. This is typically the case when there is a deep asymmetry in military power between the rebels and the state. The Red Brigades, for instance, were a small group vis-à-vis the Italian state during the 1970s. They could not aspire to liberate parts of Italy, even though they had some popular support. However, the group caused havoc by using underground attacks against security forces and Italian institutions. Given the disparity in resources, the Red Brigades opted for terrorist attacks. A number of other diverse, complex, and colourful examples are analysed in the following chapters.

This book develops the understanding of terrorism as underground political violence in different directions, both conceptual and empirical. Our ambition is to show that this apparently simple idea has some 'organizing' power in a debate that has always been cacophonic and frustratingly inconclusive; also, that it can be used in empirical analysis to shed light on the determinants and dynamics of terrorism.

The work presented below represents the culmination of many years of individual and joint work on terrorism, in which we made progress in a piecemeal, slow, and nonlinear way. In the process, we published two monographs about Western terrorism, one on nationalist violence (De la Calle, 2015a), another on revolutionary one (Sánchez-Cuenca, 2019), plus several co-authored articles. We think it is time to transform these scattered ideas and findings into a unified analysis of the phenomenon. In our view, the power of our central thesis can only be assessed in a book format, with sufficient space to persuade the reader that our main claims are worth discussing. The final product, however, is not a mere regurgitation of our previous papers. Although we build on them, we offer a more systematic treatment of previous arguments, present new empirical evidence, and elaborate several case studies that illustrate the main arguments.

The book has benefited from the comments of many colleagues. In a sense, this is 'slow-cooked' work. In general, we have found some healthy scepticism and even some resistance to some of the ideas presented here. This has forced us to sharpen our claims. We are particularly grateful to two anonymous reviewers and to our editor, Dominic Byatt, who provided invaluable advice. Also, we obtained very useful suggestions in a workshop on the manuscript held in June 2021 at the Carlos III-Juan March Institute of Social Sciences and would like to thank the lead commentators Robert Fishman, Guillermo Kreiman, Luis F. Medina, Isik Ozel, and Francisco Villamil, as well as the other participants. Early drafts of different sections of the manuscript were presented at University College London and Stanford University, where we obtained challenging and useful feedback. Research stays at Stanford University's Center for Advanced Study in the Behavioral Sciences (CASBS) (De la Calle) and Oxford University's Nuffield College (Sánchez-Cuenca) gave us the opportunity to complete the manuscript. Paul Rigg, as usual, made an excellent job of reviewing the English.

Contents

Introduction	**1**
1. Clarifications: What Terrorism Is Not	**14**
1.1. On Classifications and Natural Kinds	15
1.2. Typologies of Violence	17
1.3. Areas of Ambiguity	21
1.4. Inadequate Conceptions	23
1.5. Mixed Definitions	35
1.6. Conclusions	36
2. Terrorism as Underground Political Violence	**38**
2.1. Territorial Control	39
2.2. The Underground: Violence and Space	42
2.3. Terrorism and Underground Political Violence	44
2.4. A Conceptual Map of Terrorism	49
2.5. State Terrorism	71
3. Asymmetry, Territorial Control, and Rebel Tactics	**76**
3.1. Asymmetry	77
3.2. Asymmetry and Territorial Control: The Actor-Sense	80
3.3. Asymmetry and Rebel Tactics: The Action-Sense	89
3.4. Conclusions	100
Appendix. The Measurement of Terrorism and its Implications	102
4. Variations on Territorial Control	**114**
4.1. Tupamaros	116
4.2. ETA	125
4.3. Shining Path	137
4.4. Conclusions	148
5. Within-Group Territorial Variation	**150**
5.1. The Israeli-Palestinian Conflict	151
5.2. The Islamic State	173
5.3. Conclusions	187
Concluding Remarks: Terrorism: Back and Forth	**189**
References	196
Index	210

Introduction

1.

In September 1982, a group of around 30 members of the Maoist organization *Sendero Luminoso* (Shining Path, SP) for the first time entered the Peruvian village of Lucanamarca, in the province of Víctor Fajardo. Lucanamarca is a rural mountain settlement of about 2,500 inhabitants, whose main source of economic activity is cattle breeding. On this first day, the *senderistas* planted a red flag and called the population to participate in an open assembly. The guerrillas introduced themselves and informed everyone about the ongoing revolution and the SP's economic plans, which included redistribution of land and cattle. The *senderistas* left after the assembly but, in the following weeks, made several other visits. Eventually, they announced themselves as the village's new authority and asked for compliance. Shortly afterwards they started to organize local life and forced several men to take part in armed operations in other localities. The SP created a school for the people in order to indoctrinate them. When the organization considered that Lucanamarca was ready, it announced that, from 1 January 1983, the area was a 'liberated zone'. Leonardo Misaico, the local judge (*juez de paz*), was killed by *Sendero* a few weeks later.

It is worth providing some background information on the leader of the SP in Lucanamarca, Olegario Curitomay. Curitomay had attained secondary education but failed to enter university, and his main activity was selling cattle. His wife died while she was giving birth to their daughter. The girl only lived one year; according to some sources she died of malnutrition (Falconí, Jiménez, and Alfaro, 2007: 80). After these tragic events, Curitomay joined *Sendero*. Previously, his family had confronted the Huancachuari family, the largest cattle owners in Lucanamarca (Falconí, Jiménez, and Alfaro, 2007: 100). The head of the family, Marciano Huancachuari, was accused of having exploited his cow herders; the SP killed him, his wife, and his son-in-law in February 1983.

Underground Violence. Luis De la Calle and Ignacio Sánchez-Cuenca, Oxford University Press.
© Luis De la Calle and Ignacio Sánchez-Cuenca (2024). DOI: 10.1093/oso/9780198904816.003.0001

2 Underground Violence

These killings provoked a peasant rebellion against *Sendero*. Several guerrillas were captured and killed, including Olegario Curitomay, who was beaten, shot, and burned in a public square. The reprisal of the guerrilla was brutal. On 3 April, a group of between 80 and 100 guerrillas, some wearing uniform, some bearing firearms, most axes, machetes, and knives, raided the area for around eight hours, killing numerous people in their advance before arriving at Lucanamarca at 4 p.m. Once there, they gathered numerous inhabitants in the public square, including children and women, and killed 18 of them. The final toll is unclear; according to the Peruvian Truth Commission, 69 lost their lives that day.[1]

This was the SP's worst massacre. In the so-called 'interview of the century', the SP's leader, Abimael Guzmán (aka *Camarada Gonzalo*), was asked about Lucanamarca. He spoke with great clarity:

> Confronted with the use of armed bands and reactionary military action, we responded decisively with one action: Lucanamarca. Neither they nor we will forget it, of course, because there they saw a response that had not been imagined. There more than 80 were annihilated, this is the reality, and we say it, here there was excess … [But] our problem was to give a bruising blow to restrain them, to make them understand that the thing was not so easy. On some occasions, such as this, it was the Central Leadership itself that planned the actions and ordered everything, that is how it was … I reiterate, the principal thing was to make them understand that we were a hard bone to chew, and that we were ready to do anything, anything. (Degregori, 1998: 143)

Guzmán showed no remorse. He believed that *Sendero* had to regain its authority by imposing a heavy penalty on the rebellious peasants. The guerrilla had to make them understand who the new ruler in the area was and what the consequences of disobedience were. Guzmán admits that there might have been excesses that day, but he approved of the operation and its intent.

By the late 1980s, *Sendero* considered that conditions were ripe for the culmination of the 'popular war' through systematic attacks on the capital city (Lima) that would trigger a mass uprising and would lead the SP to seize power (Burt, 1998). Violence peaked during the first half of 1992. The ongoing campaign in Lima was accelerated in two ways. On the one hand, the SP infiltrated the shanty towns surrounding the city; acting underground, it engaged in sabotage and political agitation, as well as trying to

---

[1] See https://www.cverdad.org.pe/apublicas/exhumaciones/info_lucanamarca01.php (accessed 31 July 2023).

secure public order through attacks against petty criminals and drug addicts. Burt (1998) analyses the presence and actions of the SP in Villa El Salvador, where *Sendero* killed a renowned local politician and activist, María Elena Moyano, for her open criticism of the SP, on 15 February 1992. On the other hand, the Maoist group sought to terrorize the inhabitants of Lima and demoralize security forces by means of car bombs. According to the Peruvian Truth Commission, 37 car bombs were detonated in Lima during the first six months of 1992, creating the impression that the SP might win.[2] The most lethal attack was the car bomb that exploded in Tarata street, in Miraflores, an upscale neighbourhood in Lima, just two days after the self-coup undertaken by the president, Alberto Fujimori, with the consent of the military. The car exploded at around 9 p.m., destroying an entire building: 25 people died, five disappeared, and 155 were wounded. All the victims were civilians and included children, such as 12-year-old Vanessa Quiroga.

The perpetrators had to improvise, since the initial target, a nearby bank, was being watched by security agents. The SP however decided to continue with the operation by abandoning the car among Tarata street's residential buildings. Guzmán himself considered the resulting massacre to be a mistake. During his trial, he denied any responsibility for the attack and said openly that it should never have happened.

The similarities and differences between the Lucanamarca and Tarata massacres are worth exploring. Regarding similarities, the two attacks targeted civilians and provoked a high number of fatalities. Further, both attacks presupposed a distinction between the direct and indirect targets of the violence. Thus, in the Lucanamarca case, the violence was aimed at teaching a painful lesson to the peasants who defied the SP's authority. Those killed were the direct targets, but the message was addressed to the local population who lived in *Sendero*'s liberated zones. Likewise, in the Tarata bombing, the 25 civilians who lost their lives were the direct targets, but the indirect target, the audience, was Lima's civil population.

There are also some striking differences between the two massacres. Weapons were different in each case: firearms, axes, and machetes in Lucanamarca; an improvised explosive device in Tarata. The Lucanamarca attack was conducted by over 80 recruits, some of them wearing uniforms; while the Tarata operation required very few people, less than 10 in total, wearing plain clothes to blend into the urban landscape. More importantly, the Lucanamarca massacre was linked to a campaign over territory: it was undertaken

---

[2] See http://www.cverdad.org.pe/ifinal/pdf/TOMO%20VII/Casos%20Ilustrativos-UIE/2.60.%20TARATA.pdf (accessed 31 July 2023).

in the open, in a zone that *Sendero* claimed to be liberated from state control. Thanks to these conditions, the operation unfolded over a whole day. By contrast, the Tarata bombing was a strictly covert or underground operation. Acting in the capital, where the SP lacked territorial control, the attack was fully clandestine and ephemeral, with no development in time, since otherwise security forces would have neutralized those involved.

We argue in this book that these differences go a long way in explaining why we tend to associate attacks like Lucanamarca with guerrilla insurgency and attacks like Tarata with terrorism. Even though the victims of both tragedies were civilians, and the targets went beyond those who were killed or wounded by the violence, Lucanamarca is a typical guerrilla operation, and Tarata a no less typical terrorist attack. The key difference is the 'under the ground' condition of the car bomb, as opposed to the 'above the ground' attack on the local peasants. Terrorism, we surmise, is, above all, clandestine violence.

2.

Rather than becoming entangled in perpetual discussions about overarching definitions of terrorism, we aim here for a parsimonious understanding of the phenomenon. By that we mean a set of principles that explain why we call some types of violence terrorism and not something else. This requires an analysis of the violence that is allegedly terrorist, trying to identify the factors that make this violence different or unique. As said, we claim in this book that the defining feature of terrorism is the fact that this violence is politically motivated and perpetrated underground, under conditions of clandestinity.[3]

We are not the first to note the close connection between underground violence and terrorism; in Chapter 2 we highlight numerous authors who have made this point before. Sometimes the thesis is taken for granted or presupposed in the analysis of violence. One example among many possible others helps to make the point. In his analysis of Jama'at al-Tawhid wal-Jihad (JTWJ), the forerunner of Al Qaeda in Iraq, Lister (2015) introduces this comment:

> Through 2004–06 the JTWJ demonstrated a consistent expansion of its fight against coalition forces in Iraq, with the group having evolved from a terrorist organization whose activities were limited mostly to large urban bombings and rural

---

[3] We are aware that 'clandestinity' is a neologism, but the use of this term will help us to economize on language. We could talk about the 'undergroundness' of the violence, but this sounds even more artificial.

IED attacks to a more organized insurgent force that was beginning to demonstrate a capacity to influence localized dynamics and control territory, albeit often below the surface. (**265**)

The distinction between terrorism and insurgency, which is not explicitly theorized in Lister's book, is clearly based on the assumption that the group was terrorist while underground, but became insurgent once it gained territorial control.

Let us look at another example, this time from non-academic circles. In January 2023, members of al-Shabaab (a large jihadist armed group fighting in Somalia to impose Islamic rule) exploded a bomb in Mogadishu, in the mayor's office, before storming the place. The attack was described by the mayor's deputy in these terms:

'As they have been wiped out from some regions they had to come here to wage a terrorist attack to show "we are present, we are still alive"', says Isse Mohamud Gure, the deputy mayor of Mogadishu. 'But these acts of terrorism are just the last kicks of a dying horse'.[4]

The fact that the public official describes the attack as terrorist (as different from the attacks that took place far away from the capital, in the regions) is most likely because it took place in an urban setting, in which the perpetrators acted underground. The aim was not to occupy the capital, but rather to carry out an urban attack to demonstrate its power to hurt. By acting in the capital, controlled by the state, al-Shabaab's members were heavily constrained in operational terms: their only way forward was to use underground tactics. Presumably, this is why the official called them terrorist.

By focusing on how the term is used when talking about various forms of violence, it becomes apparent that whether the attack is carried out clandestinely or the armed group acts underground is of paramount concern. Our understanding of terrorism deviates in significant ways from the dominant views in the field. In international law, terrorism is often equated with civilian victimization. In academia, some social scientists and security experts concur with the idea that terrorism is violence against civilians, whereas others define terrorism as a form of violence that presupposes the distinction between the direct and indirect target of the violence. The lack of a shared conceptualization has prevented a cumulative body of knowledge. After so many years of conceptual disagreements, those in the field seem fatigued, and the debate

---

[4] *Financial Times*, 'Somalia rebuilds: "the glass is now half- full"', 16 April 2023.

6 Underground Violence

on the nature of terrorism has waned. These days, most empirically minded researchers circumvent the issue by accepting at face value the conceptualization that is employed in the existing datasets on terrorism. However, the criteria used by coders should not be the last word on the matter—not least because the coding procedures themselves are usually ill-defined and opaque (see the Appendix to Chapter 3).

In our view, the conceptual discussion is unavoidable. We cannot make progress unless there is solid ground for shaping the concept of terrorism in a certain way. For some authors, terrorism is such an irremediably vague and charged concept that it is unfit for analytical, rigorous research. We disagree. The term exists for a reason. It captures a specific and important form of violence. Besides, some folk or commonsensical intuitions about terrorism are useful and illuminating (terrorism is the weapon of the weak, terrorism is urban guerrilla, terrorism is employed in highly asymmetric conflicts, etc.). As shown in the coming chapters, these intuitions stem ultimately from the underground nature of terrorism.

Even if we succeed in providing a thorough understanding of the nature of terrorism, how can we evaluate its adequacy compared with rival views? On what grounds can we say that a specific view on terrorism is better, or more helpful, than others? Two complementary criteria can be offered as a preliminary answer. On the one hand, the consistency and systematicity of the conception matters. For instance, if we stick to the definition of terrorism in terms of civilian victimization, Al Qaeda's suicide mission in 2000 against the USS *Cole*, a US navy destroyer, in Yemen, cannot be coded as a terrorist event, since the target was military. This is odd, because this attack is broadly considered by the media, pundits, and academics to be a terrorist deed. Likewise, this definition implies that civilian victimization taking place in civil war contexts, where the armed parties try to establish their authority using some mix of public goods and repression, should be considered terrorism. But if we were to include all this violence as terrorism, then our estimates about the global trends of terrorism, as well as our ideas about insurgencies, would be transformed dramatically. In our proposed conceptualization, based on clandestinity, we think that the USS *Cole* attack was terrorist because it was underground, while we think that much of the violence exerted by insurgencies against civilians over issues related to territorial control is not terrorist (it takes place in areas controlled by the insurgency and therefore above the ground). In this regard, it might be said that our conception is more respectful of the ways in which most people talk about terrorism. The included and excluded cases according to our conceptualization broadly coincide with what is usually regarded as the core of terrorist violence.

On the other hand, we can apply a methodological criterion based on the explanatory power of the different views. Specifically, we can take advantage of what the 19th-century philosopher William Whewell called the 'consilience of inductions', that is, the capacity to provide a unified explanation of phenomena that in principle were considered unrelated or independent of each other.[5] Thus, our conceptualization can make sense of some distinguishing features of terrorism that are not observed in other types of violence. In this context, we highlight three aspects or extensions of terrorism that have no counterpart in other types of violence and that can be explained in terms of underground violence: international terrorism, lone-actor terrorism, and state terrorism.

Regarding international terrorism, we argue that when armed groups act beyond their domestic borders, the resulting violence is always terrorist in nature. The reason for this is easy to grasp: when armed groups act far away from their territorial base, they are forced to act underground if they do not want to be easily caught. When Palestinian armed groups committed attacks in European countries in the 1970s, their actions were carried out in utmost secrecy. International attacks are terrorist because the perpetrators, regardless of territorial control at home, must act underground in an alien country.

Lone-actor armed activity must be clandestine by definition. Individuals acting alone cannot have territorial control and therefore their attacks will have to be secret or underground. Although this may seem obvious, the reason why we associate lone-actor violence with terrorism is precisely because that violence can only be clandestine, given the constraints faced by a single individual. The fact that many lone-terrorists are linked to a network of activists does not alter the fact that the attack is executed by a single individual.

Finally, state terrorism has been the subject of a long controversy. We distinguish state terrorism from state repression. According to our conceptualization, state terrorism occurs when the state launches secret or covert operations against its rivals, that is, when it operates under conditions of clandestinity. For those familiar with the much-acclaimed film *The Battle of Algiers* (1966), state terrorism would be epitomized by the planting of bombs by covert security officers in buildings where pro-independence sympathizers were supposed to live and hide. In addition to being heavily repressive in

---

[5] 'Accordingly, the cases in which inductions from classes of facts altogether different have thus jumped together, belong only to the best established theories which the history of science contains. And as I shall have occasion to refer to this peculiar feature in their evidence, I will take the liberty of describing it by a particular phrase; and will term it the Consilience of Inductions' (Whewell, 1847: 65).

8 Underground Violence

its treatment of separatist prisoners (openly violating their legal rights), the French military establishment also carried out terrorist attacks against inimical constituencies by exploiting the advantage of secrecy that allowed it some measure of deniability.

State-backed secret operations are archetypal when the state carries out attacks beyond its borders, that is, when the state acts underground. From an operational point of view, the killing of a Palestinian leader in Europe by Mossad is indistinguishable from the killing of an Israeli diplomat in Europe by a Palestinian armed group. Hence, we consider that *both* attacks are terrorist in nature.

It is worth noting that we refer to international terrorism, lone-actor terrorism, and state terrorism not because of the status of the target (who may be combatants or not), but because the perpetrators act underground. By uncovering what these three types of terrorism have in common, namely the clandestine conditions under which the violence is executed, we come closer to an intuitive, but nonetheless comprehensive, understanding of the phenomenon. Or, to put it in another way, our approach has considerable power in terms of Whewell's 'consilience of inductions'.

3.

A fully satisfactory view on terrorism cannot be developed without addressing its relationship with other forms of violence. The first issue is whether terrorism is something different from guerrilla or insurgent violence. To settle this, we need a theory about the production of violence, that is, a theory about the conditions under which various forms of violence can be carried out. Acting underground, as opposed to gaining territorial control, is, for us, the key factor in explaining the production of rebellious violence.

The critical question is under what conditions rebel leaders choose terrorism over other armed strategies. Our answer is straightforward: clandestine violence occurs when there is a large asymmetry between the actors involved in the violence. In asymmetric settings, the weaker side (usually, the rebels) will act covertly because of their lack of territorial control. Territorial control implies a certain degree of military power, or a capacity to conquer space. When this military power does not exist, underground violence may be the only available option. It is not for nothing that terrorism is often described as a 'weapon of the weak'.

Asymmetry may be a property of the conflict (such as when we say that the conflict between the Irish Republican Army (IRA) and the United Kingdom

(UK) over the status of Northern Ireland was an asymmetric contest) or of the conditions under which a particular attack takes place (such as when we say that a guerrilla that wants to detonate a bomb in the capital city has to act in the enemy's territory, under extreme asymmetric conditions).

To cope with the many complex issues that arise in the analysis of asymmetry, we exploit a distinction between the actor- and the action-sense of violence. From the point of view of the actor, the armed group may control territory or remain underground. From the point of view of the act of violence, the attack may be carried out using indirect tactics such as bombings and kidnappings, or more direct tactics that encourage violent confrontations between the armed actors—such as in battles, sieges, skirmishes, and ambushes.

To illustrate this distinction, the Red Army Faction (RAF) in Germany (also known as the Baader-Meinhof gang) is an excellent example of the harsh constraints under which a fully underground group operates (actorsense). The RAF never gained territorial control in the Federal Republic of Germany of the 1970s. Germany was one the most developed countries in the world and had a highly effective police force. As Aust (2008) makes clear in his detailed reconstruction of the group, members of the RAF spent much of their time searching for safe houses and trying to elude constant police vigilance. Given its clandestine nature, the RAF could not but launch terrorist attacks, that is, acts of violence that are consistent with the perpetrators operating clandestinely. This is, therefore, an instance of pure terrorism: a terrorist group employing terrorist tactics.

There is no reason, however, to expect that terrorism is restricted to underground groups. Groups with territorial control may employ terrorist tactics when the constraints are such that the attack can only be carried out from the underground. Let us return to ISIS, which is a clear case of an armed group with territorial control. The range of violence that we observe is now much wider than in the RAF. ISIS developed a full army with tanks, artillery, and infantry that was able to engage in military battles with national armies. But it also committed terrorist attacks in the enemy's territory, for instance in Iraq's capital city. When attacking in Baghdad, ISIS was under similar constraints to those of any clandestine group. Thus, an insurgent group with territorial control may engage in terrorism (in the action-sense) when it is forced to act clandestinely.

We elaborate below on these distinctions and provide numerous examples from armed groups of disparate regions and periods. It goes without saying that the distinction between clandestinity and territorial control is not a stark one. There are grey areas between these two pure or ideal types. Territorial control is a matter of degree rather than kind. Moreover, there are surrogates of territorial control (such as safe havens or sanctuaries) that should be considered. We examine these questions in detail and seek to accommodate the complexity of the real world without entirely sacrificing our theoretical framework.

4.

Even if our conceptualization on the nature of terrorism is deemed plausible and internally consistent, it might be argued that this is a purely theoretical exercise with minor implications for the empirical analysis of the phenomenon. We hope to convince the reader that this is not the case. On the one hand, we test two general propositions that follow from the conceptual framework, moving from conceptualization into theory building and testing. On the other, we use the framework and the theory to account for the variation we find in armed groups regarding territorial control and clandestinity.

The first proposition we test is about the relationship between violence and economic development. Our theory establishes that the greater the asymmetry between the state and the armed group, the more likely that the armed group is underground. This is a hypothesis about the actor-sense of terrorism. To measure the level of asymmetry, we use the Gross Domestic Product (GDP) per capita of the country in which the armed group was created, assuming that the higher the level of economic development, the more powerful the state is and, therefore, the greater the asymmetry between the state and the armed group. Economic development enters here as a proxy for state capacity.

In the literature on civil war, GDP per capita has a robust and negative effect on the occurrence of conflict. Thus, civil wars are disproportionally concentrated in poor countries. We posit that the relationship between underground groups and state development is inverse: the richer the country, the more likely that if an armed group is created, it will be underground. In poor countries, the state often cannot prevent armed groups from gaining territorial control. The resulting insurgencies provoke deep conflicts with the state, producing, in many cases, a civil war. In richer countries, if an armed group is formed, it will most likely be underground. The state does not lose territorial control within its borders, but nonetheless an armed group challenges the state's monopoly of violence. In this regard, we should expect a positive relationship between the formation of underground groups and state capacity.

This positive relationship is eventually attenuated at the highest levels of development. In the most-developed countries, the state is sufficiently powerful to make domestic armed groups, territorial or underground, unfeasible. This means that for very high levels of GDP per capita, we should expect domestic peace. Of course, the country may suffer international attacks, or a lone-actor may provoke a massacre, but, given the state's strength, an armed organization cannot survive for long.

When the two parts of the proposition are put together, what we obtain is a non-linear hypothesis about development and underground groups. The relationship should be a concave one, with an inverted-U shape. Underground groups are more likely in states with medium or high levels of development, but not in those with the highest development levels, where the state enjoys the full monopoly of violence.

Our second testable proposition refers to the action-sense of terrorism. According to our theory, underground groups are greatly constrained in the choice of tactics. Specifically, they can only employ tactics that are consistent with being underground. In other words, clandestine groups cannot but use terrorist tactics. By contrast, groups with territorial control can choose between terrorist and guerrilla tactics. To test the relationship between territorial control (or lack of it) and tactical choice, we focus on two tactics, detonating improvised explosive devices (IEDs) and facility attacks (aimed at the occupation of space, such as seizing a building or a village). IEDs are a feasible option for underground groups. Thus, we should find that clandestine groups use bombings to a greater extent than territorial groups. The reasoning is the inverse to that of facility attacks: the latter should be more frequent in territorial groups than in those that are clandestine.

We further investigate two extensions of the hypothesis. First, when rebels act in a country's largest cities, we should observe a greater proportion of IEDs, since these attacks, in most cases, are underground (they take place at the enemy's territorial core). And secondly, clandestine groups should be more prone to carrying out international terrorist attacks than territory-controlling armed groups, given that for the latter it is costlier to divert resources from the fight for local control.

Chapter 3 offers compelling evidence in favour of all our theoretical expectations. Using different samples of armed groups, different time periods and different statistical specifications, our findings clearly show that rebels resort to terrorism when they are facing acute asymmetries of power against their rival states. This is confirmed for both the actor- and the action-senses.

Having shown that the theory generates testable hypotheses that are confirmed thanks to the analysis of a large sample of armed groups (actor-sense) and of attacks (action-sense), we proceed to cross-sectional and longitudinal comparisons. Regarding the former, we examine three cases of territorial control: the Tupamaros in Uruguay (1966–73), a pure case of a fully clandestine, revolutionary group; Euskadi ta Askatasuna (ETA, Basque Homeland and Freedom) in Spain (1968–2011), an underground, nationalist group that enjoyed for many years a sanctuary or safe haven in the south of France; and the Shining Path in Peru (1980–95), a revolutionary group with territorial control that combined guerrilla and terrorist violence. We move from pure clandestinity to territorial control, focusing on this dimension to explain the different dynamics of violence in each case.

Regarding the longitudinal comparison, we study the internal variation of violence and territorial control in two cases: the Palestinian movement and ISIS. In both cases, there is considerable historical variation in territorial control. As for Palestinians, we observe the full panoply of insurgent possibilities after the 1967 Six Day War: Fatah's guerrilla camps first in Jordan and then in Lebanon; terrorist infiltrations in Israel; international terrorism (indelibly associated with several dozen hijackings in the 1970s); the emergence of Hamas, a domestic terrorist group in the occupied territories after the first Intifada; the terrorist campaign of the second Intifada; the transformation of Hamas into a group with territorial control in the Gaza Strip; and the guerrilla battle between Hamas and Fatah in 2007. As can be seen, there is ample room to exploit the modulations of armed struggle on the Palestinian side in terms of gaining or losing territorial control, safe havens, and the like.

ISIS makes up another complex case in which terrorism and guerrilla are intertwined in several ways through time. The precursors of ISIS started as an underground group in Iraq in the aftermath of the US invasion in 2003. After the premature 'mission accomplished' US partial withdrawal, ISIS gained some level of territorial control in the Anbar province during 2007. This triggered the US military surge during the first half of 2008. Perfectly timed with the so-called Sahwa uprising by which Sunni tribal leaders cut their ties to jihadist militants in exchange for easier access to the federal budget, the surge smashed ISIS' liberated areas and forced the group to become clandestine again.

Two additional events came to alter the balance of power between ISIS and its enemies. First, the Syrian rebellion quickly began in 2011 and opened up opportunities for war-hardened jihadist militants to cross the border and seize territory around Eastern Syria, with Raqqa eventually becoming their territorial stronghold and a sanctuary for Iraqi militants. And second, President Obama decided to pull out US troops by October 2011, again offering new opportunities for an insurgent surge. With Sunni leaders infuriated with the level of graft and sectarianism displayed by the Iraqi administration, an uneasy coalition of jihadist, tribal, and former Baathist members coalesced, leading ISIS to seize territory and capture Mosul in June 2014. The rest of the story is recent and well-known. In sum, terrorism was widely used by ISIS even when it developed a formidable army, including tanks, artillery, and other heavy weaponry.

The analysis of the variations across and within armed groups regarding tactics reveals the relevance of the distinctions based on our theory about the ways in which armed groups organize. The production of violence is ultimately determined by the territorial control (or lack of it) of the armed group.

5.

This book is deliberately brief. Our main goal is to bring some analytical clarity to the complex study of terrorism, without alienating those readers less interested in intellectual vendettas and obscure academic debates. And, conversely, we want to fill the book with substantive, meaningful illustrations without losing sight of our theoretical framework. At the very least, we expect readers will find it useful to apply our theoretical lens when interpreting contemporary episodes of rebellion in the world.

The book has five chapters beyond this introduction. Chapters 1 and 2 take issue with the academic debates around the definition of terrorism and identify some common features that are usually associated with the phenomenon both by the public and by scholars. Chapter 1 reviews the two main definitions and shows their main shortcomings. Chapter 2 develops our alternative conceptualization based on underground violence. In Chapter 3 we draw observable consequences of our theory and test them using large-n data. This chapter comes with an Appendix in which we discuss how to measure terrorism and show how consequential this may be by providing a replication exercise in which the apparent lack of results is reversed with a simple, more coherent operationalization of terrorism.

Chapters 4 and 5 complement the statistical evidence with narratives that leverage cross- and within-group variation regarding clandestinity and violence. The book ends with some concluding remarks in which we discuss how a research agenda based on our conceptualization of terrorism might be advanced.

1
Clarifications

What Terrorism Is Not

This chapter critically discusses the two dominant conceptualizations of terrorism. The first suggests that the most salient characteristic of terrorist violence is civilian victimization, while the second argues that terrorist violence is coercive, based on the distinction between the direct target of violence and the indirect or target audience. There is much to commend about both theories, since each captures a large chunk of what terrorism is about. However, we contend that neither is able to uncover the generative mechanism of terrorism nor to account for some of the most basic ways in which we talk about terrorism.

On the one hand, while civilian victimization is certainly produced in many terrorist attacks, terrorism is far from being a form of violence that only targets civilians. There are numerous counterexamples of groups and attacks that target security forces and that have always been considered terrorist (in the academic literature, in policy analysis, in the media). Broadly speaking, the equation between terrorism and civilian victimization makes sense for international terrorism, but not for domestic, which is by far the most frequent.

On the other hand, while it is true that terrorism, in most cases, functions by drawing a distinction between the direct and indirect target, many other forms of violence (those that are based on coercion or the power to hurt) operate similarly. Therefore, this is insufficient to single out the specificity of terrorism.

The combination of the two conceptualizations (civilian victimization using coercive violence) does not overcome the criticisms that we make of each conceptualization separately. By showing the limitations of these theories, we lay the groundwork for our own view, based on the clandestinity of the violence, which is fully developed in the next chapter.

Underground Violence. Luis De la Calle and Ignacio Sánchez-Cuenca, Oxford University Press.
© Luis De la Calle and Ignacio Sánchez-Cuenca (2024). DOI: 10.1093/oso/9780198904816.003.0002

1.1. On Classifications and Natural Kinds

Entities, either natural or social, can be grouped in many ways. These groupings constitute classifications or taxonomies. In one of his tales, Jorge Luis Borges talks about a Chinese encyclopaedia in which animals are classified according to dislocated categories, such as 'trembling animals', 'animals that belong to the Emperor', 'loose dogs', 'Sirens', 'domesticated animals', and many others. Borges's tale became famous, among other things, because Michel Foucault used it in the introduction to his book *Les mots et les choses* (1966). The Chinese encyclopaedia's bizarre classification helped him to make the point that knowledge is embodied in what he called an 'episteme', a configuration of power forces that makes a certain approach to reality possible. Classifications reflect the dominant episteme in a certain historical moment.

Borges's classification is so shocking because it precludes any possibility of making sense of it. It is devoid of any practical or scientific value. It does not allow us to improve our interactions with the animal realm, nor is it based on any theory of the animal species. Classifications are often driven by our practical and intellectual interests.

We might ask whether a particular classificatory scheme has some sort of precedence, whether it is more basic than others. This very question assumes that there might be classifications that are not only useful or convenient, but also enlightening, that is, that shed some light on how reality works and is structured. Philosophers have debated and argued long on this matter. Can entities be grouped according to natural kinds, that is, kinds that 'carve nature at its joints' as Plato put it two thousand years ago?

In his classical book on philosophy of science, Hempel (1965: Ch. 6) distinguished between artificial and natural classifications; only the latter have some explanatory power, stemming from their integration in a theoretical framework. Thus, Mendeleev's periodic table generates predictions (that have been confirmed) because it is based on the atomic theory of elements. It provides a classification of the elements according to their constitutive or generative parts: their atomic structure. Likewise, the Cladistic classification of species is more natural than the Linnean one because it is based on phylogeny (evolutionary theory) rather than on morphological characteristics that may be misleading when tracing the 'true' differences between species.

Whether 'natural' kinds exist in the social world is deeply contentious. Let us begin by examining a core issue in political science, the nature and variety of political regimes. The broadest classification divides them into democracies and dictatorships. Are these regimes 'natural' political kinds? What is the distinction supposed to shed light on? We differentiate democracies and dictatorships because we value some properties of democracies (such as political equality, toleration, and freedom) that are absent in dictatorships, or because we are interested in understanding why some regimes have certain consequences: for instance, democracies avoid famines (Sen, 1999: 16); democracies do not fight against each other (Russett, 1993); and democracies allow for peaceful alternation of governments (Popper, 1945: 110). Given these positive features, dictators have been reluctant to define themselves as such, at least since World War II. Communist regimes usually portray themselves as 'popular democracies', as opposed to liberal (Article 1 of the Chinese constitution establishes that China is a 'democratic dictatorship'). On the opposite side of the ideological spectrum, Franco's dictatorship in Spain claimed to be an 'organic democracy', free of the 'unnecessary' political divisions created by parties.

No matter how legitimate these arguments may look, when it comes to making decisions about particular cases, the idea of a 'natural' political kind is problematic. To begin with, our conceptions about democracy have changed. Today, if a country excluded women from suffrage rights, it would not be accepted in the democratic club. But Switzerland before the 1970s qualified as a democracy even though several cantons did not allow women to vote. Since participation in politics is a continuous property, the minimum participatory threshold to consider a country fully democratic is hard to establish. This problem is particularly pressing regarding categorical indexes of democracy, since they do not allow for intermediate levels of 'democraticness'. Hence, the Democracy Dictatorship database (Cheibub, Ghandi, and Vreeland, 2010) opts to not impose conditions on participation (since the authors hold a purely Schumpetarian view of democracy that only cares about competition); in contrast, Boix, Miller, and Rosatto's (2013) database introduces a somewhat arbitrary rule: a country may be democratic if at least half of the male population can vote. This condition, however practical, does not look like a natural joint.

Furthermore, 'natural' kinds in the social realm alter the agents' behaviour. Using Hacking's (1999) terminology, we deal here with 'interactive kinds' rather than with 'indifferent kinds': in the former, the entity may react to the classification scheme (either to enter into it or to escape from it). Thus, as democracy became the hegemonic regime type at international level, many dictatorships opted to hold rigged or biased elections as a way to circumvent the pressure from Western countries and international organizations (Levitsky and Way, 2010; Schedler, 2013).

Many of the problems relating to the conceptualization and measurement of democracy, or political regimes more generally, resurface in the debate on terrorism. Politicization of the term, ambiguity about its boundaries, alternative measurement procedures, and historical meaning change are also present in our case. To cope with these difficulties, we rely on Dupré's (1993) 'promiscuous realism', a philosophical stance that does not deny the existence of objective differences in the world but, simultaneously, accepts the claim that multiple legitimate classifications are possible. This classificatory pluralism reflects the ontological complexity of the world. If the world is irremediably complex and heterogeneous, the very aim of having a consistent and complete typology of the world becomes chimerical. We are going to leverage this position to advance our own taxonomy of political violence. We will see that there is no unique way to conceptualize terrorism. Terrorism is predicated at different layers of reality (from actions to conflicts); and we need to make room for this plurality of senses in our elucidation of the term. Among other things, the acceptance of this promiscuous reality makes a dictionary-like definition of the term impossible.

1.2. Typologies of Violence

Political violence comes under a wide variety of forms. The possibilities for taxonomy are multifarious. One initial consideration is whether we should work with the existing categories and then suggest some classificatory scheme that makes sense of the differential characteristics of these categories, or whether we should proceed in a purely deductive fashion, formulating novel categories or kinds according to the theoretical criteria used in the taxonomy. In other words, should we reject the existing labels and start from scratch, or should we take advantage of them and classify the existing forms of violence, wars, genocides, state repression, terrorism, and the like, according to some taxonomical criterion? To discuss the pros and cons, we briefly examine Tilly (2003) (an example of the former) and Kalyvas (2019) (an example of the latter).

According to Tilly, political violence should be organized according to two characteristics: the salience of short-term damage and the extent of coordination among violent actors. The first criterion refers to how violent actions are; that is, whether violence merely accompanies the action (as if it were an accidental trait) or whether the action is aimed to be violent. The second criterion captures the level of coordination required for the exercise of violence,

18   Underground Violence

going from the highly decentralized production of violence to the existence of centralized organizations. By combining the two criteria in different degrees, Tilly suggests seven categories: (i) violent rituals, (ii) coordinated destruction, (iii) opportunism, (iv) brawls, (v) individual aggression, (vi) scattered attacks, and (vii) broken negotiations. Tilly (2003: 18) argues that traditional categories (interstate war, civil war, and the like) fail to constitute 'a distinct causal realm with its own laws'; to rephrase it in the terms of the previous section, the traditional categories, in Tilly's view, do not identify the 'natural' joints of violence.

But how are we going to judge, in the social world, whether our classifications carve the true joints of the phenomena? Is there anything remotely close to the predictions made by Mendeleev in the periodic table of elements? The best we can do is to assess whether classifications enhance our understanding of how violence operates in different settings. But what if these settings are defined in an entirely new way, unrelated to the folk categories we use in ordinary life? How can we then adjudicate between alternative classifications?

Tilly's attempt is a risky one. If the new taxonomy is not fully convincing, it will remain as an idiosyncratic exercise. Indeed, as far as we know, Tilly's typology has not been used in subsequent empirical research. His ideas are just too far removed not only from folk categories, but also from existing theories and datasets. If we wanted to test hypotheses based on Tilly's taxa, we would need to fully restructure data collection. On the other hand, there are good reasons to pay attention to old categories. In many cases, they exist for a reason: there have been recurrent episodes in the past that generate a pattern that is reflected in traditional categories. Besides, some of the folk categories even acquire legal status (e.g., war, genocide) and play a role in how violence is exercised.

This is not a plea for conceptual conservatism. We agree that there exists room for refining and redefining the existing categories, merging some of them, introducing new types that were blurred in an over-broad category, and so on. But ignoring our common understanding about types of conflict comes at a cost.[1]

---

[1] Our position is in some ways analogous to that of Rawls (1971) in his concept of 'reflective equilibrium'. When elaborating his theory of justice, he sought an equilibrium between our moral, considered judgements and the main tenets of the theory. The process of equilibrium formation is circular: we start from our most basic intuitions about fairness to build the theory of justice, but as the theory advances, we refine and filter the original judgements. At some point, the theory and the judgements are at peace with each other: then we have a reflective equilibrium. In our conceptualization of terrorism, we try something similar: our understanding stems from some deep intuitions about what terrorism is and what it is not, and then the conceptualization is used to refine and filter the original intuitions.

Kalyvas's (2019) taxonomy does not get rid of existing categories. He starts from 11 kinds of violence: (i) interstate war, (ii) civil war, (iii) state repression, (iv) genocide, (v) ethnic cleansing, (vi) intercommunal violence, (vii) organized crime/cartel violence, (viii) military coup, (ix) mass protest/rebellion, (x) political assassination, and (xi) terrorism. Let us assume that these 11 kinds are the most relevant. Kalyvas introduces two dimensions, the state vs. non-state condition of the perpetrator, and the state vs. non-state condition of the target of violence. The resulting 2 × 2 matrix shows the affinities between the 11 kinds of violence (see Table 1.1).

The two criteria go a long way in revealing different kinds of violence. But they are not sufficiently precise to separate out the various kinds coexisting within a single cell. In some cases, this is not particularly problematic. Thus, in the state acting against the civilian population, it might be argued that both genocide and ethnic cleansing are subtypes (special cases) of state repression.

However, in the case of non-state groups attacking the state, distinctions are harder to draw. Here, we surmise, the main anomaly stems from terrorism. One initial clue about the different scope of terrorism in contrast to other kinds of violence comes from the very word we use for it, an 'ism' word. The other kinds of violence refer to a certain type of phenomenon, a certain type of conflict, with delimited geographical and time boundaries: they are embodied in concrete nouns such as war, genocide, and the rest. They represent, so to say, an ontology of conflicts. Even if many complexities must be dealt with in the process of identifying conflicts, we can establish the area and the period in which interstate wars, civil wars, rebellions, coups, state repression, genocide, and ethnic cleansing occur. We tend to assume that these are episodes of violence located in space and time (they constitute separated, or at

Table 1.1 Kalyvas's (2019) classification of political violence

	Target: state	Target: non-state
Perpetrator: state	Inter-state war	State repression Genocide Ethnic cleansing
Perpetrator: non-state	Organized crime/cartels Mass protest/rebellion Military coup Political assassination Civil war Terrorism	Intercommunal violence

least separable, conflicts). Terrorism, by contrast, is a much more ambiguous term. The 'ism' suffix points to a higher level of abstraction. Thus, it is not by chance that terrorism may refer both to a certain armed group (such as when we say that the Provisional IRA was a terrorist group) and to a certain kind of tactics (such as when we say Hezbollah has carried out terrorist attacks outside of Lebanon). The 'terrorism' kind cannot be reduced to a conflict (a set of episodes of violence bounded in space and time). A consequence of this fact is the possibility of terrorism crosscutting other categories. Due to the versatility of the concept, terrorism may be found in various types of conflicts. This would explain why there also exists 'terrorist' as an adjective, apart from the abstract noun: we talk about terrorist violence, terrorist groups, terrorist tactics, terrorist attacks, and so on. This adjectival form of the term has no exact parallel in the words we use to define types of conflicts. Given this multi-dimensional usage of the term, it is no wonder that we find terrorism all over Kalyvas's 2 × 2 table. We start with an obvious example: political assassinations and terrorism are not exclusive kinds. Some assassinations, in fact, are typically terrorist, such as when the Red Brigades killed Aldo Moro, the general secretary of the Christian Democratic Party, in 1978, or when People's Will killed Tsar Alexander II in 1881. More importantly, terrorism can be produced in the context of civil war, and a growing literature has sought to disentangle the relationship between the two (see Chapter 3 and its Appendix). Thus, the conflicts in Iraq and Syria over the last two decades are civil wars according to all the existing definitions, but several of the actors involved in these conflicts are labelled 'terrorist'; likewise, the external intervention of Western countries is presented as part of the war against terrorism.

Further, it is unclear that the target of terrorism is always the state. There are cases where terrorism is used against social groups. During the Troubles, for example, Unionist paramilitary organizations carried out a high number of sectarian attacks against Republicans (and Catholics more generally). These attacks were aimed against a community, and they resemble intercommunal violence to a greater extent than violence against the state. However, they are usually regarded as terrorist.

Finally, Kalyvas's typology assumes that terrorism can never stem from the state; but this is a highly controversial point. We will argue that, under very specific circumstances (those of covert action by secret services or mercenaries that replicate the conditions of clandestinity), the state can commit terrorist attacks.

Our main contention is that, due to its very special nature, terrorism cannot be confined to a single cell in Kalyvas's 2 × 2 typology of violent conflicts.

We need to introduce other criteria apart from the perpetrator's and target's state/stateless condition. This does not imply that the typology is useless, but it strongly indicates that a clean, well-ordered taxonomy in such a complex realm as political violence is probably unfeasible. To return to Dupré's (1993) 'promiscuous realism', we must be ready to accept some degree of disjunction in the criteria we use to characterize the different kinds of violence. That is, we cannot aim at providing something akin to Mendeleev's periodic table regarding violence. There are simply too many dimensions involved in the generation of the kinds of violence and several of them are cross-cutting.

1.3. Areas of Ambiguity

The main hurdle in the formulation of a conceptualization is the political contamination of our beliefs about what kind of violence is terrorist. As is well known, the word itself comes with a particularly heavy political load. 'Terrorism' has become a catchword for illegitimate (unacceptable) political violence.[2] Insofar as the range of the 'non-legitimate' changes historically, so does the conception of terrorism (Stampnitzky, 2013). In Stampnitzky's reconstruction of the field of terrorism studies, she notes how the term was still used in the 1960s to refer to a certain kind of state activity against the civil population; it was in the 1970s, with the expansion of Palestinian, nationalist, and revolutionary terrorism in many developed countries, when the term mutated and became associated with a certain type of insurgent or rebel behaviour. Lacking a firm anchor, the meaning of terrorism has varied, making this field of study an 'interstitial project' (Stampnitzky, 2013: 138), neither fully academic nor purely political. Her conclusion is that terrorism is not a stable concept and therefore cannot be a basis for a rigorous theoretical body.

Since 'terrorism' has a derogatory intent, terrorists themselves invent other words, just as dictators prefer to be called by other names (see section 1.1). A notable exception is al-Suri, Al Qaeda's ideologue, who accepted the terrorist condition of the attacks he was promoting in his mammoth treaty *The Military Theory of the Global Islamic Resistance Call* (Lia, 2007: 382).[3] However, most terrorists opt for expressions such as 'revolutionary warfare', 'national liberation fighting', 'anti-imperialist struggle', 'urban guerrilla', 'resistance', or 'holy war'. By using these expressions, they imply that they are involved in

---

[2] An exception here is Ted Honderich, who has argued for the possibility of a morally justified terrorism. See Honderich (2008) for his defence of Palestinian terrorism against Israeli civilians.
[3] According to Hoffman (2006: 21), anarchist terrorists accepted the 'terrorist' label.

22   Underground Violence

some kind of just or legitimate war, fighting against oppression, exploitation or moral corruption—hence the popular dictum, 'one man's terrorist is another man's freedom fighter'. In a curious twist, terrorists sometimes employ the very word 'terrorism' against their enemies. The Greek Revolutionary Organization 17 November wrote in a document that 'if anybody, today in Greece, routinely practices terrorism, that is the ruling class together with imperialism seeking to perpetuate the system of working-class exploitation' (Kassimeris, 2001: 115). Likewise, an Al Qaeda statement issued in October 2001, during the bombing of Afghanistan, asked: 'Is it possible that America and its allies would kill and that would not be called terrorism? And when the victim comes out to take revenge, it is called terrorism. This must not be acceptable.'[4] Bill Ayers, once a member of the Weather Underground, goes even further, arguing that they were not terrorists because their actions did not fit the prevailing definitions of terrorism in the public discourse:

> Terrorists terrorize, they kill innocent civilians, while we organized and agitated. Terrorists destroy randomly, while our actions bore, we hoped, the precise stamp of a cut diamond. (Ayers, 2003: 263)

Is it possible to avoid the political implications of the term? Some terrorism experts act as if they were exorcists, trying to eliminate the 'political devil' from their field of study through definitional incantations; the assumption is that the supposedly objective tone of a dictionary entry can expel the bad spirits (political value judgements) (see, again, Stampnitzky, 2013: 198–200). Schmid and Jongman (1988) surveyed the field and collected over 100 definitions. They asked experts to fill out a questionnaire and found 22 recurring themes in their answers (use of violence, political motivations, terror, victim-target differentiation, coercion, publicity, etc.). Out of this, they proposed a complex and long definition that sought to include as many of these themes as possible. This inductive approach is unlikely to do the job (see also Weinberg, Pedahzur, and Hirsch-Hoefler, 2004). Using the minimum common denominator of existing definitions does not mean that the resulting definition will reveal the generative principles of terrorism, that is, the reasons why we regard certain attacks or armed groups as terrorist.

Interestingly, the debate on definitions has lost steam in recent years, if only because cross-national datasets on terrorism have been made available

---

[4] 'Text Statement from Al Qaeda', *New York Times* (9 October 2001), https://www.nytimes.com/2001/10/09/international/text-of-statement-from-al-qaeda.html.

(LaFree, 2019); researchers have turned to statistical analysis of the existing data without paying much attention to the type of violence included in these datasets. Efforts on conceptualization have tended to disappear due to the tacit assumption that terrorism is simply what datasets on 'terrorist attacks' include (an exception is Richards, 2015). However, datasets start from definitions with very little theoretical elaboration and therefore reproduce many of the shortcomings of inductivism. The definitions employed are notoriously vague (see, for example, Sheehan (2012: Appendix) for a list of definitions used in the main datasets). The ambiguity of the definitions has implications for the decisions made on the events to be included in the database. In a sense, scholars who ignore the conceptual debate by running regressions with the existing datasets are but delegating the definitional problem to the coders. In the Appendix of Chapter 3 we offer some more detailed examples of the problems that are endemic when the quality of the data is taken for granted.

1.4. Inadequate Conceptions

Having clarified what should count as a satisfactory explanatory taxonomy, we argue next that the two most widely mentioned characteristics of terrorism lack precision or empirical adequacy to form the basis on which a conceptualization of terrorist violence might be built. These two characteristics are the target of the violence (civilians vs. combatants) and the coercive nature of the violence (hit one to terrorize the many). We hold that these characteristics, either separately or combined, fail to capture what makes terrorism a unique type of violence.

Killing Civilians

Many authors have defended the view that what differentiates terrorism from other forms of violence is killing civilians (among many others, Abrahms, 2006: 42, 2012: 369; Boot, 2013: xxii; Carr, 2002: 6; Coady, 2021: 19; Cronin, 2009: 7; Goodwin, 2006: 2028; Jones and Libicki, 2008: 3; Kamm, 2008: 157; Lake, 2002: 17; McCormick, 2003: 486; Nacos, 2016: 37; O'Leary and Tirman, 2007: 6; O'Neill, 2005: 33; Stepanova, 2008: 11; Stern, 2003: xx). A typical example from an influential article in the field: Kydd and Walter (2006: 52) define '"terrorism" as the use of violence against civilians by nonstate actors to attain political goals'.

24   Underground Violence

Some authors, particularly philosophers, go further than this, adding that in terrorism civilians are innocent, or are killed randomly, or both. Michael Walzer defines terrorism as follows:

> Terrorism is the deliberate killing of innocent people, at random, in order to spread fear through a whole population and force the hand of its political leaders. (Walzer, 2004: 130)

In *Just and Unjust Wars*, Walzer argued that 'randomness is the crucial feature of terrorist activity' (1977: 177). Other philosophers followed the lead (Cohen, 2008: 103). The reference to innocence is problematic from a methodological perspective, as it entails inescapable value judgements. In his 'Letter to Americans' (Ibrahim, 2007: 200), Osama Bin Laden held that American civilians are not innocents, for they freely choose governments that commit all sorts of atrocities against Muslims. If the goal is to elaborate a theory of terrorist violence, the presence of value judgements (such as moral innocence) is a source of confusion. Philosophers, of course, are entitled to discuss the moral dimension of terrorism, but there is no reason to incorporate their conclusions, whatever they are, in the conceptualization of terrorism.

As for the randomness of the attacks, this is a matter of degree and should be analysed under the lens of the selectivity of violence.[5] Even in the attack against the World Trade Center, a case for non-randomness can be made. After all, Al Qaeda might have decided to crash the planes in London, Beijing, or, for that matter, any other US city different from New York. The fact that they were aimed at the USA (and at New York) is not a random decision.

We know, besides, that terrorists choose targets based on ideological, ethnic, or religious traits (as in Palestinian attacks against Israeli security forces and civilians); these attacks may be more or less selective, but clearly are not random or fully indiscriminate. More importantly, we also observe highly selective terrorist attacks against individuals who behave in a certain way (for instance, a judge who has imprisoned a particular group's members). There is no empirical or theoretical basis to conclude that terrorism is indiscriminate violence (see De la Calle and Sánchez-Cuenca, 2011b).

We do not rule out the possibility of shifting the usage of the term 'terrorism' to refer to any kind of civilian victimization (as in Carr, 2002, or

---

[5] The random condition of terrorist violence is mentioned in some definitions: see, for example, Canetti-Nisim, Mesch, and Pedahzur, 2006: 485; Ross and Gurr, 1989: 406.

Goodwin, 2006). But this comes at a price. Terrorism is now a pattern of target selection that may be observed in every type of political violence. Although we think that the question about why civilians are targeted in conflicts of any type is an interesting and legitimate one (Balcells and Stanton, 2021; Asal, Phillips, and Rethemeyer, 2022), this fails to identify either a kind of violence in itself, a kind of conflict, or a kind of armed actor.

The definition of terrorism as civilian victimization relies upon the 'principle of distinction' between combatants and non-combatants as stated in International Humanitarian Law. This principle was formulated in the context of inter-state wars in which two (or more) clearly identifiable armies fight against each other. Since the nature of war has changed substantially and, more importantly, since most armed conflicts in recent decades are intra-state, the traditional boundaries between combatants and non-combatants have become murkier (see Melzer (2014) for a review). Broadly speaking, combatants can be characterized as those who bear arms and take part in hostilities. This, however, does not settle the issue (Coady, 2021: Ch. 4). In the case of urban violence, for instance, should the police be considered combatants? What about the special case of members of the military who are targeted when they are off duty or when they do their routine administrative work in times of peace? On the other hand, arc all those who are part of an armed group combatants, even those who only help with logistics, intelligence, or propaganda?

The panoply of special cases is indeed wide. For the sake of simplicity, it will suffice to distinguish between civilians on the one hand, and 'armed people' on the other. By armed people we refer to members of paramilitary groups as well as to members of police forces and the military, both in times of war and peace, whether on or off duty.

Given this distinction, is it helpful to make terrorism equivalent to the targeting of civilians by non-state armed groups? Our answer is in the negative, for two reasons: civilians are killed systematically in other forms of violence and terrorist groups often target security forces. We elaborate on each part of the answer.

It is a well-established fact that the main perpetrator of violence against civilians is the state. This holds for all kinds of warfare activity, either inter-state or intra-state. Bombing civilian populations is particularly deleterious, as the Allies' aerial campaigns against Germany and Japan at the end of World War II attest (more than one million German and Japanese civilians were killed). According to Downes (2008) and Valentino (2004), a state targets civilians mainly when it is involved in a prolonged war of attrition and the state can only win through a heavy sacrifice of domestic troops, or when the goal is territorial conquest and the local population is an obstacle to the state's control of the territory (killing civilians will cause displacement of the population).

Repression is the purest case of civilian victimization by the state. Sometimes, repression is carried out in an arbitrary, random-like way (as in Stalin's purges); however, at other times, repression is targeted against a specific group, resulting in genocide or mass killings.[6] Many authors rule out by fiat the possibility of state terrorism. For those who share this view, the fact that the state kills non-combatants is irrelevant. We address this issue in greater depth in the next chapter. At this point, we would like to emphasize that the exclusion of the state's repressive violence is ad hoc from the viewpoint of a conception based on civilian victimization; alleging 'adhocness' in this context means that the reasons for excluding the state are not grounded in a theoretical argument about the nature of terrorism. In other words, it is unclear why a definition that establishes the status of the target as the defining characteristic of terrorist violence should include the condition that the violence to be analysed must be exclusively non-state. In our own conceptualization of the phenomenon, the (partial) exclusion of the state follows from the very definition we provide. Here, however, the exclusion is arbitrary.

Apart from the contentious point about state violence, the main objection is that we possess ample evidence of civilian victimization by non-state actors that is normally not taken as terrorism. Thus, we do not use the term terrorism to refer, for instance, to sectarian violence in the context of ethnic conflict, pogroms, or, more generally, mass atrocities by non-state actors. Scholars have defined 'mass atrocities' as the killing of more than 1000 civilians in a certain period of time (this includes genocides). Although mass atrocities are mostly committed by states, the existing databases list at least 40 mass atrocities by non-state actors during the period 1989–2018 (Anderton and Brauer, 2021). As far as we know, people do not refer to non-state mass atrocities as terrorist violence.

Even more importantly, we have plenty of evidence about the attacks on civilians in the context of insurgencies and guerrilla groups. According to Balcells and Stanton (2021: 47), 'violence against civilians occurs in the context of many different types of conflict and contentious political activity, varying

---

[6] Interestingly, Valentino (2004: 84–7) considers that a certain type of mass killing should be labelled 'terrorist': specifically, when the systematic targeting of civilians is driven by an attempt to coerce the enemy. In his view, this covers both state and insurgent violence. In this conceptualization, the two criteria we are examining (targeting civilians, coercing the enemy) are combined (see section 1.5).

across categories of contentious political action'. In the same vein, Weinstein (2007: 198) writes:

> The killing of civilians is a common consequence of armed conflict. Some of this violence is the unintended result of large-scale fighting between warring parties. Some follows directly from conflict-induced famine, malnutrition, and disease. But much of the violence directed at noncombatant populations in the course of war is intended. Armed groups target civilians as they organize their militaries, solicit resources to sustain the fighting, build bases of popular support, and weaken the support networks of opposing groups.

The academic literature on civil war rarely calls this type of violence 'terrorist'. A brief summary of the main theories that have been advanced to account for civilian victimization in the civil war context is useful to understand why this violence is different from that of terrorism. All the theories hinge upon the relationship between insurgencies and the local population. When it comes to creating a political order that replaces that of the state, the insurgents may try different strategies. They may seek people's collaboration in exchange for state-like services (imposing order, exerting justice, providing public goods, implementing social policies) or they may coerce people through the use of violence. Given the fragile authority of the new rulers, the defection of the local population represents a daunting challenge. If some locals join 'the enemy', and cooperate with the state, the insurgents' authority may be seriously eroded. This is at the core of Kalyvas's (2006) analysis of violence against civilians in civil wars. Reducing a rich and complex argument to its bones, indiscriminate violence is always a second best (as it usually backfires) and is motivated by a lack of information about the local population's allegiances. Selective violence, by contrast, is intended to punish informers and denouncers, with the goal of deterring others. In Kalyvas's theory, this violence is particularly frequent in those zones in which the insurgents are dominant but do not have full territorial control, their authority being contested by the enemy.

Other theories have focused on organizational constraints and levels of resources (Weinstein, 2007). Insurgent groups that are rich in resources can afford to repress the local population since they are not heavily constrained by the need to recruit locally. Instead, groups that are poor in resources tend to develop more consensual and collaborative arrangements with the local population. In a similar vein, De la Calle (2017) has argued that armed groups will carry out more attacks against civilians in areas where they aim at controlling territory as a way to impose local compliance, whereas they will be more restrained when operating in (urban) areas where they need to rely on networks of support to organize attacks.

Metelits (2010) introduces an additional layer of complexity by looking at variation across insurgent groups within conflicts. In her view, it is the presence of competition among paramilitary forces that generates the killing of non-combatants. When the armed group has near-monopoly power in a particular area, cooperation with the local population is feasible. However, when a competitor enters the insurgent group's area of control and challenges its access to resources, the group, in order to impose order, may victimize civilians. To use one of Metelits's case studies, the FARC in Colombia committed greater violence against civilians when the paramilitaries (the 'paras') entered the conflict. Similarly, Balcells (2017) has shown that civilian victimization is greater during a civil war when levels of political polarization were larger before the conflict starts; she finds, for instance, that in the Spanish Civil War, more civilians were killed in municipalities in which the Left and the Right had obtained a similar electoral share in the 1936 elections, four months before the conflict erupted.

This cursory review of some of the studies that have been conducted to analyse the behaviour of insurgent groups towards non-combatants in civil wars shows that the literature takes for granted that violence against civilians is an essential part of civil conflicts. This violence is rarely interpreted as terrorist violence.

Thus far, we have shown that states as well as insurgent groups target civilians, sometimes in an indiscriminate fashion. The definition of terrorism as violence against civilians cannot distinguish among the various kinds of violence aimed at civilians. The definition is certainly more plausible if the only violence to be considered is non-state, but even so it has to cope with communal violence, mass atrocities, and insurgent groups' systematic violence against the civilian population in the context of civil wars.

On the other hand, it is unclear whether terrorism is *only* violence against civilians. Terrorist violence is frequently aimed at combatants (that is, military, police, and members of rival paramilitary groups). Turning to the Global Terrorism Database (GTD), a simple tabulation of all lethal attacks by type of target (99,136 incidents) shows that almost 40 per cent of these attacks were aimed at the military (20.45 per cent), the police (16.42 per cent), or terrorist/non-state militias (2.54). 40 per cent is simply too high a figure to be considered as an exception to a general trend.[7]

---

[7] We restrict the analysis to lethal attacks for the sake of comparison with other datasets (see below). If all attacks are considered, the percentage is somewhat lower, 31 per cent, but still too high to be dismissed as a mere exception.

Suicide missions are typically included in the repertoire of terrorist tactics. According to the GTD, 50.8 per cent of lethal suicide attacks target combatants. In the case of lethal non-suicide attacks, 38.6 per cent target combatants. This difference is statistically significant and indicates that suicide attacks, despite their terrorist condition, are systematically aimed at combatants (see Chapter 5 for ISIS' use of suicide missions for military purposes).

It might be argued that the GTD's coding rules are simply too broad, so that the database unwittingly covers a portion of insurgent violence (see the Appendix to Chapter 3). The Domestic Terrorism Victims dataset (DTV; see De la Calle and Sánchez-Cuenca, 2011b) offers a finer test, as it records all individual fatalities caused by terrorist attacks in Western Europe for the period 1965–2005 (n = 4,955), identifying key demographics such as victims' jobs. Table 1.2 provides information about the number of fatalities and percentage of combatants killed by the eight most lethal armed groups in Western Europe before 2005. In four of them (PIRA, ETAm, GRAPO, and Red Brigades), the number of combatants killed represents well above 50 per cent of all lethal attacks.[8] There is very little doubt that the groups included in the table are terrorist. Were we to decide to eliminate them from the universe of terrorism, the whole field of study would have to be rearranged.

Table 1.2 Percentage of combatants killed by the eight most lethal armed groups in Western Europe

	Country	Fatalities	Percentage of combatants
PIRA (Provisional Irish Republican Army)	UK	1,648	65.05
ETAm (Basque Homeland and Freedom, military branch)	Spain	772	60.10
UVF (Ulster Volunteer Force)	UK	529	12.29
UDA (Ulster Defense Association)	UK	245	14.29
INLA (Irish National Liberation Army)	UK	130	38.46
NAR (Armed Revolutionary Nuclei)	Italy	117	17.09
GRAPO (First of October Anti-Fascist Resistance Groups)	Spain	85	77.65
BR (Red Brigades)	Italy	53	60.38

Source: DTV.

---

[8] Abrahms (2006) suggests that a group qualifies as terrorist when more than 50 per cent of the attacks are aimed at civilians. We think that this threshold is arbitrary. Besides, it has some counterintuitive consequences. Based on the data of Table 1.2, we should conclude that ETA, the PIRA, or the Red Brigades were insurgent groups, but not terrorist—something that goes against our most basic intuitions on the nature of terrorism.

30 Underground Violence

Table 1.3 Victim status by type of terrorism in Western European countries

	Total	Secessionist terrorism	Revolutionary terrorism	Fascist terrorism	Vigilante
Combatants	45.8% (2,083)	59.7% (1,708)	57.0% (196)	18.0% (62)	11.8% (117)
Non-combatants	54.2% (2,456)	40.3% (1,154)	43.0% (148)	82.0% (278)	88.2% (876)

Source: DTV.

The variation in the targeting of combatants within terrorist groups is enormous. Some groups are below 20 per cent, others above 60 per cent. The fact that all of them are usually labelled 'terrorist' implies that the status of the victim is not the generative mechanism for this kind of political violence.

Table 1.3 displays the general patterns of target selection in Western European countries according to the perpetrators' ideology. Four ideologies are distinguished as a function of the ultimate goal sought by the terrorists: (i) secessionist or nationalist violence, aimed at the separation of a region from state territory, (ii) revolutionary violence, aimed at provoking a mass insurrection against the system, (iii) fascist terrorism, aimed at creating the conditions under which a military coup would be welcomed by society, and (iv) vigilante terrorism, aimed at preventing the state from changing the status quo. Two opposite patterns emerge: on the one hand, secessionist and revolutionary terrorism that predominantly target combatants, and, on the other, fascist and vigilante terrorism that target almost exclusively non-combatants. The differences in targeting among the various ideological types of terrorist groups are probably larger than any difference we can find between insurgency and terrorism (see also Figure 3.4).

In sum, the definition of terrorism based on targeting civilians is a non-starter. Firstly, we find ample evidence about targeting civilians or non-combatants in other types of violence (e.g., mass atrocities, civil wars). Secondly, some groups that are universally regarded as terrorist attack combatants on a systematic basis, sometimes in a greater proportion than non-combatants.

Coercive Violence

A second approach to the definition of terrorism is to distinguish between the direct target of violence and the audience that contemplates the violence and may fear the same outcome if it does not comply with the perpetrators' demands (Braithwaite, 2013; Burleigh, 2008: xiii; Clutterbuck, 1977: 21; Crelinsten, 2002: 83–4; Crenshaw, 1995: 4; Frey, 2004: 7; Hoffman, 2006: 40; Krueger, 2007: 14; Lee, 2011: 205; Richards, 2015; Rubinstein, 1987: xvi; Schmid and Jongman, 1988: 28; Wilkinson, 1985: 12). As an illustration, we offer Enders and Sandler's (2012: 4) definition: 'Terrorism is the premeditated use or threat to use violence by individuals or subnational groups to obtain a political or social objective through the intimidation of a large audience beyond that of the immediate victims.'

What matters most here is the coercive nature of the violence. By exerting violence, the terrorists do not try to destroy the state or society. However, thanks to the limited violence against direct targets, the terrorists instil fear or terror in the audience that contemplates the violence. In one of the most influential and comprehensive books in the field, *Inside Terrorism*, Bruce Hoffman defines the term as 'the deliberate creation and exploitation of fear through violence or the threat of violence in the pursuit of political change' (2006: 40). In this sense, it is obvious that Al Qaeda, for example, was not trying to exterminate the population of the United States by launching the 9/11 attacks. The direct target was those who were working in the World Trade Center or in the Pentagon, while the main target was American society and its authorities. In this context, it is often argued that the goal of attacking the direct target is ultimately to terrorize the main target. The main target is frightened or terrorized by what happens to the direct one.

If the main target reacts to the attack aimed at the direct target it is because the violence has a communicative dimension (Crelinsten, 1987). This raises the idea of violence being a message that the perpetrator sends to the audience target. If this communicative element were absent, the audience target would not be able to react to the attack. However, from the fact that the terrorist action must be intelligible for the indirect target it does not follow that terrorism is only about conveying a message. Even when the message has been conveyed 'effectively', it is often the case that the terrorists keep repeating the same actions (for instance, the series of hijackings by Palestinian armed groups, or the series of attacks against British soldiers in Northern Ireland by Republican forces). This persistence is not related to communication, but to imposing a cost on the enemy. Nuances apart, it seems that the basic distinction between the two targets is clear and can be applied to many instances of terrorist violence. As in the previous section on civilians, we argue that this characterization of terrorism in terms of two targets covers too much, in the sense that violence that is seldom regarded as 'terrorist' falls under the definition, but also that it covers too little, since not all terrorist violence fits the definition.

We start by noting that differentiating between two types of targets is not exclusive to terrorism. In fact, the possibility of separating a direct and a main target is very common in any form of coercion. Coercive violence consists of imposing a cost on someone through violence (or the threat of it) to force the person to act as the coercer wants. In the case of collective actors (such as ethnic and ideological groups, societies, or states), coercive violence typically works by killing some members of the collective to induce others to make a certain decision that otherwise, in the absence of coercion, they would not make. As Kalyvas (2006: 26) says about coercive violence in general, it 'is intended to shape the behavior of a targeted audience by altering the expected value of particular actions'.

Political violence that is not a pure manifestation of military power fits the logic of coercion. In *Arms and Influence*, Thomas Schelling distinguished between military power and the power to hurt: in his characteristic style, 'there is a difference between taking what you want and making someone give it to you' (Schelling, 1966: 2). Taking what you want corresponds to military power; making someone give it to you corresponds to the power to hurt. Similarly, Kalyvas (2006) talks about two overarching aims of violence, extermination and compliance, which roughly correspond to military power and the power to hurt respectively. Extermination requires the destructive capacity of military power; compliance is granted through coercive violence.

The important point here is that this mechanism is present in terrorism, but not only in terrorism. Most forms of violence involve the logic of coercion and terror, including those of wars and guerrillas (Biddle, 2021: 31–2). War is often a more complex process than simply conquering territory and annihilating the enemy. Although there are wars that are driven by using the destructive capacity that stems from brute military power, war often involves bargaining and coercion. As said, conflict based on the war of attrition logic is based on coercion, but is not necessarily terrorism. In a war of attrition, the contest is won by the party with the greater capacity to endure. In a strict sense, 'attrition warfare is essentially siege warfare: wars generally lacking in maneuver or movement, which are instead dominated by static, linear, or trench operations' (Downes, 2008: 60). But attrition is also used to conceptualize punishment operations against the enemy as well as counterinsurgency warfare in the fight against guerrillas. Attrition strategies, whether in interstate war, insurgent conflict, or terrorism, rely on coercion: a cost is imposed on the enemy in each period, conditional on the enemy not surrendering. The cost endured by each party is based on the distinction between the direct and main targets. The main target, assessing the harm done on the direct target, decides whether to continue or quit.

The two atomic bomb attacks on Japan are examples of the logic of attrition, pushed to its limits. It is clear that the USA did not intend to exterminate the Japanese population. Rather, the attack was a message, in the starkest possible form, to the Japanese government and Japanese society about the consequences of not surrendering. The attack, therefore, presupposed the distinction between the direct and main target, and the bombs were certainly aimed at instilling fear in the population. According to the standard explanation, the USA resorted to attrition strategy because the expected human cost of an invasion of Japan was unacceptably high. For revisionists, Japan might have surrendered by other means and the ultimate target of the explosion of the atomic bombs was not Japan, but the Soviet Union (Alperovitz, 1995). However, even if this more complex historical interpretation is correct, the decision to use the bombs still relies on a distinction between the direct targets (the civilians of Hiroshima and Nagasaki) and the ultimate target (the Soviets, who became aware of the USA's nuclear power). There are many other campaigns of coercive violence against civilians caused by state armies, including Hitler's *Blitz* in 1940–41 or the Allied aerial campaigns in World War II. More recently, the ongoing war in Ukraine, even though it was initially one of conquest triggered by Russia, has become a war of attrition in which the Ukrainian counteroffensive now incorporates a so-called 'sneak and peek' campaign aimed at wearing down the Russian troops.[9] Whether these campaigns of violence are to be considered terrorism is highly debatable. If they are regarded as terrorism, then terrorism seems a pervasive component of warfare activity.

This unrestrained expansion of the concept of terrorism can be limited if state violence is eliminated from the definition. We ultimately agree (for reasons that will be apparent in the next chapter) with those who reject the idea that the state's coercive violence is terrorism. But, as in the case of civilian victimization, the exclusion of the state is done here arbitrarily, since it does not follow from the proposed conceptualization in terms of the direct and indirect targets of the violence.

Even if we assume that the reduction to non-state violence is in some ways warranted, it is still the case that guerrillas and insurgencies often use attrition or coercive violence against both the state and the local population. Regarding the state, for instance, the insurgents who fight in irregular civil wars (Kalyvas and Balcells, 2010) engage in constant harassment of enemy forces by undertaking hit-and-run tactics that are part of an attritional or

---

[9] See *Financial Times*, 3 September 2023 (https://www.ft.com/content/0560e2fc-d9a9-417c-b5e3-bc279dfb2bb6).

coercive strategy. If we were to regard these tactics as terrorist, the universe of terrorism, again, would expand beyond recognition. And regarding non-combatants, we can return to the cases that were discussed previously about killing civilians to deter people from collaborating with the enemy or to induce compliance with the new rulers. In either case, there is an unmistakable coercive dimension, in the sense that a few killings may serve to 'teach a lesson' to all others who may be tempted to switch sides (as our opening Lucanamarca story well illustrates). This type of violence, which is frequent in most civil wars, is not usually considered terrorist.

Finally, we would like to highlight that there are some aspects of terrorist violence that are not well captured by the logic of coercion. Typically, those who claim that terrorism is coercive violence tend to argue that terrorist violence generates fear or terror (hence the very term 'terrorism'). However, neither coercion nor terror is strictly necessary for the understanding of terrorism. This is seldom admitted in the conceptual discussions on terrorism.[10] Particularly in cases of revolutionary terrorism (aimed at regime change), violence is intended to mobilize an apathetic population rather than trying to force the state to make concessions (Rubenstein, 1987: xvii). Revolutionary terrorists believe that by killing members of the state apparatus or the bourgeoisie they (i) establish a path that the masses will follow, (ii) reveal the vulnerability of the system, and (iii) contribute to raising class consciousness (Sánchez-Cuenca, 2019: 34–7). Revolutionary groups do not aspire to change policies by extracting concessions from the state. Rather, they seek to create the conditions for an insurrection that will smash the state or even end with capitalism and the bourgeois social order.

Propaganda by the deed (or armed propaganda), which is the most common strategy followed by revolutionary terrorist groups, works on the assumption that violence will attract followers to the cause and will mobilize a community of support. As the Red Brigades explained in a text on their strategy of violence, 'urban guerrilla plays a key role in the political deconstruction of the regime and the state. It directly hits the enemy and paves the way for the resistance movement. Around the guerrilla the resistance movement is created and organized.'[11] It is worth noting that the motto that Italian armed groups used in the 1970s was not 'to kill some in order to terrorize the many', which is often taken as the epitome of terrorism, but,

---

[10] One exception is Coady (2021: 45), who argues that 'common as the fear reaction may be, it does not seem to be true that this is what terrorists invariably aim at'.

[11] Brigate Rosse, 'Risoluzione della Direzione Strategica', April 1975. Reproduced in Prette (1996: 54). Our translation.

significantly, '*colpiscine uno per educarne cento*' (hit one to educate a hundred.) Here, violence is supposed to have an educational role for the masses; the pedagogical value of violence has very little relationship with coercion or terror. Obviously, the attacks of the Italian armed groups revolted many and caused terror in much of the population, but that was not the main goal of the terrorists; what they were trying to bring about was the conditions for an insurrection and the ensuing collapse of the state apparatus.

We do not claim that coercion is always absent in revolutionary terrorism. In some episodes, such as the kidnapping of Aldo Moro, the terrorists asked for the release of prisoners in exchange for the Christian Democrat politician. In this case, coercion was key to the act. But even in this case, the leaders of the Red Brigades were thinking of the kidnap as a tool to intensify and deepen what they called 'the internal contradictions of the state'.

This also holds for Al Qaeda, since some of its attacks do not respond only to the logic of coercion, as mobilizing followers is also crucial. The 9/11 attacks included motives that might be framed as coercion (Al Qaeda was targeting the USA to force American troops to withdraw from the Arabian Peninsula), but, clearly, a no less important motivation was the sheer spectacularism of hitting the financial core of the USA, in its most global city, New York, and ultimately emboldening and/or radicalizing Muslims all over the planet. Al Qaeda's attacks were intended to provoke a war against Western powers that would attract radical Islamists everywhere. From this perspective, Al Qaeda is but another instance of revolutionary terrorism (Ryan, 2013). The bottom line of the argument is that coercion is not the only conceivable purpose of terrorist violence. Some terrorists kill to mobilize supporters and to trigger a general insurrection against the system. Therefore, a view of terrorism that defines the phenomenon in terms of coercion is an incomplete one that cannot make sense of terrorist violence as a mechanism to trigger mobilization.

1.5. Mixed Definitions

It might be argued that we have examined only partial characterizations of terrorism. Some may agree with the two conclusions we have reached so far, namely that terrorism as violence against civilians on the one hand and terrorism as coercive violence on the other, cover too much; but terrorism might still be defined as a combination of the two characteristics (i.e., coercive violence against civilians), with the intent that this will cover terrorism, and nothing but terrorism. An example of this type of definition might be

Primoratz's (1990: 135): terrorism is 'the deliberate use of violence, or threat of its use, against innocent people, with the aim of intimidating them, or other people, into a course of action they otherwise would not take' (see also Bjørgo, 2005: 2; Combs, 2018: 7; O'Neill, 2005: 33). Primorazt's reference to 'innocents' must be understood as referring to non-combatants.

There is something appealing about this approach. In fact, Downes (2008) has argued that attritional strategies and civilian victimization are closely associated. Thus, a definition along these lines reflects the relationship between the two characteristics: coercion and civilian targeting.

From a purely logical point of view, we have raised two objections regarding each of the two characteristics. The first is lack of precision: the definition based on each characteristic is insufficient because the same traits can be found in other types of violence. The second is about ignoring the variation we find in terrorism: as a matter of fact, terrorists kill combatants *and* non-combatants, and terrorists use violence for coercive *and* mobilization purposes. From this perspective, this more stringent definition (coercive violence against civilians) leaves too much terrorism 'outside': terrorist attacks aimed at security forces and terrorist violence aimed at mobilizing supporters do not fit the suggested definition. Since these two are essential (or just too frequent) components of terrorism, we think that the precision of the combined definition comes at too high a cost.

1.6. Conclusions

Despite the political battle over the meaning of terrorism, we think there is room for an analytical approach that avoids many of the traps along the way. We are searching for a conceptualization that does not deviate too much from our most basic intuitions about the phenomenon. The main problem is that these basic intuitions are often buried under academic definitions. However, if we examine how people refer to terrorism in different contexts and at different times, we can identify the basic intuitions and build a conceptualization of terrorism that makes sense of the ways in which we talk about terrorism.

Thus, we deem the definition of terrorism as attacks against civilians to be mistaken because it is inconsistent with some basic uses of the term. For all we know, no one questions the terrorist label applied to the Red Brigades even though most of the fatalities caused by this organization were members of the security forces. And, exactly for the same reason, we think that defining terrorism in terms of coercion is inadequate: the violence of the Red Brigades was aimed at mobilizing the revolutionary subject rather than at coercing the Italian state.

Of course, there is a strong association between terrorism on the one hand, and killing civilians and coercive violence on the other. This is why so many definitions have focused on these characteristics. But these associations are far from perfect and do not constitute a sound basis for a conceptualization of the phenomenon.

Having clarified what terrorism is not (it is not necessarily violence against civilians, and it is not only coercive violence), we advance in the next chapter an understanding of terrorism in which the key theoretical factor is clandestinity. Terrorism, in our view, is, above all, underground violence.

2
Terrorism as Underground Political Violence

Our central theoretical claim is that terrorism should be primarily understood as underground violence rather than civilian victimization or coercive violence. What makes terrorism unique is that it does not require physical occupation or control of space. Terrorism is intrinsically linked to secret, covert action. Most insurgent violence, by contrast, is about gaining territorial control and the creation of a liberated zone in which the rebels become the new authority and challenge the efficacy and legitimacy of the state.

An understanding of terrorism based on clandestinity does not clash with the previously discussed notions that terrorist groups sometimes target civilians, or that they use violence to coerce audiences. But it prevents the application of the concept to civilian targeting and coercive violence when the attack is not secretly carried out. At the same time, our definition does embody instances of terrorism not included in those conceptualizations, such as attacks against combatants, or violence pursuing mobilization goals—as long as the attack is perpetrated under the rules of clandestinity.

Terrorism is politically motivated violence carried out secretly by actors without territorial control. This conceptualization is not an arbitrary or idiosyncratic imposition; rather, it builds on a broadly used public understanding of terrorism. In other words, it is not that we set up our definition and then rule out by fiat instances of violence that sit outside of our definition. To the contrary, we survey the field and the most common uses of the term and come up with a definition that embodies the core ideas contained in the concept. As will be seen, our proposed conceptualization has some unifying power, in the sense that it helps to provide a comprehensive view of the phenomenon by accounting for many of its apparently disconnected features. It does so, moreover, without breaking with many of the traditional views on the nature of terrorism. Finally, it is eminently practical, as it generates some observable consequences that can be empirically tested (as shown in Chapter 3).

Underground Violence. Luis De la Calle and Ignacio Sánchez-Cuenca, Oxford University Press.
© Luis De la Calle and Ignacio Sánchez-Cuenca (2024). DOI: 10.1093/oso/9780198904816.003.0003

We begin by analysing the characteristics that make underground violence so unique: secrecy and immediacy. The lack of control over space imposes severe constraints, including non-recognizability (the perpetrators do not wear uniforms) and very short-lived attacks. Secondly, we more deeply explore the concept of territorial control and how to analyse and measure it. Thirdly, we present a basic distinction in the analysis of violence between the actor- and the action-senses. With this conceptual apparatus, we proceed in section 2.4 to present the resulting conceptual map on terrorism, contrasting terrorist violence with related types of violence. Lastly, we show that this conceptual map makes room for the possibility of state terrorism, which we define as underground repression.

2.1. Territorial Control

To understand the nature of clandestinity and underground violence, we need to figure out first its reverse side: the significance and strategic relevance of having territorial control. Territory is the most basic ingredient of the state. In his lecture *Politics as a Vocation* (1918), Max Weber famously said that the state 'is a human community that (successfully) claims the monopoly of the legitimate use of physical force within a given territory. Note that "territory" is one of the characteristics of the state' (1946: 78). The object of much violence in human history, under the form of either inter-state or intra-state wars, revolves about the control of territory. Territory is an essential asset for many different reasons, including natural resources, geostrategic influence, demography, and, most importantly, the space in which to build structures of political dominion.

Territorial control is hence the most important aspiration for states and insurgencies alike. Insurgencies need territory liberated from the state's authority to have a safe space in which they can train recruits, store weapons, plan operations, and establish links with the local population. In the most favourable scenario for the rebels, they become de facto rulers in populated areas. The rebel army acts as a sort of proto-Leviathan by imposing order, extracting rents from the population, and providing some public services. At its peak, the Liberation Tigers of Tamil Eelam (LTTE) controlled a large portion of the Tamil-dominated regions in Northern and Eastern Sri Lanka. The group was able to build fortifications to defend its territory and develop an organized army with over 16,000 members. The LTTE is one of the few insurgent groups worldwide that has had warships and even aircraft. In its replacement of the state, the LTTE developed courts of law, a postal

40 Underground Violence

service, a police force, and a public broadcasting service (Hussain, 2010; Stokke, 2006).

However, in most cases, rebels' territorial control is fragmented or incomplete (Kalyvas, 2006: 210–12). This may happen in areas under dispute, in which there is dual power and it is unclear who will become the new authority (for example, where the state rules during the day, and the rebels during the night), or in areas in which one party has an advantage in the control of local life but the rival is not completely absent (thus, civilians can establish contact with both parties).

In the past, the most common form of rebels' territorial control was in the countryside. However, as most societies have experienced an accelerated process of urbanization, much of the conflict has moved to cities (King, 2021). A paradigmatic example is ISIS' control of Mosul in Iraq and of Raqqa in Syria, as well as several minor cities (see Chapter 5). Likewise, Hezbollah was able to have effective territorial control in the Shi'ite slums of South Beirut during the Lebanese civil war (Jaber, 1997: 146). Another potential urban example is the no-go areas in Belfast and Derry during the early phase of the Troubles, in which Republicans had effective control of certain neighbourhoods. It was simply too risky for security forces to enter those areas. To end this anomalous situation, in 1972 the UK dispatched a large army contingent to the two cities to regain state control ('Operation Motorman') (Smith, 1995: 110).

Territorial control is a gradual rather than discrete property (Kalyvas, 2006: Ch. 7). The low end of the continuum corresponds to the underground. Two intermediate possibilities are worth mentioning. On the one hand, it may be the case that an armed group is unable to 'liberate' territory from state control but, nonetheless, possesses a 'safe haven' beyond the national border. Thus, the group has a base, but it is located beyond the theatre of operations. Thanks to this base, it can train recruits, set up camps, and store weapons without having to hide from the state. The group does not have territorial control as such, but the safe haven acts as a surrogate for it. Many examples can be given. Let us take the African National Congress (ANC). The initial plans of the ANC's armed branch, the Umkhonto we Sizwe (MK), created in 1961, were effectively to bring down the South African regime via guerrilla warfare, but it was crushed by the state in less than four years (Barrell, 1992; Legassick, 2003: 284). The Soweto Uprising in 1976 changed this status quo by offering the MK a large cohort of potential recruits, plus some fresh ideas about moving the fight from the countryside to the main cities. In a remarkable statement, military leader Comrade Mzala noted in 1981 that 'any strategic perspective would be moving from insufficient, nay, false, premises if it did not recognise that South Africa is above all else an industrial capitalist society' (Legassick, 2003: 287); however, he still argued that rural guerrilla warfare was the best way to strike at industrial society's weakest flank—the countryside. Guerrilla warfare continued to be a non-starter, as the organization failed to build bases within South Africa. During the 1980s, the ANC was not able to control territory within South Africa, but it had camps in Tanzania and Angola. It is estimated that the ANC had around 10,000 guerrillas outside the country (Moorcraft, 2018: 345–6). Not having a territorial base in South Africa, the violence, mostly urban, was oriented to 'armed propaganda', a quintessential goal of terrorism (Legassick, 2003: 291). As late as 1986, Ronnie Kasrils, a member of the MK's High Command, conceded that 'urban areas are a vital terrain of our struggle ... we should utilize our urban strength, our township strength, our working-class strength as a springboard'; but still not rule out rural guerrilla warfare (Legassick, 2003: 293; see also Simpson, 2009). The ANC was an underground group,[1] but its bases in neighbouring countries contributed to its growing numbers and ensured its survival.

Likewise, during the 1970s, the Palestinian Liberation Organization (PLO) had to act underground within the borders of Israel, but it had camps and bases in Lebanon (and earlier in Jordan) (see Chapter 5). In the case of Euskadi ta Askatasuna (ETA) in Spain, ETA never gained territorial control, but the French Basque Country was a sort of safe haven for the group until the mid-1980s (see Chapter 4). The existence of an outside safe haven falls short of powering the armed organization with the same resources offered by seizing territory inside the borders of its rival state. But it nonetheless helps the group to recruit more easily and sometimes to launch guerrilla-like cross-border attacks, as we will see in the next chapters.

On the other hand, we have nomadic or roving groups. They do not have territorial control, but they are not fully underground either. A good case in point is the Spanish *Maquis* under Franco (1939–52): the rebels hid in the hills, descended to the villages to attack security forces or collaborators with the dictatorship, and escaped back to the mountainous terrain (Serrano, 2006). They were not able to establish permanent residency in the hills, as they were forced to move when chased by the security forces.

Some specific conditions associated with territorial control can be mentioned in order to distinguish armed groups with and without territorial

---

[1] See Mangashe (2018) for a vivid, first-hand account of the MK's clandestine operations inside South Africa.

control. In particular, we consider that an armed group is guerrilla when at least one of the following conditions is met (De la Calle and Sánchez-Cuenca, 2012):[2]

a. The rebels have the capacity to set up camps or bases within the country's borders in which they store weapons, train recruits, and plan attacks.
b. The rebels have the capacity to establish stable roadblocks, disrupting the flow of goods and people within the country.
c. The rebels have the capacity to rule the civil population in the localities they seize (e.g., extracting rents and providing some public goods such as 'justice', security, and/or social services). To be recognized as the new authority, insurgents may wear uniforms and carry arms in the controlled areas.

The conditions are ranked according to how demanding they are. The first condition does not require any level of interaction with the local population, and the controlled area may even be uninhabited. The second condition assumes some degree of control over the local population. The third, in turn, implies full control over the local population, that is, rebels' governance. Weinstein (2007: 164) defines rebels' governance as (i) a monopoly of violence in the territory, (ii) the establishment of institutions to regulate relations with civilians, and (iii) taxation and hierarchical decision-making systems. Arjona (2016) goes further by distinguishing between 'rebelocracy' (full involvement of the insurgents in civilian life, going beyond taxation and security) and 'aliocracy' (the insurgents only get involved in taxation and security). Any form of a stable rebel social order is a strong indicator of territorial control.

Territorial control, no matter how low, is a crucial achievement for any armed group. It has obvious logistical advantages and makes the expansion of the group possible, setting a more serious challenge to the state.

2.2. The Underground: Violence and Space

Underground violence can be easily defined in negative terms: it is the kind of violence that takes place in the absence of territorial control. Underground

---

[2] Biddle (2021: 317–20) proposes an index of holding ground based on four characteristics: duration of firefights, proximity of attackers to defenders, incidence of counterattack, and incidence of harassing fires and unattended minefields. Given the wide variety of tactics and situations in irregular warfare, we think that these criteria cannot be applied everywhere, and it is hard to measure them in most conflicts.

violence does not require effective control of the space in which the armed group acts. The paradigmatic example is that of an improvised explosive device (IED). The artefact can be planted secretly and detonated from a distance, by remote control. The operation does not require physical control of space; it is sufficient if the perpetrators are not discovered or denounced. Likewise, a sniper who fires at a politician or a police officer may also be regarded as an underground act: it does not require occupation of space. By contrast, the movement of troops to gain a new position, or to seize a building or a settlement, is a complex endeavour that can only succeed through occupation of space. Most military action, in the context of inter- or intra-state warfare, corresponds to a fight for control of space.

Underground violence has some characteristics of its own. On the one hand, the perpetrators cannot be identifiable, since they act in a hostile area, which is normally under the enemy's control. At the very moment in which they are recognized, they risk being immediately arrested or killed. Hence, secrecy and disguise are absolutely crucial. It is no surprise then that those involved in underground operations never wear uniforms, armbands or any other signal that might make them identifiable and therefore vulnerable to security forces. It is precisely because guerrillas have some physical control of space and may participate in assaults that they can wear uniforms. Members of Fatah in the late 1960s might have worn military uniforms in their camps in Jordan or in the battle of Karameh in 1968 against the Israel Defense Forces, but had to use plain clothes when they infiltrated Israel for underground activity (see Chapter 5).

On the other hand, the absence of space control in underground operations makes them ephemeral. They cannot last for long because otherwise security forces might capture or kill the perpetrators. A bomb explosion or a shooting are events that lack a temporal development; they presuppose some sort of immediacy. If the attack is prolonged, it cannot remain clandestine or underground. By contrast, guerrilla operations may last for longer; thus, a battle between insurgents and the state's army can develop over several hours or even days. In a battle, movements are essential, but movement takes time. In underground attacks, movement is severely limited and therefore the attacks cannot last.

When the perpetrators are willing to die, the attack may be prolonged, although this depends on the capacity of the security forces to bring them down. In the 2016 Nice attack, a truck driver ran over the crowd celebrating the Bastille day, killing 86 people and wounding hundreds. The attack lasted for five minutes exactly, the time the police needed to neutralize the perpetrator (Klausen, 2022: 430). In the November 2015 Paris attacks, the

44 Underground Violence

shooting of the people in the Bataclan lasted for 15 minutes. The operation extended in time because the terrorists took around 120 hostages. Obviously, in the case of hijackings and kidnappings, the operation has an important temporal dimension (the terrorists can stay in the enemy's territory because they hold hostages). These, however, are exceptions rather than the rule and their exceptional nature can be explained without having to go beyond the theory of underground violence.

Because of these special characteristics related to space and time, underground violence is highly disruptive, even more so when it occurs in times of peace, breaking the social order suddenly and unexpectedly. Hence its dramatic impact on the public (the target audience), which is often not commensurate with the actual damage caused by the violence (Mueller, 2006).

Acting underground imposes severe constraints on the range of violent tactics that are feasible. Coordination and mutual support among the perpetrators is considerably difficult. It is no wonder then that underground attacks are carried out by small groups or even by individuals acting alone. Moreover, the necessity of acting secretly restricts the kind of weaponry that can be employed. Broadly speaking, underground attacks entail low levels of military power. These characteristics, as shown below in greater detail, make underground tactics quite idiosyncratic.

2.3. Terrorism and Underground Political Violence

Our main theoretical claim establishes that *terrorism is underground political violence*. The political qualification is an important one. While we think that terrorism is underground violence, not all underground violence is terrorist. Unlike other forms of underground violence, terrorism is political. By that we simply mean that the violence is driven by political goals. Very broadly speaking, this presupposes that the terrorists seek some of the following: regime or policy change, territorial autonomy or secession, or the prevention of any of these. Regime change is the trademark of revolutionary groups; it may be highly varied from an ideological perspective, ranging from the classical Anarchist or Marxist group to jihadist groups fighting for Islamic rule. Secession is characteristic of nationalist groups with irredentist claims. These goals are not mutually exclusive; some groups may be revolutionary and secessionist simultaneously, like ETA, a secessionist group with a Socialist ideology, or Hamas, a nationalist Palestinian group with an Islamist ideology.[3]

---

[3] Groups fighting for territorial goals do not always manage to seize and hold territory. See Castan Pinos and Radil (2020) on this issue.

The boundaries of the political are not always easy to delimit. It is hard to decide, for instance, whether some religiously motivated underground attacks are political. In general, we see no objection to the inclusion of jihadist underground violence as terrorism, since the political goals are obvious (establishing an Islamic regime, toppling infidel governments, expelling foreign troops). However, there are forms of violence that, being religiously motivated, have only remote political implications. An interesting case in point is the sarin gas attack in the Tokyo underground in 1995 by Aum Shinrikyo, an apocalyptic Buddhist sect (Lifton, 2000). Obviously, the belief in the end of the world may have political consequences, but it is not so easy to be more specific. Although Aum Shinrikyo is usually covered in works on terrorism (see, for instance, Hoffman, 2006: 119), we are reluctant to follow suit. We agree that, from a security point of view, the authorities should be as concerned about Aum Shinrikyo as about any other group with a potential for violence, but, from an analytical perspective, a religious cult does not belong to the general category of political violence.

It is crucial to be clear on the importance of the political orientation of the violence since, otherwise, terrorism might be conflated with other forms that are similar in operational terms but obey a rather different constellation of motivations and determinants. Criminal organizations, for instance, commit violence for private reasons. Their violence, even if it may look similar to terrorism when they do not control territory, is driven by a non-political logic. Nonetheless, it is sometimes the case that criminal organizations decide to act for political reasons. When the Italian mafia killed high-profile public officials, as it did with the assassination of judges Giovanni Falcone and Paolo Borsellino in 1992, it was crossing the line, going from the private criminal business to political terrorism. But perhaps the most extreme case is the launching of a terrorist branch by the Medellin drug cartel, the so-called *Extraditables* (the Extraditables). Pablo Escobar funded and organized an underground group to carry out attacks against state officials and civilians to prevent the extradition of noted members of the cartel to the United States (Jamieson, 2005: 167–8). Political leaders, members of the government, judges, and journalists were targeted between 1989 and 1993. There was an explicit political goal, the prevention of extraditions by the Colombian state and, therefore, the resulting underground violence qualifies as terrorist. It is also well known that armed groups (including terrorist ones) enter into criminal activities, often related to drug production and trafficking, to fund their organizations (Asal, Milward, and Schoon, 2015).[4] These complications

---

[4] It is also the case that terrorist attacks have a positive effect on organized crime (Kreiman and Spadafor, 2022).

apart, the general point should be clear: there are different motivations for undertaking clandestine violence. Even if the boundaries between politically motivated armed groups and criminal organizations may be porous and difficult to operationalize, the conceptual distinction is not particularly problematic. This distinction is relevant insofar as the determinants of criminal groups and terrorist organizations may be entirely dissimilar.[5]

Terrorism, understood as underground political violence, is also different from underground operations carried out in the context of warfare for purely military reasons. Secret or covert operations are not alien to warfare. In a literal sense of the underground, subterranean warfare through tunnel making has been well studied (Richemond-Barak, 2018). In World War I, the trench war was heavily affected by tunnel construction. Tunnels allowed for mining operations, penetration in the enemy's territory, as well as capture of the front line (Jones, 2010). These were subterranean operations (in a purely physical sense) but also underground ones, in the sense that they were covert actions that took the enemy by surprise. Something similar can be said about blowing up a bridge in the enemy's terrain to block its advance or retreat. As long as this is a secret operation, it can be regarded as underground.

We exclude this type of action from terrorism, since they can be fully explained by their military value. There is no political motivation involved in these actions (although the conflict these actions are a part of may have political roots). Whether an underground or above-the-ground attack is more convenient is decided on purely military criteria.

A typical case in point is military sabotage in the context of war. Sabotage is defined as 'a mission (conducted via individual act or as part of a campaign) to secretly disarm, obstruct, or destroy enemy war materiel or infrastructure for military advantage' (Powell et al., 2021: 5). The reference to the secret nature of sabotage makes clear its affinity with underground terrorist operations. Sabotage has been well studied in naval affairs. Powell et al. (2021: 6) exclude Al Qaeda's 2000 attack against the USS *Cole* on the grounds that it was a terrorist attack rather than an act of war. Although the authors do not make explicit their definition of terrorism, it can be presumed that it is precisely the political intent of the terrorist attack that makes the USS *Cole* incident different from typical naval sabotage. Sabotage operations are covert; they are carried out by commandos, usually belonging to special operations units that can be as small as terrorist cells, and are forced to act

---

[5] This also applies to other forms of violence that share many characteristics with terrorism but, ultimately, are not politically motivated, such as incel violence (see Hoffman, Ware, and Shapiro, 2020), which we do not consider terrorism.

under strict clandestinity. What makes violence terrorist is, therefore, the combination of an underground operation and political motivation.

Let us examine in greater depth the intimate association between terrorism and the underground. This association is often implicit in detailed analyses of violence. In an analysis of ISIS' evolution, Hashim (2018: 236) introduces this comment:

> Control over territory allows the nonstate actor to build bases, to experiment out in the open with little fear of disruption, and to evolve from simpler or more 'primitive' methods of warfare, such as terrorism, to more advanced methods, such as guerrilla warfare, and ultimately to mobile semiconventional warfare.

Other authors make this association more explicit, tying the use of terrorism to the lack of territorial control. In his early work on insurgency, Walter Laqueur (1976) clearly distinguished between rural and urban guerrillas. In his view, 'the normal use of "urban guerrilla" is a euphemism for urban terrorism' (403). And, more importantly, 'Urban terrorists cannot normally establish "liberated zones"' (404). Ariel Merari is one of the first scholars who developed the distinction between guerrilla and terrorist groups in terms of territorial control. In his own words, 'the most important difference is that unlike terrorism, guerrilla tries to establish physical control of a territory' (Merari, 1993: 224). Likewise, Donatella Della Porta has written extensively on terrorism as clandestine violence (Della Porta, 1995); more recently, she has argued against the use of the very term 'terrorism', by introducing a generic category of clandestine political violence (Della Porta, 2013).

In his thorough organizational analysis of terrorist groups, Jacob N. Shapiro defines terrorism in terms of secrecy and lack of territorial control:

> Terrorist groups are, for the most part, small organizations operating somewhat secretly without the power to take and hold territory. The need for secrecy—which arises because such groups typically cannot exclude government forces from the areas where they operate, nor effectively fight back against security force efforts to capture or imprison their members—imposes a host of organizational challenges and constraints. (Shapiro, 2013: 2–3)

Many other examples can be found in the literature. DeNardo (1985: 39) states that 'the terrorists explode their bombs and issue demands from the underground without mobilizing anyone in public demonstrations'. Hoffman (2006: 35) distinguishes between guerrillas, insurgents, and terrorists: terrorists 'do not function in the open as armed units, generally do not attempt to seize or hold territory, deliberately avoid engaging enemy military forces in combat, are constrained both numerically and logistically from undertaking concerted mass political mobilization efforts, and exercise no direct control or governance over a populace at either the local or the national level'. Weinstein (2007: 17), in turn, distinguishes conflicts according to whether the rebels seek to gain control or not, and retains the term 'terrorism' for the latter. Smelser (2007: 91) writes that 'terrorist episodes are often carried out by clandestine groups'. Bergesen and Lizardo (2004: 38) define terrorism as 'a scattered and random event performed by clandestine groups of often small numbers'. Drake (1998: 2) says that terrorism is 'the recurrent use or threatened use of politically-motivated and clandestinely organized violence'. Kilcullen (2009: 12) establishes the link between terrorism and the underground when he refers to 'a classical terrorist organization (which draws its effectiveness from the motivation and cohesion of a small number of people in clandestine cells)'. Kahler (2009: 104) adds the political dimension to the underground condition: 'Unlike criminal networks, whose collective purpose is obscure, terrorist networks are political in their aims. Because their actions are, by definition, violent and illicit in the eyes of at least some governments, their actions must also be clandestine.'

Our conceptualization of terrorism as underground political violence has several advantages over the alternatives that were discussed in the previous chapter. To begin with, it makes room for variation in targets. There is nothing anomalous about underground armed actors targeting security forces. But, at the same time, our view provides a simple reason why terrorism and civilian victimization are so often associated. Given the above-mentioned constraints of the underground, soft targets (those who entail low risk for the perpetrators, such as civilians) may be selected more often than hard targets (such as security forces). As discussed below, the underground is especially constraining in international terrorist attacks, when those who carry out the attack act in a foreign country, that is, an unfamiliar terrain in which their isolation is particularly pronounced. These unfavourable conditions go a long way in the explanation of why civilians are the preferred target in international terrorist attacks. There are strong reasons, then, for expecting a positive association between terrorism and civilian victimization.

Secondly, the underground nature of terrorism is independent from the strategic goals that the perpetrators are pursuing. Most of the time, terrorists use coercive tactics that rely on the power to hurt and, therefore, on forms of violence that presuppose the distinction between the direct and indirect targets of violence. But our conceptualization also embodies the patterns of violence of those clandestine groups whose attacks aim at raising consciousness and mobilizing constituencies.

Third, our conceptualization is agnostic about the nature of the perpetrators, unlike many definitions that rule out the participation of states by fiat. We therefore avoid the typical ideological charge that the terrorist scholars are usually biased against the rebel side by not identifying states as terrorist. Because we think that the use of terrorism is driven by a high asymmetry in power between the armed actors (see Chapter 3), it is only natural that rebels will end up triggering more terrorist attacks than states. But this is a logical consequence of the argument, not an arbitrary decision.

Finally, it is also the case that by understanding terrorism as underground political violence, many of the disjointed characteristics associated to terrorism fit each other, revealing in this way the unifying or organizing power of the conceptualization we propose. This will be apparent in the next section, where we offer a map of violence that puts terrorism in its proper place compared with other types of violence. The map is complex, requiring some careful study. Yet, this is crucial for revealing the full explanatory power of our conceptualization.

2.4. A Conceptual Map of Terrorism

In the previous chapter we mentioned that the very term 'terrorism' is peculiar when compared with other nouns used to refer to conflict (genocide, guerrilla, war, and so on). Whereas conflicts are represented by concrete nouns, 'terrorism' is an abstract one. The adjective, 'terrorist', can be applied to a variety of settings, as in 'terrorist attacks', 'terrorist conflicts', 'terrorist groups', 'terrorist operations', and the like. Ordinary language is telling us here something deep about the nature of the phenomenon, namely that the term is a protean one that cannot be reduced by linguistic fiat to one of its possible senses. It is precisely because terrorism is polymorphous that we need an 'ism' word to name it.

If there are various irreducible senses of terrorism, then we have to give up on the possibility of establishing a dictionary-like definition of the word. We must come to terms with the uncomfortable fact that we do not talk about terrorism in a single sense. For the sake of simplicity, two senses will suffice to capture most of what is said about the phenomenon: the action- and the actor-senses. The action-sense has to do with certain attacks that we consider terrorist regardless of the identity or nature of the perpetrator.

The actor-sense, however, assumes that certain perpetrators are (inherently) terrorist. At this level of abstraction, the distinction may sound tautological: terrorists are those who commit terrorist acts and terrorist acts are those carried out by terrorists. But, as we will see throughout this section, the action- and the actor-senses do not fully overlap and therefore tautology is avoided.

Interestingly, the distinction between the two senses can be illustrated through the different ways in which terrorism is conceptualized in national legal codes. Although countries have been unable to find common ground for an official, universal definition endorsed by the United Nations (Saul, 2019: 40), many have sought to establish their own definitions. In the common law systems, terrorism tends to be defined in the action-sense, as a certain type of violent act (see Golder and Williams (2004) for a comparative review). In the USA, for instance, terrorism is defined in section 2331 (Chapter 113B, Title 18 of the US Code) as acts that violate the criminal laws of the USA and are intended '(i) to intimidate or coerce a civilian population; (ii) to influence the policy of a government by intimidation or coercion; or (iii) to affect the conduct of a government by mass destruction, assassination, or kidnapping'. Although this is the dominant definition, section 2656F of Chapter 38, on annual country reports on terrorism, introduces the actor-sense when it refers to terrorist groups in foreign countries. Both the USA and the EU maintain and update lists of foreign terrorist groups. These lists, however, are subject to political and geostrategic considerations (de Jonge Oudraat and Marret, 2010): the USA, for instance, did not want to include the Provisional IRA (PIRA) due to pressure from the Irish lobby, and the EU excluded Hezbollah because of France's interests in Lebanon.

European penal codes, particularly those of countries that possess direct experience with protracted domestic terrorist conflicts (such as ETA in Spain, the Red Brigades in Italy, and the Red Army Faction in Germany), tend to emphasize the actor-sense. In Spain, article 570 of the Penal Code defines a terrorist group as a criminal group aimed at subverting the constitutional order or the alteration of public peace. In Italy, article 270 of the Penal Code also defines what a terrorist group is and specifies that, in order to qualify as terrorist, the violence displayed by the group must be aimed at causing grave harm to the country, its institutions, or international organizations. In Germany, section 129 of the Criminal Code states that criminal organizations whose aims or objectives are murder, genocide, crimes against humanity or against personal liberty, are considered terrorist. In this legal approach, being a member of such a group is already a criminal offence. This is clearly based on the actor-sense, on certain armed groups being terrorist.

In the actor-sense, therefore, we look for groups that can be described as terrorist. Our main point here is that these are groups that do not gain territorial control and remain underground. In principle, this may be the case either because they are not interested in becoming a full insurgency with territorial control or because the enemy is so powerful that it prevents the armed groups gaining territorial control (see Chapter 3). The fact is that if they are clandestine, they are bound to use terrorist methods.

The actor-sense is frequently employed in the literature on political violence. It is based on the analysis of the organizations that produce terrorist violence. The unit of analysis is the actor rather than the act. In game-theory approaches, formal models analyse the interaction between a state and a terrorist group (as in Bueno de Mesquita, 2005). There is also a literature in which terrorist groups are examined as case studies (among many others, Berger, 2006; Dartnell, 1995; Heghammer, 2010; Kassimeris, 2001; Sánchez-Cuenca, 2001), as well as comparative, large- and small-n analyses in which the unit of observation is the terrorist group (to mention a few, Asal and Rethemeyer, 2008; Burstein, 2018; Cronin, 2009; De la Calle, 2015a; Jones and Libicky, 2008; Sánchez-Cuenca, 2019; Shapiro, 2013). In the previous section, almost every quotation in the list of authors who emphasize the link between terrorism and underground violence corresponds to the actor-sense. There is then a strong case to be made for the autonomy of the actor-sense of terrorism, based on characteristics of the organization, namely being underground versus holding territorial control.

The action-sense requires less of a justification since it is, arguably, the dominant one in the literature on terrorism (for instance, see Kydd and Walter, 2006). Terrorism is regarded as a special kind of tactic that can be adopted by any armed group. The nature of the perpetrator is not a relevant consideration; what matters is the kind of violence employed. Terrorism is used when the conditions are such that the armed group has minimum military power and relies on the power to hurt. If we think about what kinds of attacks can be carried out when military power is minimum, the examples that come to mind are IEDs, selective shootings (including snipers), assassinations, hijackings, kidnappings, and small-scale ambushes. All this falls short of a military confrontation with the state army, or large-scale armed assaults. Compared with military bombs, which are industrially produced and used in the context of war, IEDs are handmade and employed in irregular wars, but also in times of peace, to disrupt the social order. The fabrication of IEDs does not require military power as such, and the devices are detonated by surprise. Selective shootings can be carried out with just firearms. A sniper can act alone and shoot from the roof of a building. Both hijackings and kidnappings can

52   Underground Violence

be organized by small teams without military technology beyond firearms. An ambush of a police patrol or a military convoy requires some minimum degree of military organization. Our point is that all these tactics are associated with terrorism because they are consistent with acting underground.[6]

These tactics contrast with those that are employed in guerrilla conflicts, based on military skirmishes, ambushes, raids, seizing of buildings and villages, armed assaults and even small-scale battles in the open. The boundaries with terrorist tactics may be fuzzy; an ambush can be observed both in the context of terrorism and in the context of guerrilla warfare. But even if this description cannot but be impressionistic given the sheer complexity and variation of violence, the general theme seems clear: the conditions for most guerrilla tactics are more demanding in terms of military power and effective control of space. Precisely because the use of guerrilla tactics entails some form of military power, the tactics have an offensive side that is absent when terrorism is employed. Thus, armed groups that use guerrilla violence can aim at expanding their base of operations and at gaining control over new space. Terrorist tactics, by themselves, are insufficient to achieve territorial control: a bomb explosion may be useful to destroy a building and spread terror, but if the goal is to seize a village, the rebels' physical presence is necessary; and this can only be achieved by using some type of guerrilla tactic.

The two senses of terrorism do not fully overlap; if they did, the distinction would be irrelevant; that is, we would reach the same conclusions from either side of the coin, the actor- or the action-sense. The imperfect overlap accounts for some of the unavoidable ambiguities that come with the term 'terrorism'.

Our main thesis can be formulated as follows: *all the violence perpetrated by armed underground groups is terrorist, but not all terrorist violence is carried out by underground groups.* More specifically, when non-underground groups act under the constraints of clandestinity, they resort to terrorist attacks. Terrorism, then, can be understood as the political violence of underground groups plus the violence of non-underground groups which, under particular circumstances, act underground.

To fully analyse the consequences of clandestinity, we employ a 2×2 table with the actor-sense in columns and the action-sense in rows (Table 2.1) (see De la Calle and Sánchez-Cuenca, 2011a for an initial formulation). Representing the different possibilities as cells in a table may convey the wrong

---

[6] The fact that these tactics can be employed for non-political purposes (see, e.g., Richards, 2015) is not really an objection, since we limit ourselves to the analysis of political violence.

Table 2.1 The intersection of the two senses of terrorism

		Actor sense	
		Underground	Territorial control
Action sense	Coercive violence (IEDs, hijackings, selective shootings, etc.)	Pure terrorism	Terrorist violence carried out by insurgent groups
	Military power (battles, raids, seizing villages, etc.)	Proto-guerrilla	Pure guerrilla

idea that these are fixed categories. The matrix, useful as it is, does not capture the fluidity and dynamics between the various categories of violence. As will be seen below in the comments on each cell, an armed group can navigate between the four of them in different stages and, likewise, an armed group can combine in complex ways several of the possibilities outlined in the table. We start by focusing on the pure cases of Table 2.1, those of the main diagonal, and then we move into the more challenging cases, those of the secondary diagonal.

Pure Terrorism

In the first cell, we have underground groups that carry out coercive violence with a minimum of military power. The result is pure terrorist violence. Here, the rebels do not have territorial control and the kind of coercive tactics they employ are consistent with the group being underground (IEDs, selective shootings, hijackings, and the other aforementioned attacks).

The examples of fully underground groups that never gain territorial control and carry out attacks that we associate with terrorism are numerous. In the leftist or revolutionary tradition, the wave of anarchist terrorism during the 1875–1925 period is a perfect instance of underground violence based mainly on bombings and assassinations. According to Sánchez-Cuenca's (2019) dataset, there were 191 fatalities in Western countries (excluding Russia) during this period. Violence was conceived as a form of propaganda—'the propaganda by the deed' doctrine, as formulated by Bakunin (1971: 195–6); see also Linse (1982)—aimed at mobilizing the working class in an insurrectionary uprising against bourgeois society. The attacks were intended to 'open the eyes' of the oppressed and reveal the vulnerability of the state. Anarchist terrorism was particularly intense in France, Italy, Spain, and the

54   Underground Violence

United States (being milder in Germany and pretty much absent in smaller Western nations).

From an organizational point of view, the anarchists always acted secretly. There were no formal organizations with a hierarchical structure, but loosely connected networks of activists and even a significant presence of lone-actors, who sometimes moved from one country to another (see below on lone-actors). A couple of illustrations help to make the point. Santo Caserio was an Italian who killed the French President, Sadi Carnot, in 1894, avenging the execution of the anarchist Emile Henry; he acted by himself, under his own initiative (Merriman, 2009: 206). Likewise, Michele Angiolillo was another Italian who killed the Spanish Prime Minister, Antonio Cánovas del Castillo, in 1897, in reprisal for the repression of fellow anarchists in the Montjuich prison in Barcelona (Núñez Florencio, 1983: 59–60).

Consistent with their clandestine condition, most anarchist attacks employed IEDs: according to the dataset, 86 per cent of all deaths were due to bombs. A further 8 per cent were killed through selective shootings. In fact, the anarchists invented the car bomb, first used in the infamous Wall Street bomb attack of 1920 (38 fatalities) (Davis, 2007; Gage, 2009). Decades later, other revolutionary or left-wing groups followed a similar selection of tactics, including the Tupamaros in Uruguay, the GRAPO in Spain, the Red Brigades in Italy, and the Red Army Faction in Germany. These were all underground groups whose main technologies of violence comprised bombs and selective shootings.

In the ethnonational family, ETA is a paradigmatic example of an underground, long-lasting terrorist group. It never gained any territorial control in the Basque Country. Although ETA enjoyed significant social support in specific areas of the Gipuzkoa province, the presence of the state prevented the formation of a 'liberated zone' (see Chapter 4). In the case of the Provisional IRA, despite the short-lived experience of the no-go areas (see above), the PIRA was, to all effects, an underground group too. The PIRA came close to gaining territorial control in the southern part of Armagh County; because of the risk of ambushes and landmines, the British army had to use helicopters to transport troops (Harnden, 1999: 19). PIRA's use of mortars and missiles in this area indicates a certain level of military power resembling that of guerrillas. The power of the PIRA in south Armagh was due to (i) the absence of Protestants, (ii) the strong support for Republicanism among Catholics, and (iii) the border with the Republic of Ireland, which worked as PIRA's 'sanctuary' or safe haven.

Another notable case in the context of national liberation struggle is the Irgun (the *Irgun Zvai Leumi*, National Military Organization), which was an underground, secret organization, founded in 1931 in British Palestine. As Menachem Begin wrote in his memoirs, *The Revolt*, in Israel 'there was neither mountain nor forest for the rebels to hide in. We were completely exposed to the enemy's eyes. [...] We were, in short, everyday citizens indistinguishable from other citizens' (Begin, 1972: 105–6).

Similar statements can be found among other underground groups. In a completely different historical, ideological, and geographical context, the Tupamaros in Uruguay wrote in one of their founding documents, using 'Che' Guevara's terminology: 'Uruguay lacks the geographical conditions for a rural guerrilla. [...] There is nowhere in the country to make the creation of an enduring rural guerrilla *foco* possible' (Torres, 2002; our translation) (see Chapter 4). Zawahiri, Al Qaeda's leader following the killing of Osama Bin Laden, reflected in these terms about the prospects of a guerrilla movement in Egypt: 'the River Nile runs in its narrow valley between two deserts that have no vegetation or water. Such a terrain made guerrilla warfare in Egypt impossible' (Gerges, 2009: 87).

In the case of Irgun, clandestinity had some peculiarities. Only a few dozen activists were fully underground; the vast majority were 'ordinary people' leading 'normal lives', who participated in secret operations when they were called. Begin (1972: 108) calls this type of peculiar organization an 'overt underground', since people moved freely from the underground to the open and vice versa. Irgun's tactics, particularly before 1944, were quintessentially terrorist: bombings and selective shootings. The attacks were part of an attrition strategy aimed at increasing the cost of the British authorities to remain in Israel (van Tonder, 2019: 40). These were combined with sectarian attacks against the Arab local population (for instance, in June 1939, Irgun exploded a bomb in one of Haifa's markets, killing 18 Arabs). The conflict escalated in 1944, when Begin issued his proclamation of revolt. In the following years, Irgun expanded and began to act like a militia by displaying guerrilla tactics. However, its most horrific and devastating attack was a typical terrorist act, the bombing of the King David Hotel on 22 July 1946, in a building which had become Britain's administrative headquarters: although some warning calls were made before the blast, the building was not evacuated, which resulted in 91 fatalities (including 17 Jews). The bomb was not intended to defeat the British army, but rather to break its will.

In the Islamist variety of terrorism, it is also possible to find clandestine groups such as Jemaa Islamiyah in Southeast Asia (Hastings, 2010) or al-Jamaʾa al-Islamiyah (the Islamic Group, IG) in Egypt (Kepel, 2003: Ch. 12). The IG tried to gain control of urban territory in Imbaba, on the outskirts of Cairo: in 1992, the sheikh Gaber proclaimed that Imbaba was a liberated

56 Underground Violence

republic, but Mubarak's response was to send 14,000 troops, and arrest 5,000 people. During the 1992–7 cycle of violence, the IG acted as an underground group, carrying out assassinations, selective shootings, and some bombings aimed at Egyptian authorities, secular intellectuals, security forces, tourists, and Copts (Hafez and Wiktorowicz, 2004).

More controversially, the 'pure type of terrorism' might also be exemplified by the French Resistance. Of course, the very suggestion that the Resistance was terrorist may sound unacceptable to those who use the term for political reasons, assuming that 'terrorism' is always a derogatory word. The problem is compounded because the Vichy regime referred to resisters as 'terrorists'. Some of the resisters, however, proudly accepted the 'terrorist' label (Millington, 2018). In any case, from a purely analytical point of view, the terrorist condition of the French Resistance seems an inescapable conclusion. It was an underground organization that, for political reasons, involved itself in operations of sabotage and harassment of the invaders, as well as in punishment operations against Vichy collaborators. In Paris it was a fully urban underground movement; in the countryside, the *Maquis* (as in Spain; see above) were organized as roving bands that operated in the hills and in forests, with no permanent territorial base.

The Resistance was not the same everywhere. In Italy, the main activity was developed by partisans acting as guerrilla groups in mountainous terrain. But there was also an urban guerrilla group, the GAP (*Gruppi di azione patriottica*, Groups of Patriotic Action), founded by the Italian Communist Party, that was fully underground and carried out typically terrorist attacks (i.e., bombings and assassinations). Because of their secret nature, they were defined as 'soldiers without uniform' and their armed activity was framed in terms of terrorism (Peli, 2014: 4–5, 14, 27).

There are two limiting cases that illustrate the fully underground condition of pure terrorism: international terrorism and lone-actor terrorism. This is violence that, because of its very particular conditions, cannot but be associated with terrorism. We briefly examine each in turn.

We understand by international terrorism those attacks in which the perpetrators act out of their own country.[7] When the perpetrators go abroad,

---

[7] For a long period of time, from the 1970s to the 1990s, the empirical analysis of terrorism focused on international attacks. The first dataset of terrorist activity, ITERATE, only registered international events. These were defined as attacks in which more than two nationalities are involved, either because the target's nationality is different from the perpetrator's nationality or because the perpetrators are from different nationalities or they act out of their national country (see, for instance, Rosendorff and Sandler, 2005: 172). This definition of international terrorism is problematical, equating an attack against a foreigner in the perpetrators' country with an attack out of the perpetrators' country (see Sánchez-Cuenca and De la Calle (2009) for a more detailed analysis). The opportunities and constraints, as well as the political consequences, of killing a foreigner in the perpetrators' country are quite different from that of killing abroad.

disguising themselves among the population is harder, as there is no network of safe houses, intelligence is more difficult to collect, and acquiring weapons is riskier. As mentioned previously, most international terrorist attacks target civilians, simply because these are soft targets and/or because the terrorists seek maximum publicity for their deeds. The prevalence of civilian victimization in international attacks is one relevant reason why international organizations and state agencies (as well as a high number of experts) tend to define terrorism as targeting civilians (see Chapter 1, section 1.4); these are, moreover, the attacks that attract the greatest attention. Thus, domestic terrorist deeds, because they are relatively 'normal events' within a sustained campaign of violence, or because they are contemplated as a local issue, or simply because they are seen as being under the prism of guerrilla movements, tend to be overlooked in the public and legal discussion on the nature of terrorism. This is very unfortunate, since international attacks represent less than one-fifth of all terrorist attacks, constituting a strongly biased sample from which no general conclusions should be inferred.[8]

For our purposes, the most interesting aspect of international terrorism is that it represents underground violence in its purest form. When the terrorists act abroad, their connection with their community of support is completely severed. By moving to another country, they are entirely self-reliant, and they have to act in utmost secrecy. The constraints of clandestinity bite with maximum intensity, forcing the terrorists to use pure terrorist tactics. A paradigmatic example is the suicide bomb attack by Hezbollah in the Israeli Embassy in Buenos Aires on 17 March 1992, killing 29 people in response to the Israeli assassination of Hezbollah's general secretary, Sayyed Abbas Mussawi. Hezbollah's cell travelled from Beirut to London to Ciudad del Este (Paraguay), where they recruited some Shi'ite locals who acted as a local support cell in the Buenos Aires operation (Bergman, 2008: 172).

A significant number of international attacks come in the form of hijacking. This was particularly frequent in the late 1960s and early 1970s, with many attacks carried out by Palestinian groups (see Chapter 5). Hijackings had a huge communicative impact, making the Palestinian cause known all over the world. The fact that some of these attacks ended in civilian massacres was crucial in boosting the deeds' visibility.

Beyond Palestinian groups, there are groups that operate mostly at international level. An interesting case is ASALA (the Armenian Secret Army for

---

[8] Enders, Sandler, and Gaibulloev (2011) decompose the Global Terrorism Database (GTD) attacks into domestic and transnational using ITERATE's peculiar definition of international terrorism. Even with their expansive criteria, the percentage of transnational terrorism represents only 19 per cent of all attacks in the 1970–2007 period (after excluding from the calculations almost 20 per cent of all attacks in the original sample on the grounds that they are not purely terrorist; most of them are domestic attacks).

the Liberation of Armenia) (Kurz and Merari, 1985): tellingly, the group described itself as a 'secret' organization, conveying that it acted underground. It used to have a base in Lebanon and received help from Palestinian organizations. During its early years, in the late 1970s, the main target of their operations was Turkish diplomats. In a second phase, they broadened their targets to Western countries that had previously acted against ASALA. Kurz and Merari (1985: Appendix 4) report 91 attacks for the period 1981–4, 85 of them out of Lebanon and only six in Lebanon. This means that 93 per cent of the attacks took place in countries other than the country in which they had their operational base. It should not be a surprise that most of these attacks consisted of bombings.

The organization that immediately comes to mind for international attacks in the 21st century is Al Qaeda. We focus here on central Al Qaeda, leaving aside local branches or affiliates that act as Islamist insurgencies at the domestic level on behalf of, or in the name of, central Al Qaeda. Our main contention is that central Al Qaeda represents a unique case of a truly transnational or global organization—unlike ISIS, it has never tried to seize and rule territory on its own. This uniqueness, however, has more implications for the actor-sense of terrorism than for the action-one. Because of the transnational orientation of the group, its relationship with territory is quite different from the vast majority of terrorist organizations. From the action-sense, however, Al Qaeda is not so problematical.

Regarding the actor-sense, Al Qaeda presents three differential characteristics. Firstly, it lacks a specific national affiliation. It was born out of the experience of the mujahideen combating the Soviets in Afghanistan. In 1984, Abdullah Azzam created the Services Bureau, a network to recruit foreign fighters and to train them for the struggle in Afghanistan. Four years later, Al Qaeda itself was founded. After the withdrawal of the USSR in 1989, Al Qaeda redirected its activities, becoming a kind of rebel hub for organizing the fight against corrupt and secular (infidel) regimes in Muslim countries (Cragin, 2008). Al Qaeda established its headquarters first in Pakistan in 1988 and then in Sudan in 1991, and remained there until 1996. In that year, it moved back to Afghanistan, under the protection of the Taliban. After the US invasion of Afghanistan in 2001, it moved again to Pakistan in 2002, to the Federally Administered Tribal Area (FATA). The organization, therefore, had various territorial bases, but these were safe havens or sanctuaries rather than controlled or liberated territory. As they were under the protection of Islamist regimes in Sudan and Afghanistan, there was no reason to act there. It was only after 2001, once Al Qaeda settled in Pakistan's FATA, that it worked with the Taliban by launching attacks in Afghanistan (Gunaratna and Nielsen, 2008).

The existence of a safe haven was absolutely crucial for the development of Al Qaeda. As Thomas Heghammer (2010: 108) explains:

> The arguably most important lesson from the history of al-Qaida is that unhampered access to territory can dramatically increase a terrorist group's military capability. For a start, the safe haven allowed al-Qaida to quietly plan operations on its own schedule with virtually no outside interference. Moreover, it allowed Bin Ladin to build a core organization with a relatively high degree of bureaucratization and functional task division, which in turn improved organizational efficiency. Most important of all, territorial access enabled Bin Ladin to set up an elaborate military educational system, the like of which has never been seen in the hands of a transnational terrorist organization.

The group, moreover, did not develop the kind of relationship with the local population that is observed when a guerrilla holds territorial control. Al Qaeda trained people who were dispatched to various places such as Bosnia, Chechnya, Egypt, Somalia, and Yemen. Despite the emergence of numerous Islamist insurgencies during the 1990s, there was not a single case of Islamist rebels taking power beyond Afghanistan. While there were great hopes among Islamists regarding the Algerian civil war, where the GIA subjected the country to a blood bath in 1997–8, the insurgents were eventually defeated. It was this utter failure to overthrow the secular regimes that led Bin Laden to reconsider the strategy, moving into clandestine or underground operations against Western targets and becoming a global terrorist group (Gerges, 2009; Holmes, 2005: 168; Kepel, 2003: Introduction; Sageman, 2008: 42). To this nearly universal failure, Heghammer (2020: 493) adds the role played by the harsh repression of the local jihadi movements by the national Arab governments in Al Qaeda's shift to the global scene.

Secondly, the nationality of Al Qaeda members is not associated with a particular country. The leaders and recruits come from many different countries, including, among others, Afghanistan, Algeria, Egypt, Jordan, Libya, Saudi Arabia, and Yemen. This makes Al Qaeda a truly multinational organization (Gunaratna, 2002: 1).

Thirdly, Al Qaeda combines national and global aims. The ultimate goal, the formation of a World Caliphate, is a global ambition in itself. On the path to the World Caliphate, Al Qaeda may select some intermediate campaigns over others (expelling US troops from Saudi Arabia, helping the Taliban in Afghanistan, etc.); but all are subordinate to the ultimate goal. This is quite different from a domestic group attacking abroad for domestic reasons, such as, for instance, the GIA carrying out attacks in French territory in the context of the Algerian civil war.

By acting in this way, Al Qaeda has created a sort of multilevel governance structure, with central Al Qaeda on top and several regional branches beneath it (Gartenstein-Ross and Joscelyn, 2022: Ch. 8). To some extent, this has been an organizational innovation in the history of terrorism, later replicated by ISIS in direct competition with Al Qaeda. Central Al Qaeda has specialized in international attacks, but its regional or national branches adapt flexibly to the terrain and the political conditions. Al Qaeda in Arabian Peninsula (AQAP) offers a nice illustration of this flexibility, in line with our theoretical expectations. AQAP was an underground group that launched a typical campaign of urban terrorist attacks during 2003 and 2004 in Saudi Arabia (Heghammer, 2010). The Saudi security forces were able to halt the offensive, which only lasted for 18 months. After this defeat, AQAP was revived in 2009, acting mainly in Yemen. After the Arab Spring, AQAP became a formidable insurgency with territorial control in areas of Yemen, including cities, and participated in the civil war as one of the contending parties (Knoll, 2017). This example shows the versatility of Al Qaeda and its capacity for adaptation to changing circumstances: underground in an effective state, guerrilla-like in a weak one.

Central Al Qaeda's attacks against American and Western targets, from the truck bombs against US embassies in Kenya and Tanzania in August 1998, to the suicide attack against the USS *Cole* in Yemen in October 2000, to the multiple attacks on 9/11 2001, fit well the mould of international terrorist operations. Thus, from an action-sense, the international attacks launched by Al Qaeda were undeniably terrorist (including the attack again on the USS *Cole*, which was a military target): they were secret operations that employed improvised explosive devices (and hijackings on 9/11).

The main point to be taken is that international attacks represent the purest instance of underground violence. The perpetrators act in complete isolation, detached from their own cultural and social references. The constraints of clandestinity are particularly tight in this case.

Something similar can be said about lone-actor terrorism. Because of the unique characteristics associated with underground operations, terrorism is the only form of political violence that can be carried out by a single individual (McCauley and Moskalenko, 2014).[9] Other forms of political violence (guerrilla activity, genocide, riots, mutinies, intercommunal conflict, and the like) are all inherently collective endeavours that require the coordination

---

[9] This includes assassinations carried out by a single individual (if there was a political motivation, as opposed to vengeance). In the dataset on assassinations analysed by Jones and Olken (2009), 59 per cent of all assassinations correspond to solo perpetrators (the sample is formed by 298 cases, covering the period 1875–2004).

and cooperation of multiple people. If terrorism is different, it is due to its secret nature.

Spaaij (2010: 856) defines lone-actor ('lone-wolf') terrorism as 'terrorist attacks carried out by persons who (a) operate individually, (b) do not belong to an organized terrorist group or network, and (c) whose modi operandi are conceived and directed by the individual without any direct outside command or hierarchy'. This definition is quite restrictive as it excludes attacks carried out by a few individuals—for example, other datasets on lone-actor terrorism include Timothy McVeigh, even if he was helped by another person (Gill, 2015). Not counting McVeigh's attack, the most lethal attack ever by a lone-actor is Andreas Breivik's in Norway on 22 July 2011: in two consecutive attacks, first a car bomb in Oslo and then shooting participants in a summer camp of the youth branch of the Labour Party on the island of Utoya, Breivik killed 77 people in total. The USA has a long tradition of extreme right-wing attacks by lone-actors, and also some left-wingers like Theodore J. Kaczynsky (aka 'the Unabomber'), who was able to remain active between 1978 and 1995 (Phillips, 2017). If we look further into the past, some of the late 19th-century assassinations conducted by anarchists that were mentioned above also qualify as lone-actor terrorism.

If we raise the existence of this variety of terrorism here it is simply because it illustrates the uniqueness of terrorist violence. Terrorism is the only form of political violence compatible with a single perpetrator acting alone. The reason why this is possible has nothing to do with the identity of the target or its coercive intent, but with the underground, secret condition of this type of violence.

Pure Guerrilla

The other element of the main diagonal in Table 2.1 is pure guerrilla violence. By that we refer to the violence that follows from groups that gain some degree of territorial control and launch guerrilla warfare against the state. As mentioned above, there is a grey zone between territorial and underground groups, with some ambiguous, intermediate cases.

Pure guerrilla violence can be exemplified by the *Fuerzas Armadas Revolucionarias de Colombia* (FARC). The FARC were created in 1964, out of the peasant self-defence forces in the settler communities formed by displaced people during the period of *La Violencia* (1948–57). They were under the control of Communist leaders and, because of the remote locations of the settlements, the state did not have any presence there (actually, they were called 'independent republics') (Steele, 2017: 72–8). The triggering event in the establishment of the FARC was the army's attempt to gain control of one of these settlements, Marquetalia, in 1964. The FARC was originally conceived as a defensive organization, which sought to preserve social order in these 'liberated' communities. It was only in 1982 that they adopted an offensive strategy and sought to expand territorially. The organization grew between that year and 1995. With the growing presence of the paramilitaries, competing with the FARC for territorial control, the civil war entered its bloodiest phase, from 1996 to 2005, with many civilian massacres and selective killings. However, from 2006 the state was increasingly able to impose order. The FARC were organized in 'frentes' (fronts), formed by a few hundred recruits. At its peak, in 2002, the FARC had 62 fronts across the country, a total of 28,000 recruits and some presence (from partial to full territorial control) in 622 municipalities (60 per cent of the total) (GMH, 2013: 162).

The FARC were able to launch military attacks against the Colombian army, particularly after 1995. These attacks might involve as many as one thousand guerrillas (Pécaut, 2008: 40). The guerrilla tried to become the local ruler in large 'liberated' or 'demilitarized' areas. The leader of the FARC, Manuel Marulanda, said in an interview in 1999:

> We are the authority in a large part of the national territory. You can see that for yourself on our fronts. There is a police inspection, two guerrilleros show up and the inspector tells them: I have a problem and I need your help to fix it. The authority in these areas is the guerrilla. Mayors cannot work unless they talk with the guerrilla on how to organize good government. In practice, we are a government within the government, which is why we are asking to be recognized as a belligerent force. (Aguilera, 2013: 96; our translation)

The offensive campaign of the late 1990s included attacks against army garrisons, the temporary occupation of medium-size villages, sabotage aimed at energy infrastructure, and taking military prisoners. A case in point of pure guerrilla activity was the seizing of the military base Las Delicias, in the department of Putumayo, on 30 August 1996. Several hundred guerrillas participated in the operation. They used mortars, rifle grenades, hand grenades, and firearms. The combat lasted for almost two days. The FARC killed 28 members of the army and retained 60 more as prisoners. They were liberated 10 months later, as a gesture of goodwill in the preparatory phase of negotiations with Ernesto Samper's government. In the late 1990s there were several other similar attacks against military targets (Echandía, 2000: 120).

The scale of such a guerrilla attack required complex organizational and logistical resources. The goal was to occupy an army garrison. Both the kind of weaponry and the number of combatants contrast with the constraints under which underground attacks take place. This example might convey the impression that guerrilla attacks are directed against combatants, while terrorist ones target civilians. This impression, however, is unwarranted. What makes this attack 'guerrilla' is the characteristics of the attack itself (based on some military power and occupation of the space) rather than its target.

In fact, the guerrilla's military power can be used against civilians too. A good example is the Mozambique National Resistance Movement (Renamo), created in the mid-1970s in Rhodesia to combat the Marxist-Leninist government of Frelimo (the Mozambique Liberation Front); after the transformation of Rhodesia into Zimbabwe in 1979, South Africa became Renamo's main sponsor. The war broke out in 1977, but the group only managed to establish a base in the country's central provinces two years later. In a few years it gained full territorial control and became a formidable insurgency, with over 20,000 recruits and governance structures. Militarily, Renamo was organized in battalions comprising two to three companies of 100–150 men (Hultman, 2009: 828). Its initial strategy aimed at 'suffocating' the government through the destruction of economic activity, and attacking transportation and communication infrastructures, but the larger goal was to destabilize the political system, so that the regime would eventually collapse. It is here where brutal attacks against civilians enter into the picture. Renamo was not particularly interested in punishing Frelimo's social base. Rather, it sought to destroy the structure of communal villages that Frelimo had built (Lunstrum, 2009). This included raids in which members of Renamo set fire to houses, looted villages, abducted young men (and children), raped women, and mutilated dwellers. Weinstein (2007: 232) reports 112 massacres by Renamo that each caused over 15 fatalities. Massacres were far more frequent in the Southern provinces of the country, where Renamo had a weaker presence (Hultman, 2009).

Another infamous illustration of the guerrilla's civilian victimization is the GIA (Armed Islamic Group) in Algeria. The massacres against civilians in 1997–8 were so brutal that they provoked disbelief among many observers. One of the best-known events took place in the village of Rais (around 1,000 inhabitants), on 29 August 1997, only 25 kilometres away from Algiers. At one in the morning, several trucks arrived in the village, carrying rebels with firearms, knives, axes, and IEDs. According to some witnesses, some perpetrators wore uniforms. For five hours, they beheaded and cut the throats of dozens of people, often entire families. It is unclear how many people were killed, but 200–300 is a prudent estimate. The guerrillas also abducted several women. Despite its random or indiscriminate appearance, these massacres sought to punish those who were switching sides from the Islamist forces to the government (Kalyvas, 1999). According to GIA chief Abu al-Moudhir, 'it is clear that there is no indiscriminate killing. [...] When you hear of killings and throat-slittings in a town or a village, you should know it is a matter of government partisans' (Wiktorowicz, 2001: 70). The massacres, which included burning and bombing houses, were acts of occupation of the village space. No matter how brief the occupation was, the physical presence of the guerrillas set in motion a dynamic of violence that is remarkably different from that of underground operations.

The FARC, Renamo, and GIA examples vividly reflect the differences between underground and open attacks. The guerrilla attacks that we have referred to cannot be replicated by underground groups. Renamo's and GIA's raids were multi-member operations that sought to physically occupy villages and had a temporal development. These tactics were possible because both groups had the necessary logistical capabilities, thanks ultimately to their territorial control. Terrorist violence against civilians is of a different kind, based instead on shootings and bombings carried out by a very small number of perpetrators in ephemeral operations.

Having said this, the fact is that groups with territorial control can also employ terrorist tactics. In the next subsection, we explore in greater depth the possibility of combining territorial control in the actor-sense and coercive tactics in the action-sense.

Terrorist Violence Carried Out by Insurgent Groups

Underground groups have no other option but to resort to coercive violence. The constraints of clandestinity limit the range of violent tactics that they can employ: as mentioned above, selective shootings, IEDs, hijackings, hostage taking, and similar tactics that do not require heavy weaponry. In the case of insurgent groups with territorial control, the set of feasible alternatives is broader, as their range of choice goes from conventional warfare to guerrilla warfare and terrorism. Hezbollah is an interesting example. It has featured conventional warfare (as in the 2006 war against Israel, see Biddle, 2021: Ch. 5), but also guerrilla activity and terrorism (De la Calle and Sánchez-Cuenca, 2015). Apart from international terrorist attacks, Hezbollah carried out two of the most consequential terrorist attacks ever on 23 October 1983: the suicide missions against the military headquarters of the US and French troops in Beirut. The two blasts caused 305 fatalities, 299 of which were military. The impact was enormous, as the USA and France opted to withdraw their troops from Lebanon. Although there had been previous suicide missions in the area (Gambetta, 2005: 286), these attacks made headlines all over the world and put suicide bombings on the radar of many other armed groups. Again, the target was combatants, but the attacks were unmistakably terrorist in the way they were executed: underground violence, by surprise, featuring a low number of perpetrators, aimed at breaking the will of the foreign armies.

The fact that non-underground groups can use terrorist tactics produces an asymmetry in the actor- and the action-senses of terrorism. Terrorist violence in the action-sense cannot be equated with the activity of terrorist groups in the actor-sense, since armed groups that are not terrorist can nevertheless resort to terrorist tactics. As we put it above: *all violence caused by terrorist groups (actor-sense) is terrorist in the action-sense, but not all terrorist violence (action-sense) is caused by terrorist groups.*

According to our theoretical framework, insurgent groups carry out terrorist attacks when they engage in clandestine violence (secret or covert operations). This will be the case when the insurgents act far away from their territorial base, within the enemy's territory. If they go deep inside the enemy's territory, the insurgents have to act secretly, under the same constraints of an underground group and, therefore, they cannot but replicate the tactics that underground groups employ. A fairly typical situation can be described as follows: the capital of the country is under the state's control, but the insurgents seek visible attacks there to induce terror in the population, mobilize supporters, or highlight the state's vulnerability. The attacks we are thinking of here are not military operations intended to gain physical control of the capital, but secret, surprise attacks that hurt the state.

It is important to emphasize again that the target of the attack is not the relevant feature. What matters is that the attack is conducted in a clandestine way. As mentioned, the LTTE was a formidable insurgency, with full territorial control in large areas in the north-east of Sri Lanka (Hussain, 2010). But apart from guerrilla attacks, it committed a significant number of attacks in Colombo. These attacks were underground; the LTTE did not try to gain urban territorial control in the capital. A well-known atrocity was the suicide attack against the central bank, on 31 January 1996, which killed 91 civilians and injured over 1,400 others. A truck loaded with a large bomb entered the building and the suicide attackers detonated it. In this case, the underground nature of the attack and the civilian targeting overlap. But there are occasions in which we find underground attacks against combatants. Thus, on 6 February 1998, an LTTE female suicide bomber blew herself up in the Air Force headquarters in Colombo, killing eight members of the military. According to our theory, these two attacks, despite the variation in targeting, are typically terrorist, since they were carried out under the constraints of the underground. The number of perpetrators was very low (three in the case of the Central Bank attack, and only one in the Air Force headquarters). The attacks were carried out by surprise and with immediacy. The goal was not to physically occupy the buildings, but to impose a cost on the enemy, signal resolve, and terrorize the state and society.

Similar examples can be found in many other insurgencies. Think, for instance, of the car bombs and suicide attacks in Kabul by the Taliban in 2006–7, while they were regaining territorial control in the south and east of the country (Malkasian, 2021: 170). As in the case of the LTTE, some of these attacks were aimed at the army. Thus, on 29 September 2007, a suicide bomber using a military uniform blew himself up in a bus transporting Afghan National Army personnel to work, killing 28 of them and two civilians.

Just as terrorism is not (only) civilian victimization, it is not (always) indiscriminate violence. In the previous examples, the number of fatalities was high or very high. However, it is easy to come up with cases of selective underground attacks by guerrilla groups, such as the assassination of former Indian prime minister Rajiv Gandhi by the LTTE in a small town close to Madras, on 21 May 1991 (Joshi, 1996: 29–31). Although the LTTE denied responsibility for the attack (Hopgood, 2005: 56–7), several members of the group were found guilty in court. This was an international attack, in India, out of the LTTE's territorial base. Given that the mission did not occur in Sri Lanka, the attack could only be based on a clandestine operation.

Whereas attacks perpetrated in the enemy's urban area are clearly underground, there might be greater ambiguity about selective killings of civilians in the quest for territorial control. It is well known that the bulk of the violence carried out by guerrilla insurgencies takes place in the context of rebel-civilian interaction (see the review in Chapter 1). The insurgents use coercive violence against the local population in order to impose their authority and to deter any form of collaboration with the state. Thus, those who do not abide by the rebels' rules are punished. This is typically the case in contested areas, in which the guerrillas want to establish their authority, and therefore we regard them as part of the insurgent activity and, more specifically, as part of the tactics oriented to gaining territorial control.

Let us focus for a moment on guerrillas' attempts to boycott elections run by the state. Of course, if the guerrilla has full territorial control, state officials will be unable to make voting possible. But in areas of partial or fragmentary control, when the state has the power to provide ballot boxes, the guerrilla may try to prevent the locals from participating in the elections or to boycott the vote altogether.[10] This behaviour can be observed in several Latin American insurgencies, such as the Shining Path in Peru, the FARC in Colombia, and the *Frente Farabundo Martí para la Liberación Nacional* (FMLN, Farabundo Martí Front for National Liberation) in El Salvador (McClintock, 1998). The FMLN, for example, boycotted elections in the municipalities that were under its full control. But in contested areas they sought to instil fear among civilians who were contemplating the possibility of voting. Thus, on 24 February 1988, in the municipality of Guatajiagua, a village of about 5,000 inhabitants (in the Morazán department, one of the FMLN's strongholds), the FMLN killed two peasants who had obtained their registration cards for the legislative elections of March. Actually, to make the message unmistakable, the cards were left in their mouths following their execution. According to the *New York Times*, this was 'a warning to others not to take part in the elections. Rebel units in the area have told all villagers not to vote and not to propose a candidate for mayor' (*New York Times*, 29 Feb. 1988, A15). This is a typical instance of how rebel rulers try to induce compliance in the local population. As De la Calle (2017) has shown in the case of the Shining Path, the attempt to gain territorial control is associated with an increase in civilian victimization.

Since this selective violence against civilians is intrinsically related to the guerrilla's attempt to exercise stronger influence over the local population in settings of partial or fragmentary territorial control, we think this corresponds to the pure guerrilla category rather than to the category of terrorist violence carried out by insurgencies.[11]

To conclude: the commonality between pure terrorist violence and terrorist violence carried out by insurgent groups does not stem from the status of the victims, but from the organization's underground condition. Insurgents act like terrorists not when they (indiscriminately) kill civilians, but

---

[10] Whereas guerrillas seek to boycott elections, terrorists, since they have to act within the enemy's territory, sometimes participate in elections through parties that constitute the political branch of the armed group. Many examples can be mentioned, including Sinn Féin with regard to the PIRA or Batasuna with regard to ETA.

[11] Our approach to the issue of terrorism in the context of a civil war deviates from that adopted in the literature (for instance, Stanton, 2013; Fortna, 2015). We explore this issue in greater detail in the Appendix to Chapter 3.

when they act clandestinely. This often happens when the insurgents want to hit the capital (or some other big city) within the enemy's territory. It is indeed the case that often the targets of these attacks are non-combatants, but this is not the defining trait of terrorist violence, as several examples have shown.

Proto-Guerrilla

Armed groups start underground. Some of them remain underground for their entire existence. They consider that the chances of becoming full insurgencies are slim given their thin basis of popular support or given the strength of the state. In either case, they understand that gaining territorial control is unfeasible. Some other groups, however, seek to obtain a geographical zone as their operational base, with the aim of achieving control over the area. These attempts require some preparatory work, based on the formation of support networks in the population (Lewis, 2020; Staniland, 2014).

Achieving territorial control may fail or succeed. In our classification, proto-guerrilla is a 'transition cell'; that is, it represents the inflection point at which armed groups either shift successfully from their underground status to territorial guerrillas or fail in their pursuit of territory. Given this transitional condition, proto-guerrilla is a flow or transient category; it reflects the (attempted) transformation of the group, but it is not a stable position or a final outcome. From a static point of view, proto-guerrilla is an incongruent category, for it implies the use by underground groups of tactics that correspond to groups with territorial control. However, from a dynamic perspective, this is not contradictory as long as we understand it as a transitional process.

There are many cases of a transition from underground to insurgency (Cronin, 2009: 147). The formation of the FMLN was the culmination of a previous decade of armed fighting by various underground groups (McClintock, 1998: 48–53). Likewise, Hezbollah started as an underground group during the early and mid-1980s. As Naaim Qassem, deputy secretary-general of the organization, said in an interview: 'Up until 1985, Hezbollah was not yet a single entity that could stand up and speak for itself. [...] The nature of our formation required clandestine behavior' (Jaber, 1997: 62). At the end of the decade, after its victory over Amal, the rival militia within the Shi'ite community, Hezbollah became a powerful guerrilla in South Lebanon and launched a war of attrition against Israeli occupation that ended in 2000 with Israel's withdrawal.

While the successful transition into insurgency has been studied in the cases of armed groups, cases of failure are less known. An interesting example is the so-called *Operación Primicia* (Scoop Operation) carried out by the Montoneros on 5 October 1975. Montoneros was both a broad political movement, with many thousands of followers, and the guerrilla of the Peronist Left in Argentina. Unlike the Trotskyist ERP (*Ejército Revolucionario del Pueblo*, People's Revolutionary Army), which had a rural dimension, Montoneros was a fully urban movement. On 6 November 1974, two months after Perón's death, the group went underground. Most of its attacks targeted the police, business people, and political rivals; the most widely used method was shootings. According to our own database, Montoneros killed 351 people between 1969 and 1979. Prima facie, these patterns are consistent with the perpetrators acting in the underground. However, in 1975 Montoneros escalated and decided to attack the military. The most ambitious attack was *Operación Primicia* (Reato, 2010). A large team (39 activists) participated in the assault of military barracks in the North province of Formosa (though the whole operation required the intervention of at least 60 Montoneros). The operation was highly complex from a logistical point of view. Although this was a guerrilla attack in scope, the Montoneros lacked any territorial control. Thus, to reach the target, they had to transport people and materials 1,000 kilometres north, both back and forth. They came up with a solution that looks typically terrorist: to hijack a plane and to control the Pucú airport during the arrival and escape. The preparation of the attacks was clearly terrorist in conception, but the attack itself corresponded to a guerrilla acting with territorial control seeking to occupy space. The Montoneros wore uniforms, which is never the case in underground attacks, and bore rifles, machine guns, grenades, and mines.[12] There was a lengthy exchange of fire between the Montoneros and the soldiers that resulted in the death of 12 soldiers, one police officer, and nine Montoneros. The assault became a battle that has no resemblance to clandestine attacks. In this regard, the operation was incongruent for an underground organization. *Operación Primicia* triggered a full repressive response by the state and contributed to the military coup of March 1976. The Montoneros were decimated after *Primicia* and never recovered their offensive capacity. The plan to build a Montonero army proved to be a fiasco. The plan only made sense if the Montoneros enjoyed some degree of territorial control, which they lacked.

---

[12] A detailed description of the Montoneros' attack is reproduced verbatim in Anguita and Caparrós (1998: 543–50).

Discussion

Table 2.1 describes the combinations that the pair of underground and above-the-ground generate when they are crossed in the actor- and the action-senses. The main finding of the analysis can be summarized as follows: terrorist violence is, in the actor-sense, violence that is produced by clandestine armed groups and, in the action-sense, the attacks that are carried out clandestinely. As said, the two senses do not fully overlap, and therefore they are not equivalent, because the action-sense is broader than the actor-one. As shown above, not all terrorist violence is perpetrated by underground groups; a significant chunk of it corresponds to guerrilla groups that decide to act far from their territorial bases and operate inside the enemy's territory. The 'menu of choices' is wider for groups with territorial control. Although a 2×2 table may suggest a static approach, we are aware that armed groups may evolve through different stages. This dynamic element is fully analysed in Chapter 5, where we track the temporal changes in the degrees of territorial control and in the tactics employed in the Israeli-Palestinian conflict and by ISIS.

For the sake of parsimony, our categories in Table 2.1 (pure terrorism, pure guerrilla, terrorism carried out by guerrilla groups, and proto-guerrilla) are clearly delimited. However, this is a simplification of reality, not only because it cannot reflect the dynamics, but also because real-world conflicts have become more resistant to traditional categorization. Since the end of the Cold War, both state and non-state armed actors display a messier structure, in both organizational and tactical terms. This is well reflected in the literature on hybrid warfare (Hartwig, 2020; Hoffman, 2007; Schroefl and Kaufman, 2014; Stoddard, 2023). From the tactical perspective, hybrid warfare 'incorporates a range of different modes of warfare, including conventional capabilities, irregular tactics and formations, terrorist acts including indiscriminate violence and coercion, and criminal disorder'. (Hoffman, 2007: 14) From the organizational side, the actors 'may have a hierarchical political structure, coupled with decentralized cells or networked tactical units' (Hoffman, 2007: 28).

The extraordinary blend of heterogeneous elements in hybrid warfare was originally illustrated by Hoffman (2007) with the case of Hezbollah. Yet, Hezbollah, as was mentioned previously, is amenable to our conceptual distinctions. It is not impossible to discriminate between terrorist attacks (both domestic and international), guerrilla activity, and conventional warfare, going from fully underground attacks to military battles against the Israel Defense Forces. In this sense, our claim is that the categories of Table 2.1, if properly understood as dynamic stages, should be applicable even in the messy cases in which we find superposed and overlapping layers of violence within an armed group.

Hybrid warfare blurs the traditional distinction between state and non-state violence. As we have noted, the literature on terrorism has had trouble in establishing a coherent boundary between terrorism and state repression. We close this chapter by showing that our conceptualization is also able to come to grips with this hotly debated issue, namely whether the state can commit terrorist acts.

2.5. State Terrorism

The word 'terrorism' comes originally from the repression carried out by the state in the French revolution during the 'terror years', 1793–4. Still in the 1960s, the words 'terror' and 'terrorism' were often used to refer to state violence against the civil population. Today the pendulum has completed a full swing; state terrorism has practically disappeared from academic debate. The vast majority of existing definitions establish that terrorism is non-state violence (see Chapter 1). Likewise, the terrorism datasets do not include incidents of state violence. However, it is far from obvious whether terrorist violence is exclusively non-state.

Decreeing that terrorism is non-state violence seems arbitrary. The exclusion of state violence does not follow from the dominant definitions (either civilian victimization or coercive violence). We suggest, based on our conceptual framework, an alternative approach to deal with this issue. Ironically, we share the concerns held by many experts and scholars about the very existence of state terrorism, but perhaps for different reasons. Thus, although we agree that most imputations of terrorist violence to the state are unwarranted, we still think that there is one sense in which we can speak meaningfully about state terrorism.

As Blakeley (2009: 12) has rightly argued, 'for an act to be labelled "state terrorism", its constitutive elements must be consistent with those of non-state terrorism'. However, she thinks that what makes terrorism distinct is the use of violence against a direct target in order to terrorize the audience target and change its behaviour. Consequently, she conceives state terrorism as repression aimed at maintaining order and suppressing the opposition. Since we are holding a different view on the nature of terrorism, our understanding of state terrorism is somewhat different. Specifically, we claim that, even if most state repressive action cannot be considered terrorist, when the state acts covertly,

72 Underground Violence

either against citizens in its own jurisdiction, or against individuals abroad, it acts under the same constraints of any other underground organization, and therefore is forced to employ the kind of violence that we associate with terrorism. This violence is terrorist from the action-sense perspective (the state, by construction, cannot be an underground actor). Another, more economical way to put it is the following: state terrorism is underground, covert state repression.[13]

Let us first make clear why we think that most state repression has little to do with terrorism. State repression is usually defined in domestic terms, as sanctions imposed by the state against its own citizens, trying to prevent dissent; this includes intimidation, arrests, torture, internment, executions, and even mass killings (Davenport, 2007). An archetypical case is Stalin's Great Terror in 1938–9. Conquest (1990: 290) estimates that at least 5 per cent of the Soviet population was arrested (around eight million people). Around one million were executed or died in camps. The repressive techniques used by Stalin seem completely alien to the terrorist tactics that have been described in this chapter (IEDs, selective shootings, assassinations, hijackings, and other similar examples). This is a strong reason for resisting the label 'terrorism', even though this campaign of repression is known as 'the Great Terror': the technology of violence used by the Soviet regime was completely different from that which is associated with terrorism.

However, there are other forms of repression that look astonishingly similar to terrorism. Thus, when the state becomes involved in covert operations, it behaves like any other group acting underground. In accordance with our theory, we are willing to include this state violence under the generic label of 'terrorism'.

State repression may come in two different ways, depending on the identity of the perpetrators: those who carry out the covert operation may be members either of some state agency, or of an outsourced group funded and protected by the state. The former corresponds to pure state terrorism, the latter to state-sponsored terrorism.

State terrorism probably reached its most sophisticated manifestation in the campaign of targeted assassinations carried out by the Israeli secret services. This campaign involved secret, covert operations, mostly undertaken outside of Israeli territory. When the perpetrators act out of their country, the operations might then be characterized as international state terrorism.[14]

---

[13] On the opposite side of our argument, Boyle (2017) argues that state terrorism has to be open repression, since otherwise it would have no effect on the audience target.

[14] Davenport (2007) defines state repression as state violence within its own jurisdiction. From a strict point of view, the targeted assassinations outside Israel would not fall under state repression. It follows that

Bergman (2018: xx) estimates around 1500 covert operations of all types since the creation of the State of Israel in 1948. The pros and cons of open versus covert operations were examined by the Israeli military. In 1975, for example, Mossad obtained information about a meeting of Fatah's leadership in Beirut; and an air attack was discussed. However General Shlomo Gazit opposed it by arguing: 'I told Defense Minister Shimon Peres that we must not get involved in something open like this. I was prepared to combat terrorism with full force, but only in clandestine operations that did not leave a calling card' (Bergman, 2018: 194). This distinction between open and covert state operations fits well with the conceptualization we have been using so far. If state terrorism is made of the same elements as non-state terrorism, the key factor lies in clandestinity.

A well-known episode of Israeli international state terrorism happened in the aftermath of the Munich massacre: in September 1972, the Palestinian Black September Organization (BSO) kidnapped and eventually killed 11 members of the Israeli Olympic team (plus one German police officer) during the Munich Olympics. That was a heavy blow for Israel and a huge propaganda success for the Palestinian cause (see Chapter 5). Mossad officer Mike Hariri created a secret unit, called Kidon (Bayonet), whose mission was 'operating covertly and carrying out identification, surveillance, and execution of human targets and sabotage operations' (Bergman, 2018: 148). The unit sought to find and kill those responsible for the Munich massacre (operation 'Wrath of God'), though they ended up killing Palestinian terrorists unrelated to Munich (Wael Zwaiter, Mahmoud Hamshari, Hussein Abd el Hir, Basil Al-Kubaissi, and Mohammad Boudia). All five were killed in European cities (three in Paris, one in Rome, and one in Nicosia) (Bar-Zohar and Mishal, 2015: 191–205). Two were shot dead, while the other three died in bomb explosions. In the case of Hamshari, for instance, Mossad agents were able to plant an explosive device under his desk that was activated through a phone call. These were, obviously, secret attacks on foreign soil and their operational nature was identical to BSO's attacks. In fact, in reprisal for these targeted assassinations, BSO carried out attacks in Europe against Mossad agents. One of them was Zadok Ophir, who arranged a meeting in a Brussels café with a Moroccan informer, Muhammad Rabah; but Rabah happened to be a BSO member who shot and wounded him. After several months in hospital, Ophir recovered. Ami Schechori was less fortunate: he was killed by a letter bomb while working at the Israeli embassy in London. What is the

---

state terrorism cannot be regarded exclusively as 'a chapter' of state repression: it is both covert repression and covert actions abroad.

74 Underground Violence

difference in operational terms between the bomb under the desk that ended with Hamshari's life and the letter bomb that killed Schechori? Both were underground, politically motivated attacks on foreign soil. One was carried out by an underground organization, BSO; the other, by a state acting underground. Absent information about authorship, the two attacks are perfectly interchangeable in operational terms.

Regarding outsourced groups (sometimes called 'state-sponsored terrorism'), a clear example is the Spanish state's sponsorship of a paramilitary group to combat ETA in the French Basque Country, the sanctuary of the terrorist organization (see Chapter 4). The group, the Antiterrorist Liberation Groups (GAL, *Grupos Antiterroristas de Liberación*), was created in 1983 and killed 27 people between that year and 1987 (Woodworth, 2001). Its members were police officers and mercenaries. The Minister of the Interior at the time ended up in jail for his involvement in the group (he was sentenced for the kidnapping of a French citizen, Segundo Marey, who was mistaken for a member of ETA). The killings were indistinguishable from those of ETA. For instance, on 25 September 1985, members of the GAL entered a pub in Bayonne, France, which was frequented by ETA militants, and opened fire, killing four of them; they then left the place immediately. From an operational point of view, this is identical to the attack carried out by four members of ETA on 28 November 1979: they entered a pub in Azpeitia (Gipuzkoa) and opened fire against three Civil Guards (the Spanish military police), killing them all. Since the GAL was a parapolice underground group, it acted like any other terrorist group. These are sufficient grounds, we think, to consider it a case of state-sponsored terrorism.

The same holds for the Triple A (Argentinian Anticommunist Alliance), another covert paramilitary organization created by the Argentinian state in 1973, when Perón was still in power. It was immediately after Perón's death that the Triple A's death squads, under the leadership of the infamous Minister of the Interior, José López Rega, tried to suppress left-wing subversives, including the Montoneros, unionists, politicians, and activists (Gillespie, 1982: 153–5). There are no precise figures about the total number of victims; Rostica (2011: 29) mentions 1,500 fatalities, but probably the correct figure is below 1,000.[15] Again, these death squads, acting underground under the supervision of the Minister of the Interior, have to be considered terrorist in nature.

---

[15] On the webpage Desaparecidos—an ambitious project carried out by human rights activists in Latin America—there is a list of 685 people (including full name and date of death) killed by the Triple A (http://www.desaparecidos.org/arg/victimas/listas/aaa.html, accessed 26 June 2023).

Given the strict empirical equivalence in the attacks carried out by underground groups and the covert attacks launched by states' secret services, it makes complete sense to consider that the state, under the specified special circumstances, may commit terrorist acts. In terms of Table 2.1, state terrorism belongs to a non-underground actor that nevertheless launches secret, clandestine attacks (it should be placed, therefore, in the cell described as 'terrorist violence carried out by an insurgent group', replacing 'insurgent group' with 'state apparatus'). The state is not terrorist from the actor-sense perspective, but it may launch terrorist attacks in action-sense terms.

Although it is a fascinating issue, uncovering the reasons why the state sometimes opts for underground rather than overt repression goes beyond the scope of this book. Our goal is simply to show the potential of our theory of terrorism for the very special category of 'state terrorism'. Most of what has been written on this topic has focused on the legitimacy (or lack of it) of state violence. Our suggestion is to address this issue from a different angle. By looking at the technology of repression, we suggest that state terrorism indeed exists; it corresponds, according to our view, to underground repression.

3

Asymmetry, Territorial Control, and Rebel Tactics

In the previous chapter we advanced our conceptualization of terrorism as underground violence. We have shown that this idea, compared with its alternatives (civilian victimization and coercive violence), makes sense of many of the peculiarities of terrorism. This is a much-needed exercise in concept elucidation. However, our approach goes beyond a purely conceptual endeavour. This chapter tests some of the most relevant theoretical underpinnings of our conceptualization of terrorism.

Our main empirical contention is that terrorism is most likely to be observed in contexts marked by high asymmetry between the parties. In other words, terrorist violence is expected when the perpetrators of the violence are significantly weaker than the enemy. Asymmetry in power is what forces armed groups to go underground (in the actor-sense) and to use the indirect tactics associated with terrorism (in the action-sense). Thus, in the actor-sense, we show that the greater the asymmetry between the armed group and the state, the more likely it is that the armed group is underground. In the action sense, a strong correlation is found between lower capabilities (captured by absence of territorial control) and the choice of indirect tactics: groups that do not control territory, or that act out of the territory they hold, employ typically indirect tactics such as bombings, kidnappings, and assassinations.

This chapter relies on large-n comparisons. Chapters 4 and 5 elaborate on similar themes through small-n comparisons. The use of quantitative techniques in the current chapter requires an operationalization of terrorism in the actor- and action-senses. We relegate a more technical discussion of how results change when using different operationalization rules to the Appendix to this chapter.

Underground Violence. Luis De la Calle and Ignacio Sánchez-Cuenca, Oxford University Press.
© Luis De la Calle and Ignacio Sánchez-Cuenca (2024). DOI: 10.1093/oso/9780198904816.003.0004

3.1. Asymmetry

Terrorism is chosen by the weaker party when the conditions under which it acts are maximally asymmetric. As said, it is not for nothing that terrorism has been described as 'the weapon of the weak' (e.g., Crenshaw, 1981: 387). Sometimes, the term 'the weapon of the weak' is employed to refer to guerrilla warfare, and 'the weapon of the weakest' to terrorism (as in the *Encyclopedia Britannica*'s entry for terrorism), highlighting in this way that terrorism represents a form of extreme asymmetry.

In war studies, the concept of asymmetry refers to a difference in the military power of the parties. If conflicts were only determined by levels of military power, the weak would never attack the strong. But the weak party may try to compensate for its military disadvantage, for example, by seeking greater popular support, or stronger ideological commitment (Stepanova, 2008); the weak may use the irregular tactics of guerrilla warfare, consisting of greater mobility and therefore a greater capacity for surprise attacks. In fact, the weak sometimes win: Boot (2013) analyses a sample of 381 conflicts and finds that the weak party wins 25 per cent of the time (20.5 per cent before World War II, 39.6 per cent after World War II). There are several explanations for this. Following Arreguín-Toft (2005), the weak party has a chance of defeating the strong when the former uses irregular tactics and the latter regular. Regular tactics do not always work well against weak actors. The use of full military power by the strong actor may lead to an overreaction of indiscriminate violence that alienates the local population. Alternatively, Sullivan (2007) argues that the strong actor wins when the objectives of the conflict can be achieved through brute force, while it tends to lose if those objectives require the weak party's compliance. Both explanations elaborate on the complex interplay between actors with different capabilities.

Ultimately, the difference between strong and weak parties follows from Schelling's (1966: 2) distinction between military power and the power to hurt (see Chapter 1). Clearly, destroying the enemy (direct strategy) corresponds to military power, while destroying the enemy's will (indirect strategy) corresponds to the power to hurt.

Based on these conceptual distinctions, a general and simple proposition can be formulated: *The more unequal the military capabilities of the parties, the more attractive tactics based on the power to hurt will be for the weaker party. In the extreme cases of asymmetry, the weaker party will resort to terrorism, which is based on the power to hurt under the conditions of clandestinity.*

78 Underground Violence

Before developing this simple proposition further, we introduce some examples that illustrate the main point. The examples are represented graphically in a line that reflects the degree of military power of the parties. In this continuum there are two extreme points: full military power and the absence of it. The degree of asymmetry can be simply defined as the distance between the parties on the line: the greater the distance, the greater the asymmetry.

Figure 3.1 displays a series of incompatibilities between states, as well as between states and non-state armed actors. In panel A, we have the interstate war of 2003 between the USA and Iraq. The tremendous disparity in military capabilities led to a quick victory of the USA over the Iraqi army. Although the USA was involved in a prolonged operation against insurgent groups in the country, here we only refer to the US invasion of Iraq in 2003 to oust Saddam Hussein from power. Iraq was far weaker than the USA, but it

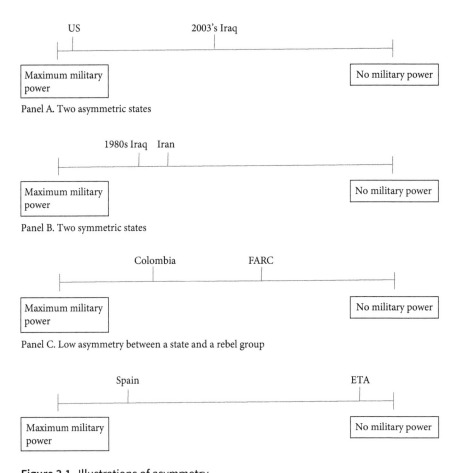

Figure 3.1 Illustrations of asymmetry

nonetheless was a state with a regular army, so we locate it around the middle of the axis.

In panel B, we again have two states, but with roughly similar levels of military power. The Iraq-Iran war between 1980 and 1988 was one of the longest and bloodiest military conflicts held by two developing countries. Note we place the Iraq of 1980 as being somewhat stronger than the Iraq of 2003 in panel A, as the sanctions imposed on the country in the aftermath of the Gulf War heavily depleted the country's security forces. Nonetheless, we put Iraq slightly ahead of Iran because of its superior equipment and better-trained soldiers; this military advantage became greater as the war unfolded, offsetting the numerical advantage of Iran (Segal, 1988: 952).

In panel C we have a mildly asymmetrical conflict between a state, Colombia, and a very powerful insurgent group, the FARC. At its apex, the FARC had thousands of recruits, it possessed some degree of military power, and held effective territorial control over large areas of the country, with the insurgents becoming de facto rulers over local inhabitants (see Chapter 2). Although it was far from being as powerful as a regular state army, it sought to develop an army structure. In this respect, the FARC was not so distant from the Colombian state.

Finally, in panel D, we have a highly asymmetric conflict between a state, Spain, and ETA, a nationalist armed group. The asymmetry in terms of military capability was overwhelming: ETA's recruits could be counted in hundreds, not thousands; it only had access to light weapons; and it lacked any degree of territorial control in its main area of operations, the Basque Country. This is why ETA is located on the far-right of the continuum, very close to a complete absence of military power. The distance between the Spanish state and ETA was definitely greater than that between Colombia and the FARC.

Terrorism, we argue, emerges when the weak actor is close to the extreme of having a total lack of military power. If the rebels cannot even launch irregular military attacks against the state, their remaining option is terrorism.

An important clarification is necessary at this juncture: asymmetry should not be considered as a fixed characteristic of a conflict, but rather as a changing trait of the situation under which the violence takes place. Thus, under certain circumstances, even actors with military capabilities can find themselves in a situation of relative weakness. Asymmetry, therefore, should be analysed at different levels, going from a particular operation to the general balance of power between two parties in a conflict.

We explore next the relationship between asymmetry and terrorism by analysing separately the determinants of terrorist groups (actor-sense) and rebel tactics (action-sense).

3.2. Asymmetry and Territorial Control: The Actor-Sense

Following a large literature stemming from Fearon and Laitin (2003), we claim that the level of asymmetry in a conflict is largely determined by state capacity. When the rebels face a strong state, territorial control is rarely an option. State capacity refers to both despotic and infrastructural power (Mann, 1993: 59): the former refers to military and repressive capabilities and the latter to the capacity to penetrate the territory and to implement decisions, and organize social and economic life. Despite the multidimensional nature of state capacity (see Hendrix (2010) for a review of different empirical indicators), economic development (that is, GDP per capita) is the variable most used to operationalize the concept. Among other things, the wide availability of data on GDP per capita for very long periods of time makes this variable particularly helpful.

State capacity is one of the most robust predictors of civil war (Fearon and Laitin, 2003).[1] Poorer countries are more likely to suffer civil conflict.[2] Poor countries do not have the ability to protect themselves from armed challengers. On the one hand, poverty can trigger grievances and a fight for scarce resources. On the other, institutional capabilities are lacking in poor countries, which facilitates armed entrepreneurs' efforts to capture territory and subdue populations. In contrast, developed countries are supposed to be 'violence-proof'. These countries are characterized by having huge military capabilities that deter challengers, and/or offer a large provision of public goods that pacify potentially aggrieved constituencies. Although scattered attacks by lone-actors or highly decentralized cells cannot be fully eliminated, the chance of observing a civil war in a developed country is near zero.

It is in between these two contexts where conflicts featuring clandestine armed groups thrive (De la Calle and Sánchez-Cuenca, 2012). Here, states are strong enough to prevent rebels from capturing territory, but not so strong as to get rid of any potential armed challenge. Regarding rebel leaders, they would like to emulate 'Che' Guevara, but they have to settle on a clandestine strategy that employs violence to coerce rivals and mobilize supporters.

---

[1] Despite the overwhelming number of studies confirming this relationship, there are some dissenting views (e.g., Djankov and Reynal-Querol, 2010). More interestingly, Besley and Persson (2011) argue that underdevelopment and conflict are parts of a larger political-economy cluster.

[2] For an alternative interpretation of the effect of GDP per capita, based on the opportunity cost of joining an armed group (the foregone income the person renounces by becoming a rebel), see Collier and Hoeffler (1998).

We test the argument about the actor-sense of terrorism in two steps. Firstly, we compare clandestine groups and territorial insurgencies with regard to economic development. Secondly, we proceed to a multivariate analysis of country/year observations in which we investigate the conditions under which each type of group is more likely to emerge.

Clandestine Rebels versus Guerrillas

According to our general argument, clandestine rebel groups are observed in countries that are more affluent on average than countries that host territory-controlling armed groups. The key variable here is whether the perpetrators of violence hold territorial control or act underground. Unfortunately, this variable is rarely included in the standard civil war datasets, which work with a quantitative criterion to identify civil conflicts: the 1000 battle-death threshold. For obvious reasons, it has been easier to collect information on conflict fatalities than on rebel presence throughout the territory. The main exception is Sambanis (2004), who included rebels' territorial control as a condition for a conflict to qualify as a civil war. Although there have been some recent efforts to use geospatial techniques to measure rebel presence (Tao et al., 2016), these have not been generalized for country-year conflict datasets.

Some scholars, however, have generated their own coding of armed groups with territorial control. We take their data at face value. Later, we re-run the analysis with our own coding, obtaining similar results and confirming the main hypothesis with different measurements of the variable.

To our knowledge, the most ambitious empirical effort to code rebel control is the Non-State Actor dataset (NSA, hereafter) (Cunningham, Gleditsch, and Salehyan, 2013). We draw on this dataset to check whether control-less rebels show different characteristics when compared to territory-controlling insurgencies. In a similar vein, we also use Asal and Rethemeyer's (2008) BAAD1 Lethality dataset (BAAD1, hereafter), which also includes a measure of territorial control.

The NSA dataset goes from 1946 to 2011 and builds on the list of conflicts included in the Uppsala Armed Conflict Data but expands the information regarding the capabilities of the rebel groups pertaining to every conflict dyad. NSA includes a variable called 'terrcon' which identifies whether rebels hold territory. Although not much information is given on the coding rules, this variable refers to control within the borders of the state the rebels are fighting against. By merging GDP per capita country information from the

Table 3.1 Territorial control and GDP per capita

	NSA data		BAAD1	
	GDP per capita at onset		GDP per capita in 1998	
	Obs	Mean	Obs	Mean
Clandestine	266	4,786.2	350	15,201.5
Territorial	172	3,361.7	42	4,861.3
T =	2.46**		5.47***	

Sources: NSA (Cunningham, Gleditsch, and Salehyan, 2013); BAAD1 (Asal and Rethemeyer, 2008); GDP per capita (Bolt et al., 2018).

Maddison Project Database[3] with the NSA dataset, we are ready to investigate whether clandestine groups are more pervasive in richer countries, compared to their territorial control-bound counterparts.

We test whether rebels with territorial control thrive more in poorer countries than rebels without it.[4] The left-hand panel in Table 3.1 shows that territory-grabbing rebels are more common in poorer countries (a GDP per capita average of 3,362 USD, compared to 4,786 USD for countries with clandestine groups). Clandestinity is clearly related to the balance of power between the contenders. NSA also includes a variable of rebel strength measuring whether rebels are 'much stronger', 'stronger', 'in parity', 'weaker', or 'much weaker' than the state. Strikingly, 55 per cent of clandestine rebels are 'much weaker' than their enemy states, compared to only 26.5 per cent of territorial rebels. In brief, the level of asymmetry between rebels and governments, as measured by country per capita income, has a large effect on the type of violence rebels carry out.

Whereas NSA seeks to be a sample of large insurgent groups (but some minor ones are also netted), BAAD1 is supposed to be a sample of terrorist groups (but some groups with territorial control are included). In total, there are 395 coded groups. BAAD1 relies on the now-extinct MIPT's Terrorism Knowledge Database, which used a very loose definition of terrorism, based on coercion. BAAD1 looks at groups that were active between 1998 and 2005 in the world and calculates their number of fatalities. Interestingly, it also reports whether these groups controlled territory. The authors define territorial control as:

---

[3] The data can be accessed at https://www.rug.nl/ggdc/historicaldevelopment/maddison/releases/maddison-project-database-2018?lang=en.

[4] We eliminate from the NSA dataset coups and anti-colonial conflicts on the basis that they have their own dynamics (for instance, anti-colonial conflicts involve affluent metropolis). However, results do not change substantially if these conflicts are included.

> the organization's ability to both (a) coerce nonmember civilians to act or forebear and (b) exclude police and military units from some defined geographic space over a period of time greater than six months. (Asal and Rethemeyer, 2008: 442)

In this sense, their definition overlaps reasonably well with some of the features we identify as control in Chapter 2. BAAD1 has 10 per cent of groups with territorial control, featuring insurgencies such as the FARC in Colombia, the Lord's Resistance Army in Uganda, the Taliban in Afghanistan, UNITA in Angola, the Naxalites in India, and the Tamil Tigers in Sri Lanka—all groups that are conventionally considered as guerrilla organizations.

The right-hand panel in Table 3.1 reports the difference of means test. Similar to the previous analysis, clandestine groups in the BAAD1 sample are more frequent in richer countries, with per capita income three times bigger than that of countries with territory-seizing insurgencies. This finding is no small feat, as the sample allegedly includes only terrorist groups. The fact that those so-called 'terrorist' groups with territorial control emerge in notably poorer countries is proof of our claim about asymmetry: when rebels face a stronger state, the best they can do is to remain clandestine and carry out a coercive, terrorist campaign.

Both NSA and BAAD1 have allowed us to check our claim without any suspicion of coding bias on our part. By the same token, both datasets also bring some coding reliability issues on the definition of control as well as sample composition problems. This is why we now proceed to offer some results with our own codification of the Global Terrorism Database (GTD). The GTD is the most comprehensive dataset on terrorism and political violence available to date, totalling near 200,000 incidents from 1970 to 2018 (START, 2019; LaFree and Dugan, 2007). GTD provides information about the nature and characteristics of the attack in terms of authorship, location, date, target, lethality, and type of action. The reader can find a detailed discussion of this database in this chapter's Appendix. Due to a loose definition of terrorism ('the threatened or actual use of illegal force and violence to attain a political, economic, religious or social goal through fear, coercion or intimidation'), it covers much of the violence that takes place in civil wars. As Table A1 in the Appendix shows, nine of the 10 most violent groups included in the dataset are insurgencies involved in civil wars, with the Taliban and ISIS on top.

Almost half of all attacks (45 per cent) in the GTD are unclaimed (Berkebile, 2017). Since the variable of territorial control is based on groups, we focus on attacks whose perpetrators can be identified. To avoid the noisy presence of short-lived groups with very little activity, we limit the analysis to rebel groups that meet some minimalist criteria of armed activity and organizational life: at least 10 attacks with at least 10 deaths in more than one year of activity. There are 277 groups with these characteristics for the 1970–2018 period. The GTD does not include information about territorial control. For each group we have tracked first-hand sources, monographs, web pages and large-n databases to find out whether the group was able to control territory within the borders of the state.[5]

Following the criteria laid out in Chapter 2, we consider that an armed group is coded as having territorial control when any of these conditions is met: (1) the armed group sets up camps or bases within the country's border, storing weapons and/or training recruits; (2) the armed group imposes stable roadblocks, disrupting the flow of goods and people; and (3) the armed group rules over the local population (extracting rents and imposing 'justice') in certain areas within the country's border.

Finally, we follow an absorption rule for those armed groups that transition from non-territorial control to territorial control (or the other way around): if there is evidence of continuous territorial control during the conflict, the group is classified as territorial even if the group started or ended as an underground organization. Short and limited spans of rebel control—such as the IRA's grip on West Belfast in the early years of the Troubles—do not qualify as territorial control, since the group remained largely clandestine during most of the conflict.

According to our coding, 105 of the 277 groups are clandestine (38 per cent), and the remaining 172 hold territory. The clandestine groups with the largest number of fatalities are the IRA (1,793 deaths), the Sinai Province of the Islamic State (1,696 deaths), Lashkar-e-Jhangvi (1,226 deaths), Lashkar-e-Taiba (1,085 deaths), Hamas (891 deaths), ETA (819 deaths), and the African National Congress (ANC) (636 deaths).[6] It also includes minor groups such as Portugal's Popular Forces of April 25 (10 deaths), the Peruvian death squad Rodrigo Franco Command (10 deaths), and the Patriotic Morazanista Front (10 deaths).

---

[5] Since we are interested in cross-national variation, we have excluded transnational groups that cannot be associated with a specific country (such as central Al Qaeda). We have also excluded what we think are the GTD's mistakes, such as the Triple A, which mixes activity from two groups with identical names in Argentina and Spain. To avoid the artificial proliferation of armed groups, we have not counted as independent groups those that are integrated in a larger organization, such as Force 17 in Fatah, or Al-Khobar in the Moro Islamic Liberation Front. In exceptional cases, we have accepted generic names, like 'Chechen Rebels', only if the level of armed activity is very high (1,640 fatalities in the case of Chechen rebels).

[6] In the case of Hamas, we describe in Chapter 5 how Hamas gained territorial control in the Gaza Strip in 2007, becoming the local ruler after defeating Fatah.

Regarding organizations holding territorial control, ISIS, the Taliban, Boko Haram, and a few other powerful insurgencies top the list of the most lethal groups (see Table A1). More intriguingly, there are some territorial groups with low counts of fatalities like the Karbi Longri Cachar Liberation Front (10 deaths), Jamaat-ul-Ahrar (16 deaths), Ansar al-Sharia (17 deaths), the Lesotho Liberation Army (19 deaths), the Patriotic Resistance Front in Ituri (19 deaths), and the Brunswijk Jungle Commando operating in Suriname (20 deaths). With some exceptions, such as the Zapatista National Liberation Front, the number of deaths by groups with territorial control is clearly underestimated in the GTD.

We use this sample of 277 rebel groups to test our hypothesis that rebel groups without territorial control emerge in states with greater state capacity. Figure 3.2 offers some visual, descriptive support for our claim. This boxplot conveys average GDP per capita (measured in the year of the group's first recorded attack) for armed groups with and without territorial control. In addition to the distribution of observations, the graph displays the mean distribution (light black) and its median value (deep black). Clandestine groups are more common in richer countries than insurgencies with territorial control.

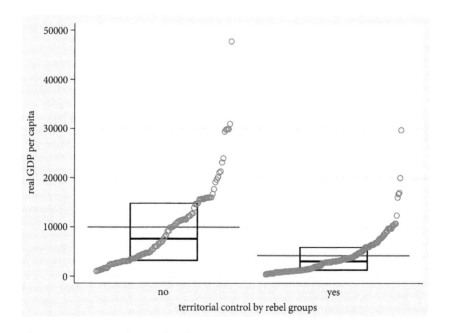

Figure 3.2 Territorial control and GDP per capita at onset

86 Underground Violence

Table 3.2 Territorial control and GDP per capita at onset

Groups	GDP per capita at onset		Number of deaths	
	Obs	Mean	Obs	Mean
Clandestine	103	9,967	105	174
Territorial	156	4,231	172	1,432
T =	7.31***		−2.60**	

We reach a similar conclusion in the means comparison of Table 3.2. Clandestine groups face states whose average GDP per capita is above 9,950 USD, whereas insurgencies with territorial control fight against states averaging less than half this number (4,231 USD). This difference can be interpreted in a very simple way: when the state faced by rebels is strong (rich), the rebels can only attack it from the underground and therefore the only feasible tactics are terrorist; when the state is weaker (poorer), the rebels have the capacity to organize as a guerrilla.

Our data also allow us to calculate the average number of victims killed by the armed groups in each type of conflict. The difference between clandestine and territorial armed organizations is in this case not only statistically significant (174 victims of clandestine groups compared to 1,432 deaths by territorial groups), but also theoretically meaningful, as territory-seizing armed groups bring about an average number of killings well above the conventional threshold of 1,000 battle deaths that is used to distinguish a civil war from lower-scale conflicts.

The Inverse U-Shaped Relationship between Terrorism and State Capacity

Our second step goes beyond a mere comparison of the levels of development in which the two types of armed groups emerge. We offer a more precise test thanks to a multivariate analysis of country/year observations showing that (i) the relationship between groups with territorial control and development is linear and negative, while (ii) the equivalent relationship in the case of clandestine rebel groups follows an inverted U-shaped form.

Two papers published simultaneously (Enders and Hoover, 2012; and De la Calle and Sánchez-Cuenca, 2012) showed that terrorist activity is associated in a non-linear way to development: terrorism is more frequent in countries with intermediate levels of development than in those that are poor or rich. Enders and Hoover (2012) proved this by analysing the number of incidents recorded by the GTD in every country/year observation. In parallel, we found the same pattern using a different research design. We also used the standard country-year panel data, but our dependent variable was conflict onset (following the analysis of civil wars, as in Fearon and Laitin, 2003). We combined standard data on civil war onset with our own GTD-mined codification of conflicts where rebels remained clandestine. Whereas the effect of GDP per capita was negative for civil war onset (the richer the country, the less likely civil war is), in the case of terrorist conflicts the effect was quadratic (more specifically, concave): terrorist conflicts concentrate at middle levels of development. In our paper we offered a theoretical explanation about these findings: in poor countries the state is weak and the rebels launch guerrilla war; in rich countries the state is strong and rebels do not take up arms or, if they do, they are immediately neutralized by security forces. It is in between, in states with medium strength, where we observe rebels who are able to take up arms, but are forced to resort to clandestine armed strategies.

In order to replicate those results with up-to-date data, we match our list of 277 armed groups coded from the GTD with a panel of country-year observations from 1970 to 2018. Unlike our 2012 study, here we seek to explain the formation of armed groups rather than conflict onset (a conflict-onset analysis yields no substantially different results). To test the hypothesis, we include GDP per capita and its square in the year in which the group carried out its first attack. If the relationship is concave (inverted-U), as the hypothesis assumes, the coefficient of GDP per capita should be positive and the one corresponding to the squared term negative. The standard control variables are included in the analysis: population size, the Polity IV index of democracy, ethnic fractionalization, ruggedness, and a Cold War dummy.

Logit estimations can be found in Table 3.3. Model 1 shows that the squared effect goes in the expected way and is significant even after controlling for other covariates. Model 2, in turn, proves the well-known negative and linear effect of GDP per capita over guerrilla formation (groups with territorial control). This is a remarkable finding, given that the set of civil wars included in the GTD is moderately biased against African conflicts and in favour of those in Latin America—countries that are on average more affluent than those from sub-Saharan Africa (see the Appendix). Model 3 includes the Correlates of War onset of intra-state wars since 1969, which is a more rigorous list of civil wars than that extracted from the GTD. We nonetheless find the same results, with GDP per capita showing its well-known negative effect on civil war onset.

88 Underground Violence

Table 3.3 Determinants of territorial and non-territorial groups in the world

	(1) New terrorist group (GTD)	(2) New guerrilla group (GTD)	(3) Civil war onset (COW)
Lag GDP pc (log)	11.84***	−0.573***	−0.520***
	(4.64)	(−4.06)	(−3.77)
Lag GDP pc Sq. (log)	−0.661***		
	(−4.50)		
Population (log)	0.660***	0.485***	0.291***
	(5.64)	(5.19)	(4.09)
Polity IV	0.0480	0.0165	−0.0120
	(1.59)	(0.60)	(−0.57)
Ethnic Fractionalization	−0.319	0.272	0.877
	(−0.36)	(0.52)	(1.39)
Ruggedness	0.263	−0.0258	0.0604
	(1.43)	(−0.25)	(0.54)
Cold war	1.222***	0.266	0.347
	(4.19)	(0.83)	(1.33)
Constant	−68.83***	−7.517***	−5.293**
	(−5.79)	(−4.22)	(−2.81)
Observations	6,367	6,367	6,367
Adjusted R^2	0.16	0.10	0.07

t statistics in parentheses; * $p < 0.05$, ** $p < 0.01$, *** $p < 0.001$

Figure 3.3 offers a compelling visual representation of our hypothesized inverted U-shaped relationship between country wealth (and more generally, state capacity) and the emergence of terrorist groups. It plots the effect of GDP per capita from columns (1) and (3) on the odds of experiencing the formation of either a clandestine (terrorist) group or a territory-seizing (guerrilla) group. It is worth mentioning that the odds are very low—an indication that we are dealing with rare events. That said, it is easy to see our main theoretical conjecture in operation, namely that the formation of guerrilla groups decreases with country per capita wealth, whereas underground groups are on average more likely to appear in middle-income nations. Of course, because states are stronger, we observe in general fewer clandestine armed organizations. For the most affluent countries in the world, armed conflict within their borders is no longer an issue (except for international and lone-actor attacks).

In sum, rebel capacity to seize and hold territory largely depends on the level of asymmetry that rebels face in the fight against their state. Weak

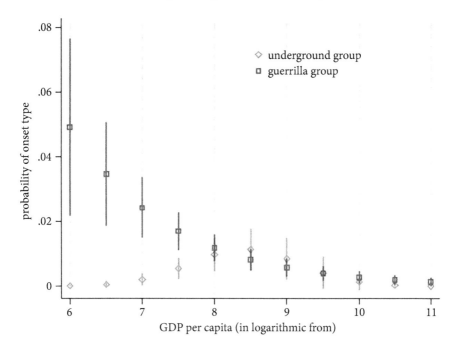

Figure 3.3 The inverted U-shaped link between GDP per capita and armed group formation

states offer many opportunities for rebels to carry out an armed campaign with a substantial level of military power. In contrast, strong states offer few openings for rebels to liberate territory and therefore the latter are forced to remain clandestine. Our next step is to show that when rebels are clandestine, their repertoire of violence significantly differs from that of territory-seizing insurgencies.

3.3. Asymmetry and Rebel Tactics: The Action-Sense

The claim we explore here is that asymmetry also explains the conditions under which certain tactics (in the action-sense) are employed by armed groups. As will be shown, these tactics are driven by the conditions of clandestinity. Note that the empirical analyses that follow are valid even if someone disagrees entirely with the conceptualization of terrorism we are advancing in this book. Our point is that the empirical regularities that we uncover can be interpreted as further support for the thesis that terrorism is underground, political violence. What we show is that there is a natural affinity between clandestinity and a set of tactics that are usually described as terrorist in nature.

We start by recalling the distinction between indirect and direct tactics: the former refer to coercive violence (power to hurt), the latter to the extermination or annihilation of the enemy (military power). Rebel groups resort to indirect tactics when they are facing extreme asymmetries in the balance of power vis-à-vis their rival states. This is consistent with the view that terrorism, from the action-sense perspective, is indirect violence perpetrated by groups operating under conditions of clandestinity.

We present two empirical tests. Firstly, if indirect tactics, such as bombings and selective assassinations, are driven by asymmetric conditions between rebels and their rival states, we should find that clandestine groups resort to these tactics more often than groups with territorial control. This does not necessarily hold for the choice of targets. According to our argument in the previous chapter, civilians are targeted by above- and underground groups alike. Secondly, if we are correct that guerrillas carry out indirect attacks in places far from their control (where the structural advantage of states is more acute), we should observe that territory-controlling insurgencies show a different repertoire of violence depending on the war theatre in which they operate.

We take advantage of changes in the coding rules of the GTD during the late 1990s to run two different analyses. We start with the analysis of the current version of the GTD and show that clandestine groups display a very different tactic profile than groups with territorial control, in line with our theoretical expectation. Drawing on previous work (De la Calle and Sánchez-Cuenca, 2015), we close the chapter with an analysis of the GTD1, the previous iteration of this database. By chance, the GTD1 categorized tactics in a way that helps us distinguish between indirect attacks carried out clandestinely and direct tactics that require territorial control. In all, both analyses below bring home the point that clandestinity has harsh consequences for rebel groups in terms of their tactic choices.

Rebel Groups and Tactics

Territorial control and tactics are intertwined. The greater the military power of the rebels, the more symmetric the combat between the armed group and the state. Once the rebels have territorial control, they can engage in military tactics, such as skirmishes, ambushes, the seizing of villages, raids, and battles. When a group is underground, these tactics cannot be sustained due to organizational and logistical limitations. Clandestine groups predominantly rely on an indirect repertoire of violence characterized by secrecy, surprise, and coercive tactics. We expect, more specifically, that clandestine groups will resort mainly to bombings—a tactic that allows small groups to counterbalance their operational weakness with cheap, high-impact actions. In contrast, groups with territorial control will rely more on guerrilla-like actions—such as ambushes, town raids, and assaults—which are necessary to maintain and increase their territorial presence.

Before getting into the analysis, we should address here the objection that territorial control may ultimately be the consequence of employing certain tactics. If this objection were true, there would then be some endogeneity, or even circularity, in the thesis that tactic choice is determined by territorial control. Essentially, the objection is that territory cannot be liberated from the state's control unless certain tactics are used. It is then tactics that explain how some armed groups end up controlling territory and not the other way around.

Briefly put, we think this objection mixes up the genesis and the consequences of an outcome. One thing is the process through which an armed group achieves territorial control, and another is whether groups with territorial control act differently from groups without it.

In this regard, we start from the assumption that almost all armed groups begin underground (Lewis, 2020: 8). For reasons discussed below, some of them remain underground, whereas others gain territorial control. Let us use a very simple illustration of how indirect and direct tactics have consequences for territorial control. Suppose an underground group is interested in attacking the police station of a village but does not aim at gaining territorial control. Given the constraints imposed by clandestinity, the rebels, most likely, will plant a bomb, to avoid any physical encounter with the police. The goal of such an attack is not to end with the presence of police in the village (the personnel killed will soon be replaced by new police officers dispatched to the area), but rather to make it costly for the state to maintain the conflict, and to send a signal about the vulnerability of the state and the strength of the rebels. Suppose now that the underground group is interested in gaining territorial control of the village: they will then assault the police station, killing some police officers and making others abandon the place, so that the rebels become the new authority. Thus, these different tactics explain the outcome—remaining clandestine or gaining territorial control.

The fact that different tactics generate different outcomes does not affect our argument. We agree that some tactics are better than others if the goal of the rebels is to gain territorial control. To seize territory, the rebels must use tactics that are consistent with this goal. But the use of these tactics does not guarantee success. As we will see in the following chapters, there are groups that strive to behave as guerrillas and fail to gain territorial control. After the failure, they revert to covert action (and indirect tactics), consistent with their underground nature. In most cases, either the group decides to act underground from the beginning, without aspiring to gain any territorial control, or the group eventually gains territorial control and becomes a guerrilla.

In sum, we openly admit that the transition from the underground to the above-the-ground condition is only possible if the rebels use tactics that make territorial control feasible. But our point is that the tactics employed when armed groups are clandestine or hold territorial control are different.

Our first test draws on the modern version of the GTD for the period 1970–2018. We use it to show that it is possible to empirically discriminate between different types of rebel groups by looking at their tactic profiles. In a remarkable contrast, the same is not necessarily true if we look at their target profiles. In other words, different types of armed actors resort to bombs differently, while there are no relevant differences regarding civilian targeting.

The simplest way to use 'events' data as a measure of terrorist incidence is to focus on attacks carried out with bombs—as this is the quintessential type of indirect, asymmetric attack. Bomb-driven events, however, may mean different things: a highly sophisticated IED design triggered to launch a military ambush and a home-made, low-powered explosive device respond to different tactical intentions. The GTD allows some recoding, as it distinguishes between industrial-made devices such as 'landmines' and 'projectiles' (rockets, mortars, missiles) and more simple triggers such as 'mail bombs' and 'remote devices'. We exclude from our operationalization of terrorism the former bomb categories, for they really belong to a different military logic of warfare (as discussed in Chapter 2).

Recoding the original GTD categories, we classify tactics into six broad categories: bombs, projectiles (and landmines), assassinations, armed assaults, attacks against infrastructure, and kidnappings.[7] We then proceed to match

---

[7] Our variable combines categories from two different GTD variables (tactics and weapons). The labels are self-explanatory, except, perhaps, in the case of 'armed assaults', defined by the GTD as follows: 'An attack whose primary objective is to cause physical harm or death directly to human beings by use of a firearm, incendiary, or sharp instrument (knife, etc.). Not to include attacks involving the use of fists, rocks, sticks, or other handheld (less-than-lethal) weapons. This also includes attacks involving certain classes of explosive devices in addition to firearms, incendiaries, or sharp instruments. The explosive device subcategories that are included in this classification are grenades, projectiles, and unknown or other explosive devices that are thrown.'

the attacks with our list of 277 groups that meet a minimal threshold of armed group's subsistence (at least 10 attacks with at least 10 deaths in more than a year of activity). For each group, we calculate the share of attacks corresponding to each tactic. We do not use absolute numbers of attacks as the dependent variable for reasons we detail in the Appendix (see also De la Calle and Sánchez-Cuenca, 2015). Suffice to say that when the attacks are measured in absolute terms, as a frequency, severe distortions are produced due to the presence of a few armed groups that carry out a very large numbers of attacks. To illustrate the distortions, let us take the six armed groups in the sample with more than 1,000 bomb attacks (four of them, the FMLN, Shining Path, ISIS, and the Taliban, are insurgent organizations engaged in long civil wars). The problem is that, given the sheer number of attacks carried out by each of these groups, they plant many bombs, but also execute many assault operations, kidnappings, and assassination campaigns. By comparing the types of attacks in absolute terms across groups, large groups appear on top regardless of the type of attack we consider. We therefore need to run the analyses using the relative weight of each tactic.

As our measure of territorial control does not have temporal variation, we limit ourselves to a cross-section analysis of the data. Table 3.4 confirms that the systematic task of coding whether armed groups remain clandestine or manage to control territory in a permanent way pays off in terms of gaining operationalizable accuracy. It shows the share of tactics depending on whether the armed group controlled territory or remained clandestine. For clandestine groups, bombs and assassinations make up the majority of their attacks, whereas groups with territorial control show more variation, with armed assaults being the most common tactic.[8]

Table 3.4 Share of tactics by territorial control

Tactics	Clandestine groups (n=104)	Groups with territorial control (n=173)	Dif-of-means test
Bombs	0.37	0.22	5.20***
Assassinations	0.21	0.06	7.51***
Armed assaults	0.22	0.35	−5.53***
Infrastructure	0.04	0.04	−0.46
Kidnapping	0.08	0.15	−4.57***
Projectiles	0.06	0.11	−2.73**

Note: Proportions do not add up to 1 because of a residual 'other tactics' category not shown in the Table.

[8] Bear in mind that the GTD is most possibly under-representing the guerrilla-like attacks perpetrated by large-scale insurgencies in remote areas, so the share of bombs for these groups is possibly overestimated.

94   Underground Violence

We next run some simple models in which we compare the effect of territorial control on the share of tactics and targets (we distinguish between civilians, government personnel, and combatants—the last of these including security forces and paramilitary members). If our argument holds, we should expect significant effects for tactics, particularly for the use of bombs, which is a kind of tactic that is particularly appropriate for groups without territorial control. By contrast, there is no ground to suppose that territorial control or its absence has an effect on targeting. As we have argued extensively in the two previous chapters, civilians can be targeted by all sorts of armed groups and under very different circumstances. The dependent variables are all measured in relative terms, as shares, to ensure that the cases are properly compared. The main explanatory variable is territorial control (value 1) versus absence of territorial control (value 0). We control for the logarithm of the number of attacks (as a measure of group resilience).[9]

Figure 3.4 displays the coefficients for territorial control over the shares of tactics and targets. In line with our expectations, groups with territorial control have fewer bombings and assassinations, but more armed assaults and kidnappings. And, as expected, territorial control does not help to distinguish between types of targets (apart from more government hits by clandestine groups). In the Appendix, we elaborate in greater detail on this issue, comparing the choice of tactics versus targets as dependent variables.

We now turn to the GTD1 rendition because it offered a clearer categorization of types of tactics capturing the theoretical distinction between direct versus indirect attacks. GTD1 totals 61,637 events and covers the 1970–97 time span. With a slightly but crucially different codification than the current version, GTD1 distinguished seven tactics: facility attack, bombing, assassination, kidnapping, hijacking, assault, and maiming. The last two were marginal in number of attacks (note that 'assault' is now one of the main categories), so we focus on the remaining five.

Again, we employ our minimal threshold of activity for a group to be included in the analysis: we only consider armed groups that have a name, that have killed at least 10 people in more than 10 attacks, and that have acted for more than one year. For the period 1970–97, there were 122 armed groups that met these criteria, 64 of which remained clandestine (see De la Calle and Sánchez-Cuenca (2015) for a more technical analysis of this data).

Facility attacks and bombings are the two most important and frequent categories in the GTD1. The GTD1 codebook defines a facility attack as follows:

---

[9] These are OLS regressions with standard errors clustered by country.

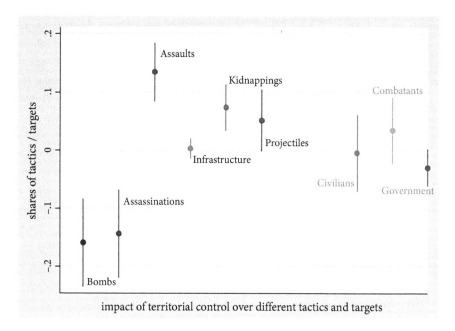

impact of territorial control over different tactics and targets

Figure 3.4 The impact of territorial control over different shares of tactics and targets (OLS models with shares as dependent variables; n=277)

Note: Predictive coefficients with 95 per cent intervals from OLS models all with country clustered standard errors and control for number of years of armed group's activity.

The objective [of the facility attack] is to rob, damage or occupy a specific installation. The term installation includes towns, buildings and in some cases, vehicles. Thus, a bank robbery is a facility attack although all its guards may have been killed. […] The occupation of a town, wherein persons may be killed or wounded, also is a facility attack since the objective was to take the town (installation), not to kill or wound persons. […] Normally, a multi-member team is involved. The operation is carried out openly—in contrast to the covert placement of bombs at night.

The features of large-team operations aiming at occupation of space are inherent characteristics of guerrilla activity. Given the requirements of this type of action, we expect to observe more facility attacks when the rebels have some territorial control. The only exception is bank robbery, which the coders categorize as facility attacks. Bank robberies can be carried out, as has often been the case, by underground and open groups alike. In fact, bank robbery is one of the main sources of financing for clandestine groups (Freeman, 2011; Horgan and Taylor, 1999).

Bombings, in contrast, are not aimed at taking over a place, but rather at destroying it. And, as the coders emphasize, the action of placing a bomb and causing it to explode is clandestine in nature. As the GTD1 codebook puts it: 'In contrast to a facility attack, which often is aimed at physically taking over the installation, a bombing is designed simply to destroy or damage it. The clandestine nature of bombing separates it from facility attacks.' Although territorial groups can also use bombings, we expect clandestine groups to more frequently employ this kind of attack.

Finally, assassinations and kidnappings are compatible with any kind of armed group. Assassinations are carried out by all violent groups. And the same can be said for kidnappings, which have largely been used either to blackmail governments in exchange for imprisoned comrades or to raise funds from well-off fellow citizens. These four categories (facility attack, bombing, assassination, and kidnapping) depict well the variation in tactics that armed groups display. We think this classification is particularly convenient because of the hypothesized association between facility attacks and territory-seizing insurgencies on the one hand, and bombings and underground groups on the other.

To explain tactical variations, we calculated, for each of our 122 groups, the proportion of facility attacks, bombings, assassinations, and kidnappings throughout its whole period of activity depending on whether it controlled territory or remained clandestine for much of its active years. Table 3.5 shows again very different patterns if we split the sample by rebel control. Whereas groups with territorial control largely rely on guerrilla attacks (59 per cent of attacks), clandestine groups are more dependent on coercive tactics such as bombings (38 per cent) and assassinations (32 per cent). Even though the current GTD covers 20 more years (1998–2018) of violence, the two versions report larger shares of assassinations and smaller shares of kidnappings by clandestine groups. The low visibility of many assassinations during civil wars may be driving this effect.

Table 3.5 Tactics and territorial control (GTD1 data)

Tactics	Territorial control		Dif-of-means test
	No	Yes	
Bombings	0.38	0.16	5.79***
Facility	0.26	0.59	−9.39***
Assassinations	0.32	0.13	5.36***
Kidnappings	0.05	0.11	−3.42***

It might be contended that tactical choice is explained by alternative factors, such as the size of the armed group or the linking of armed groups with sponsor states. In previous work, we find that our main theoretical claim holds even if controlling for these alternative arguments (De la Calle and Sánchez-Cuenca, 2015).

Geography and Rebel Tactics

Armed actors update their tactics when the balance of power changes. This has two implications. Spatially, groups employ different tactics depending on the regional balance between their capabilities and those of their rival state. Temporally, groups adapt their tactical game when they move to seize territory (and the opposite when retreating). We exploit available data to test the spatial claim in three ways. Regarding space variation, we investigate whether groups with territorial control reproduce the behaviour of underground groups when they attack in the capital. Second, we analyse whether having a sanctuary (a so-called safe haven in territory beyond the jurisdictional borders of the rebels' rival state) boosts guerrilla-like attacks by otherwise clandestine groups. Third, we check whether clandestine groups are more prone to perpetrating attacks on foreign soil than territory-seizing insurgents. Regarding time variation, we address in Chapter 5 the dynamics of conflict as a function of variations in territorial control by analysing rebel groups in the Middle East.

One specific implication that flows from our general argument is that territorial groups acting in areas under safe state control—such as the capital city—will have to operate under the same constraints of secrecy as any other underground group. Therefore, the tactical profile of territorial groups in the capital should be more like that of underground groups. Far from resembling *guerrilleros*, rebels operating in capital cities will 'look like' terrorists, even if they have other areas of the country under their control.

Not every rebel group fighting to hold territory operates in the capital city. The communist New People's Army carried out few attacks in Manila, the capital city of the Philippines (around 5 per cent of its attacks). The Tamil Tigers had very similar numbers. In contrast, the FMLN perpetrated one out of every five attacks in San Salvador, the capital city of El Salvador. We are not investigating here why some insurgencies operate in cities more than others. Instead our claim is that if rebels want to operate in cities, they have to abide by the rules of clandestinity. As the capital is usually under state control

98   Underground Violence

(except in the last stages of an insurgent's victory), the rebels have to act in secrecy. This means that, for groups with territorial control, the proportion of facility attacks should be lower in the capital than in the rest of the country, and conversely for bombings. We do not have expectations about assassinations or kidnappings, because both can be similarly carried out in urban and rural settings.

To test this hypothesis, we have created a variable that captures whether the attack took place in the two largest cities of the country in which the group acts. We can compare, therefore, whether the tactics profile is the same in these large urban centres as in the rest of the territory. In accordance with the expectation that groups fighting for territory act less in areas secured by the state, we find that underground groups tend to operate in the two largest cities (39 per cent of all attacks) much more than territorial groups (17 per cent). These differences are statistically significant. The fixation of clandestine groups with big cities is driven by their need to maximize the impact of their actions, and the optimal conditions these places offer for secretly organized, disruptive attacks.

Table 3.6 employs GTD1 data to break down these numbers by theatre of fighting. It is notable that territory-seizing insurgents carry out a greater proportion of bombings when operating in the two largest cities, in comparison to their attacks elsewhere. Facility attacks still represent the largest share, but recall that this includes bank robberies, a quintessential terrorist act oriented towards funding the armed organization. It is worth stressing that clandestine groups carrying out attacks beyond the country's two largest cities are unable to mimic a more guerrilla-like repertoire of violence, since they cannot but resort to bombings and assassinations.

These results confirm that groups with territorial control change their tactics when they decide to operate in urban settings, thus providing more

Table 3.6 Tactic profile by insurgencies (GTD1 data)

| Tactics | Theatre of fighting | | | |
| | Two largest cities | | Elsewhere | |
	clandestine	with territory	clandestine	with territory
Bombings	0.48	0.34	0.34	0.14
Facility	0.20	0.44	0.28	0.62
Assassinations	0.26	0.13	0.33	0.13
Kidnappings	0.03	0.07	0.04	0.11

fine-grained evidence that the constraints imposed by (lack of) territorial control have a large impact on the repertoire of rebel warfare.[10]

We now move to the second test, on sanctuaries. As discussed in Chapter 2, rebel groups that are fortunate enough to receive lenient treatment from a neighbouring country (out of ideological affinity or simple incapacity to kick them out) obtain a logistic boost in terms of recruitment and the range of tactics that it can choose. Hosting camps or safe houses beyond their rivals' reach increases the rebels' reserve army, enhances training, and encourages more audacious attacks across the border. In Chapter 5 we examine how the Palestinian insurgency took advantage of camps in Jordan and Lebanon to carry out hit-and-run incursions into Israel that may not have been possible in the absence of the sanctuary. Figure 3.5 presents in a more systematic fashion how sanctuaries help clandestine groups launch more guerrilla-like attacks. Compared to purely clandestine groups, those with some sort of sanctuary show a greater ability to carry out guerrilla-like attacks. But they stop far from mimicking insurgencies with territorial control.

We close with a brief look at how rebel groups behave when they operate beyond their 'natural' borders. The GTD1 collects information about the attack's location, so we coded the share of killings perpetrated by each group

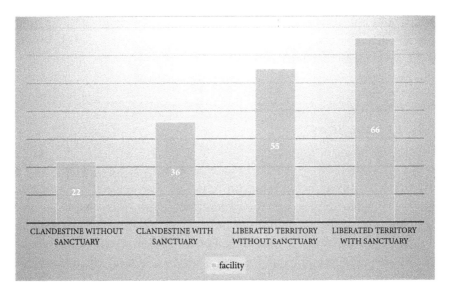

Figure 3.5 Sanctuaries and facility attacks (as percentage of all attacks), based on GTD1 data

---

[10] Similar results can be obtained using the GTD for the whole period 1970–2018. We continue using the GTD1 for consistency with the previous results.

100 Underground Violence

Table 3.7 International attacks and territorial control, based on GTD1 data

	Territorial control (without sanctuaries)		
	No	Yes	Dif-of-means test
Attacks abroad (of all attacks)	0.15	0.06	1.91*
Bombings abroad (of all attacks abroad)	0.45	0.31	1.4

beyond its country of reference. To avoid distortions provoked by groups operating in sanctuaries abroad (whose dynamics do not necessarily reproduce those of fully clandestine groups), we only select groups without that advantage. The results in the first row of Table 3.7 show that clandestine groups more than double the share of foreign attacks than insurgencies with territorial control. Although there is much confusion about the use of terrorism in civil wars, to our knowledge no scholar has conflated civil wars with international terrorist attacks. Our results suggest why: international terrorism is almost exclusively the domain of clandestine groups (ISIS, in this regard, is a noteworthy exception; see Chapter 5).

The second row of Table 3.7, regarding the prevalence of bombings in international attacks, still shows a higher percentage for underground groups, but the difference is no longer statistically significant, for good reason: once rebels act outside their countries, the constraints of clandestinity are equal for all of them, regardless of whether they have territorial control at home or not.

3.4. Conclusions

In this chapter we have theorized that clandestinity is a consequence of an extreme form of asymmetry. When the rebels are very weak vis-à-vis the state, they are forced to operate from the underground. Both the formation of clandestine groups and the adoption of indirect tactics are largely determined by an extreme asymmetric imbalance between rebels and states. Asymmetry prevents rebels seizing and holding territory and forces them to remain underground. The best tactical option for clandestine rebel groups is to resort to indirect, coercive tactics such as IEDs, assassinations, and kidnappings.

However, it is not only underground groups that engage in indirect tactics; some territorial groups also do it. We find that this usually happens when territory-controlling insurgents operate in areas under safe state control, beyond the war theatre in which they compete for territory (typically, the country's capital or other large cities). Absent territorial control, rebels resort to clandestine attacks.

The theory's main observable implication (in the actor-sense) is that underground groups have a non-linear relationship with development. These groups are more likely to emerge at intermediate levels of development: at low levels, rebels can liberate territory and create guerrilla insurgencies; at high levels, no rebel group, either clandestine or guerrilla-like, emerges given the strength of the state. In the action-sense, we have shown that the choice of tactics is a function of the degree of territorial control.

The empirical results reported here, both in the actor-sense (underground groups) and in the action-sense (indirect tactics), can be formulated without using the word 'terrorism'. These findings, however, follow from our conceptualization of terrorism. Moreover, the simplest and most natural interpretation of them is to consider that the underground groups and the tactics we have analysed in this chapter constitute an exploration of terrorist violence. We have shown that lack of territorial control has significant consequences for the resulting type of armed group and for the resulting kind of tactics employed. Briefly put, there is an obvious correspondence between the underground groups analysed here and the universe of terrorist groups, as well as between the indirect tactics examined and the universe of terrorist tactics. What these groups and these tactics have in common is that they stem from the conditions of extreme asymmetry. The greater the imbalance between the rebels and the state, the more likely it is that the rebels organize underground and resort to indirect tactics: that is, the more likely that they become terrorists and carry out terrorist attacks.

By interpreting our empirical findings in this way, we show that our conceptualization of terrorism not only makes sense of many of the constitutive characteristics of terrorism, but also generates interesting and novel empirical consequences that can be tested.

APPENDIX TO CHAPTER 3

The Measurement of Terrorism
and its Implications

Our conceptualization of terrorism has implications for the measurement of violence. These implications are implicit in much of the quantitative analysis of Chapter 3. In this appendix we address this issue more explicitly and we explore the consequences of measuring the concept in different ways. To show the importance of making sound decisions on how to operationalize terrorism, we engage in a replication exercise of a recent article that purports to refute the widely accepted thesis that terrorism is the weapon of the weak. By measuring terrorism according to our conceptualization, and keeping every other aspect of the research constant, we come to the opposite result, reestablishing our confidence in the traditional thesis that terrorism is used by weak armed groups or by groups that operate in an unfavourable context.

1. A Critique of Existing Measures

There is no straightforward operationalization of terrorism. Since we speak about terrorism in the actor- and action-senses, there cannot be a single measurement of the phenomenon. In the actor-sense, the key issue is whether the armed group holds territorial control or is underground (acknowledging that territorial control is a continuous property, its lower bound being clandestinity). In the action-sense, terrorism is about the tactics employed. Actors and tactics may not be approached with the same metric. Therefore, when it comes to measurement, we must decide which use is to be analysed.

When clandestine actors carry out clandestine attacks (upper-left cell in Table 2.1) or when territory-controlling insurgents spur armed assaults (lower-right cell in Table 2.1), the overlap between groups and actions is considerable, and empirical approaches focusing on one or the other may yield similar results. For instance, in Chapter 3 we have shown how the insight that terrorism is more pervasive in middle-income countries holds regardless of the use of data at three different levels of analysis (conflict, armed group, attacks). But this coincidence cannot be taken for granted. As there is no perfect match between the actor- and the action-senses, our conclusions will depend on the specific research questions we are trying to answer.

The actor- has received less attention than the action-sense in terrorism studies. This is unfortunate, because the actor-sense is crucial to bringing the agency of armed actors back into the analysis of conflict (Verwimp, Justino, and Brück, 2009). In Chapter 2 we provided operational criteria to distinguish underground groups from those with some degree of territorial control. Obviously, this approach demands a resource-intensive coding strategy, since the researcher must become familiar with the nature of hundreds of armed groups, but it generally generates more robust insights, as we have shown in Chapter 3.

Most research on terrorism has opted to drive in the easier lane of analysing terrorism from the action-sense, as open-access datasets in the field have traditionally focused on collecting information at the lowest possible level of aggregation: the attack or event.[11] ITERATE (International Terrorism: Attributes of Terrorist Events) pioneered this effort, covering international terrorist attacks since 1968 as units of observation. Collecting events is a daunting task; it requires highly detailed information sources, and the risk of under-reporting bias is considerable (Drakos and Gofas, 2006). This may be why, in the empirical study of civil wars, genocide, and ethnic violence, datasets usually focus on the conflict, not the event, as the unit of observation (which in some cases is disaggregated spatially and temporally).

The most comprehensive dataset on terrorism is the Global Terrorism Database (GTD) (La Free and Dugan, 2007), which is widely used in empirical studies on terrorism (a 'google scholar' search reports more than 11,000 hits). It covers data since 1970 and includes nearly 200,000 observations.[12] Around 45 per cent of all attacks have unknown authorship. The definition of terrorism guiding the selection of cases is quite broad: 'the threatened or actual use of illegal force and violence by a non-state actor to attain a political, economic, religious, or social goal through fear, coercion, or intimidation'. This definition, however, is not sufficiently precise to differentiate the various types of political violence. Hence, when it comes to operationalization,

---

[11] It could be argued that there is a still lower level, that of the victim. In our own dataset, the Domestic Terrorism Victims' dataset (DTV), which has covered Europe since 1965, the unit of observation is the person (properly identified in almost every case) who was killed by a terrorist group. 4,955 observations are included; see De la Calle and Sánchez-Cuenca (2011b).

[12] We use a GTD version that ends in 2018.

the GTD adds three criteria that can be combined in a sort of Boolean logic. An attack qualifies as terrorist if at least two of the three criteria are met:

> Criterion 1: The act must be aimed at attaining a political, economic, religious, or social goal. In terms of economic goals, the exclusive pursuit of profit does not satisfy this criterion. It must involve the pursuit of more profound, systemic economic change.
>
> Criterion 2: There must be evidence of an intention to coerce, intimidate, or convey some other message to a larger audience (or audiences) than the immediate victims. It is the act taken as a totality that is considered, irrespective if every individual involved in carrying out the act was aware of this intention. As long as any of the planners or decision-makers behind the attack intended to coerce, intimidate or publicize, the intentionality criterion is met.
>
> Criterion 3: The action must be outside the context of legitimate warfare activities. That is, the act must be outside the parameters permitted by international humanitarian law, insofar as it targets non-combatants (START, 2019).

The relationship between the three criteria and the original definition is hard to establish. Criterion 1 qualifies what the economic goals mentioned in the definition may be: they must be related to some sort of systemic economic change, but not personal profit. It may be guessed that the rationale for this is the exclusion of private goods from the terrorist agenda. Thus, Criterion 1 eliminates greed-motivated attacks, which are often observed in some civil conflicts in which the control of natural resources plays a key role (Collier and Hoeffler, 2004), and, relatedly, it also rules out organized crime. Criterion 1 may be seen as a reasonable restriction, but if there is a theoretical justification for it, then it is hard to understand why it is optional, that is, why an attack may be deemed terrorist even if it does not meet this condition, as long as it meets Criterion 2 and Criterion 3. In the case of organized crime, for instance, these two criteria (as well as the original definition) often apply: a large chunk of its violence takes place outside warfare activity and has an intimidatory or coercive intention. Therefore, it might be considered terrorist even if Criterion 1 is not met.

Criterion 2 does not seem particularly troublesome; it simply restates that the violence must have a coercive dimension. But this seems essential to the definition and, therefore, it is strange that an attack may be terrorist if it fulfils Criterion 1 and Criterion 3, but not 2. Finally, Criterion 3 is perhaps the most contentious of all. It introduces a condition about the target of the violence that is not mentioned at all in the original definition (McCann, 2023: 977). According to Criterion 3, the targets of the violence must be non-combatants. While Criterion 1 and Criterion 2 are met in around 98 per cent of attacks, there is a significant 12 per cent of all attacks that do not meet Criterion 3. However, as this is an optional requirement, 24,000 attacks against the military are included because, though they do not meet Criterion 3, they meet the other two.[13]

The ambiguity regarding Criterion 3 stems ultimately from a more general ambiguity about terrorism in the context of civil wars, which roughly corresponds to the upper-right cell of Table 2.1, that is, terrorist tactics carried out by groups with territorial control. Actually, most of the violence collected by the GTD comes from civil wars. Table A1 shows the 10 armed groups with the greatest number of attacks in the GTD, as well as the total number of fatalities.

As can be seen, all these armed actors (except for the IRA) are the main contenders in civil war conflicts.[14]. These 10 actors sum 40,302 attacks, or 38 per cent of all attacks for which the authorship is known. How the GTD filters the violence of civil war, classifying some of it as terrorism and the remaining as pure insurgent violence, is a bit of a mystery. Some attacks included in the database are far removed from a conventional understanding of terrorism. For example, in the case of the Afghan conflict, the GTD includes a battle, with hundreds of deaths and unfolding over five days, as

Table A1 10 armed groups with the highest number of attacks in the GTD

	Country	Attacks	Fatalities
Taliban	Afghanistan	8,727	37,653
Islamic State of Iraq and the Levant (ISIL)	Iraq, Syria	6,530	41,396
Shining Path	Peru	4,562	11,607
Al Shabaab	Somalia	3,797	10,518
Farabundo Martí National Liberation Front (FMNL)	El Salvador	3,351	8,065
New People's Army	Philippines	3,054	4,571
Irish Republican Army	United Kingdom	2,669	1,796
Boko Haram	Nigeria	2,665	21,702
Revolutionary Armed Forces of Colombia (FARC)	Colombia	2,490	5,661
Kurdistan Workers' Party	Turkey	2,457	5,093

[13] There are another 5,000 attacks against the military that meet Criterion 3. See McCann (2023) for a more systematic analysis.

[14] If the Troubles are also regarded as a civil war, then all 10 organizations would be major participants in civil wars.

106 Underground Violence

a terrorist incident. This is the description provided by the GTD about this supposedly 'terrorist incident':

> 08/10/2018: Assailants armed with mortars, explosive devices, and firearms attacked Ghazni, Afghanistan. At least 466 people, including 326 assailants, were killed in the ensuing clashes, which lasted until August 14, 2018. Additionally, some security personnel may have been abducted in the attack. The victims included security personnel and civilians. The Taliban claimed responsibility for the incident and stated that the attack would 'strengthen their position in talks'. In addition, the Afghan government also attributed responsibility to Lashkar-e-Taiba (LeT) and the Haqqani Network, though the Taliban insisted that they carried out the attack alone. (GTD ID code: 201808100024)

This is, clearly, an insurgent large-scale attack that bears no resemblance at all to terrorist attacks. The number of perpetrators is (at least) 326, far too high for terrorism; the operation lasts for five days, far too long for the immediacy of terrorist attacks; and the way in which the operation unfolds is completely different to the repertoire of terrorist attacks. The attack was a military operation against the Afghan army. However, the GTD considers that this attack fulfils criteria 1 to 3 and therefore is classified as terrorism. If this attack is included as terrorism, then much, if not all, insurgent violence falls under the category of terrorism.

The GTD's loose conceptualization of terrorism leads to biases across space and time. The definition is so ambiguous that the dataset may reflect political or ideological trends that are alien to the phenomenon itself. Let us briefly highlight some of those biases. With regards to the spatial distribution of attacks, it is easy to note a shift in collecting data from the Americas during the Cold War (51 per cent of attacks were from the continent) to the Middle East and South Asia, the hot spots of the so-called 'war on terror' from 2001 (see Table A2). The latter regions made up 19 per cent of the attacks during

Table A2 Geographical distribution of GTD attacks (vertical percentages)

Regions	Cold War	1990s	War on terror (≥2001)
Americas	50.8	27.9	3.3
Western Europe	24.0	16.4	3.0
Middle East and Maghreb	8.0	18.9	34.7
South Asia	10.7	21.6	42.8
East and Central Asia	0.5	2.5	0.3
Eastern Europe	0.2	4.4	2.5
Sub-Saharan Africa	5.5	8.0	13.3
Australasia & Oceania	0.2	0.3	0.1

the Cold War, but they skyrocketed to 77 per cent of the attacks during the 'war on terror'. The obvious critique is that these regions have been as war-prone during the last two decades as they were during the Cold War years, with severe (although mostly GTD-unreported) civil wars in Afghanistan, India, Pakistan, and Bangladesh. In another vein, the bias against Africa in the GTD has already been documented (Lutz and Lutz, 2013).

The case of Afghanistan is again particularly concerning. The Soviet-Afghan war (1979–89) is largely absent from the GTD, as if there had been no terrorist incidents according to the GTD criteria during this long and bloody conflict. The first attacks registered in the GTD are in 1988, at the very end of the Russian invasion. However, it makes little sense to assume that the attacks by the mujahideen were never terrorist following the GTD definitions. On the contrary: in their detailed account of the mujahideen's tactics during the war, Jalali and Grau (2001) dedicate one full chapter to 'urban combat' and register several terrorist operations as retold by their perpetrators. The US invasion of Afghanistan, by contrast, is richly covered in the GTD, with thousands of terrorist attacks each year. This imbalance between the two conflicts may be partly due to the different nature of the conflicts in the 1980s and in the 2000s, but the total absence of coverage of terrorist incidents in the first conflict is telling about the lack of consistency in the application of the GTD definitions.

As for variation over time, the rise in attacks overlapping with the spark of US operations abroad in the aftermath of the 9/11 terrorist attacks is noticeable, and more specifically, following the rise of the Islamic State and the twin wars in Syria and Iraq. Figure A1 includes another interesting trend about fatalities per terrorist attack. During the 1970s, terrorist attacks failed to produce more than one death per attack; the ratio grew during the 1980s fuelled by the civil wars in Latin America, but it skyrocketed after 9/11 and markedly during the last decade. This, of course, could be driven by a higher lethality of armed actors resorting to terrorism, but, equally, it may be the consequence of applying different coding rules in different periods.

In favour of the latter hypothesis, the GTD's collection procedures seem to be increasingly aligning the dataset with more conventional datasets on civil war. For instance, Bethany Lacina's dataset on battle deaths (Lacina and Gleditsch, 2005) offers a good approach to lethality during civil wars (we eliminate battle deaths due to inter-state wars from the dataset). If the GTD captures something different from civil war violence, we should observe low correlation between the two measures of lethality. Tellingly, the correlation is 0.38 from 1989 to 2000, but then shoots up to 0.94 after that year. This is

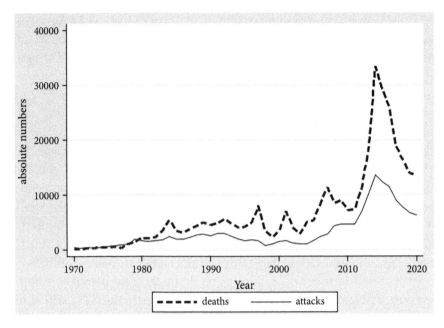

Figure A1 Evolution of GTD incidents and deaths over time

additional evidence that typical episodes of civil war combat have 'slipped into' the GTD dataset in large numbers.

Based on these considerations, we are sceptical about empirical analyses that use the GTD—as it stands—for the study of terrorism. The GTD can be compared to a rich oilfield. Crude oil has first to go through a refinement process before it can be used for industrial purposes. The 'refinement', so to say, may go in two directions: either the actor- or the action-sense. For the actor-sense, the GTD can be used when augmented with information about the territorial control of the armed groups. For the action-sense, we need to devise proxies that come close to the tactics that are associated with terrorism. The next section develops this point further.

2. A Replication Exercise

Even though most datasets are imperfect, we do not agree with the popular idea that quantitative studies of terrorism are 'doomed' (Mahoney, 2018). As repeatedly emphasized throughout this book, datasets are very useful research tools, if properly used. Therefore, we would like to show that empirical research using the GTD database could still provide fruitful findings if concise definitions of terrorism are used to curate the database.

To make our point, we need to raise a thorny issue: the use of terrorism in the context of civil war. Findley and Young (2012) used the GTD to analyse attacks in civil conflicts, finding that at least half of the GTD attacks take place in them. For reasons explained in the previous section, we argue that this is problematic given the ambiguity of the GTD's operationalization of terrorism. Other authors have provided more specific operational rules. Stanton (2013) and Fortna (2015; 2023), for instance, focus on targets. Thus, they consider that terrorism in the context of civil war corresponds to indiscriminate civilian victimization (excluding the selective civilian victimization aimed at generating compliance that was reviewed in Chapter 2). This indiscriminate violence is proxied via bomb attacks against civilians, which is the indicator chosen to measure terrorism. There is some plausibility in this way of defining 'civil war terrorism', since it is often the case that when guerrillas act in urban contexts, completely detached from their territorial area, civilians (soft targets) are operationally easier than the military or police (hard targets); moreover, if the goal is to terrorize the population or to break the will of the state, a civilian massacre may be the most efficient tactic. However, we contend that this method of categorizing terrorism in civil wars is conceptually wrong, because what makes the attack terrorist is not the target, but its underground condition.

Since a detailed examination of attacks is not feasible in a cross-sectional analysis of conflicts (with many thousands of attacks in each conflict), we need a proxy for the measurement of terrorism. Based on the argument made in Chapter 3, we think that the best proxy for terrorism is the use of bombs, regardless of whether the attack is indiscriminate or not, or whether the attack is aimed at civilians or not. Bombs are consistent with the actor operating underground. Of course, bombs can also be used in operations in which military power is employed. However, we assume that if the use of bombs is more frequent in a particular conflict, this may be a symptom of a greater frequency of underground operations.

In section 3.3 of Chapter 3 it was shown that (i) weaker armed groups resort to bombs to a greater extent than stronger ones, and (ii) a target-based codification of attacks does not yield meaningful results. In this Appendix, we take issue with Fortna (2023), who claims that terrorism (understood as 'deliberately indiscriminate attacks on civilians') is not the 'weapon of the weak' because civilian targeting does not seem to be driven by rebel weakness.[15] And it should not, we could add. In what follows, we replicate Fortna's

---

[15] Fortna (2023) is aware that not all civilian victimization in the context of civil war can be regarded as terrorist, a point we repeatedly made in Chapter 2. In her own words, selective civilian victimization 'is

110 Underground Violence

analysis using an alternative operationalization of terrorism based on the use of bombs and show in a simple way that there is a strong link between her main measures of rebel weakness and the share of bomb attacks (alternatively, there is no connection between target types and rebel weakness).

In her analysis of the 'weapons of the weak' hypothesis, Fortna (2023) relies on the Terrorism in Armed Conflict (TAC) dataset (Fortna, Lotito, and Rubin 2020), which covers 409 rebel groups over the 1970–2013 period. This dataset draws armed groups from the UCDP dataset on civil wars and then matches those actors with attacks as coded in the GTD. As the UCDP only includes groups above a certain threshold of violence (25 deaths per year), this procedure is certainly biasing the TAC against small, clandestine groups whose low-intensity campaigns remain below the radar of civil war-focused datasets. Of course, one could claim that these groups are not operating in a 'civil war' context and therefore should be excluded from the dataset. But then it is difficult to justify the use of the TAC if the researcher really wants to test hypotheses about weak armed groups resorting to terrorism. Despite the rich information embodied in the GTD, the TAC focuses only on attacks against civilians.

Fortna displays 14 different measures of 'rebel weakness' to prove her point that terrorism (understood as the number of attacks against civilians) is unrelated to rebel strength. Because the dependent variable has many zeros and is overdispersed, she runs 'zero-inflated negative binomial' models. She does not find any support for the idea that civilian targeting is empirically connected to rebel weakness, concluding that the famous statement that terrorism is the weapon of the weak is unproven.

We proceed as follows. For the sake of simplicity, the GTD attacks are classified into three target categories (civilians, combatants, and government personnel); we then add as an alternative dependent variable our proxy, bomb attacks. We then merged these numbers into the TAC dataset.

When measured in absolute terms (total number of attacks), the correlation between these different dependent variables is very high, always above 0.60 (n=1,719), indicating that TAC's armed actors with a high number of attacks against civilians also carry out a large number of attacks against combatants (p=0.73) and government personnel (p=0.78), as well as using bombs (0.90). We replicate Fortna's results but substitute our four dependent variables (civilians, government, combatants, and bombs) for her measures of

---

ubiquitous in civil wars (Stanton 2016, 30), but is not what we normally think of as "terrorism". Focusing instead on deliberately indiscriminate violence, I seek to capture the inherent randomness that makes terrorism so terrifying' (Fortna, 2023: 643).

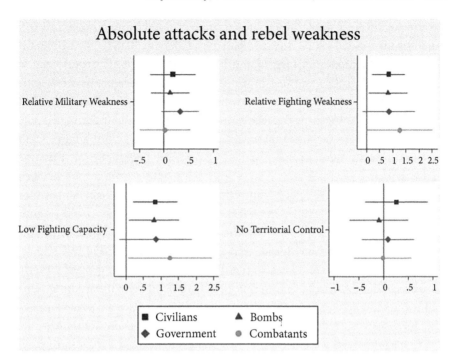

Figure A2 Absolute attacks and different measures of rebel weakness (zero-inflated negative binomial models with control variables)

Note: Predictive coefficients with 95 per cent intervals from ZINB models with all controls included.

civilian targeting.[16] However, we introduce the same controls and employ the same estimation techniques. Figure A2 reports the relationship between the total number of attacks and Fortna's most straightforward indicators of rebel weakness (results do not vary if others are chosen). The results indicate that it does not matter whether we use different types of targets or the bombing tactics, as the differences between them are weak or insignificant in every case. With these results in mind, we might conclude that rebel strength is unrelated to different indicators of violence.

However, these negative results are not particularly informative. As explained in Chapter 3, it is key to measure targets or tactics as shares and not as count variables. The reason is easy to grasp: large groups commonly generate high numbers across every variable measuring targets or tactics. The comparison in the total number of civilians killed across large and small

---

[16] We would like to thank Page Fortna for kindly sharing the replication data for her *Journal of Conflict Resolution*'s 2023 article with us.

groups makes little sense, since large groups also kill more combatants than small groups (see De la Calle and Sánchez-Cuenca, 2015).[17] By calculating the relative frequency of targets and bombs for each TAC group-year, we can rerun the models and test more carefully if weaker groups fixate more on specific targets and tactics, controlling for the number of attacks. If the dependent variables are properly measured, as shares or relative frequencies, our argument implies that weaker groups will carry out a larger share of bomb attacks than stronger armed actors. The argument, on the other hand, remains agnostic about targeting: clandestine groups may be more aggressive towards civilians because their intrinsic weakness prompts them to attack soft targets (Hultman, 2009), or, alternatively, they could be more careful because they rely heavily on the logistical support of third actors who may not sanction indiscriminate actions against civilians (De la Calle and Sánchez-Cuenca, 2013). It is also possible that clandestine groups with different ideological aims have different preferences on civilian targeting (De la Calle and Sánchez-Cuenca, 2011b), which is, in our view, a clear example of why terrorism as civilian targeting misses the point (see also Table 3.3).

Once again, even if we use other researchers' datasets (TAC, in this case), Figure A3 confirms that measures of rebel weakness are systematically related to a higher reliance on bomb attacks. In contrast, levels of rebel strength do not account for variation in civilian targeting. Interestingly, there is some evidence that weaker rebels proportionally target more combatants, although this finding is less robust than the link between bombs and rebel weakness.[18]

The results of Figure A3 increase our confidence in the 'weapon of the weak' hypothesis. Terrorism, proxied by the share of bombings relative to other tactics, is more frequent in groups without territorial control. The general lesson that we draw from this exercise is that different operationalizations of terrorism may lead to very different findings. When terrorism is proxied as mass civilian attacks, rebel strength is irrelevant. However, when terrorism is measured, no matter how imperfectly, in a consistent way with our conceptualization of terrorism as underground violence, we restore the classical idea that terrorism is driven by the high asymmetry between the rebels and the state.

---

[17] A comparison of absolute figures across highly heterogeneous armed groups is equivalent to comparing the electoral support for parties measured by the total amount of votes for each party across countries with very different population sizes. Thus, in highly populated countries, almost any type of party will gain more votes than would be the case in small countries. The only way to overcome this problem is to compare relative support cross-nationally. The same holds for the use of tactics by armed groups.

[18] Regarding territorial control, its effect on bombings is statistically weaker. However, it must be noted that Fortna's measure of territorial control is drawn from the Non-State Actor dataset (Cunningham, Gleditsch, and Salehyan, 2013), whose definition and operationalization is obscure (see our discussion about this in Section 3.2). In Chapter 3, Tables 3.4, 3.5, and Figure 3.4 show that bombings have a lower relative frequency in groups that enjoy territorial control.

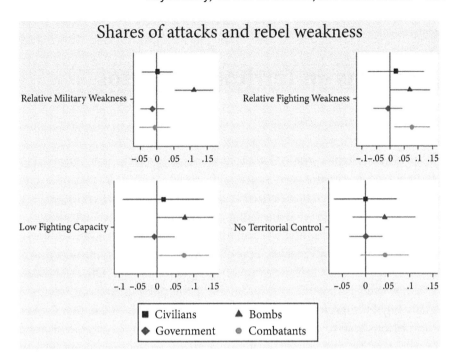

Figure A3 Share of attacks and different measures of rebel weakness (OLS models with control variables)

Note: Predictive coefficients with 95 per cent intervals from OLS models with all controls included.

Many quantitative studies on terrorism do not problematize the use of existing datasets. The operationalization of terrorism is not usually discussed, or, if it is, the measurement decisions are not based on a theoretical analysis of the phenomenon. Although datasets become a sort of 'focal point' for researchers (and the more they are used, the more well-established they seem), the fact is that datasets suffer from the same shortcomings that affect the field in general. Our point is not that we should stop using datasets like the GTD, but, rather, that the raw data they offer must be processed according to a coherent and systematic conceptualization of the phenomenon. Otherwise, statistical analyses, even if they incorporate the most sophisticated estimation techniques, cannot be fully trusted.

4

Variations on Territorial Control

The previous chapter showed that clandestinity is driven by an extreme imbalance of power between states and armed groups. Terrorism is epitomized by indirect tactics perpetrated either by underground groups or territory-controlling groups operating under conditions of clandestinity.

The analyses in Chapter 3 were all quantitative, based on large samples of armed groups. The advantages of a quantitative approach are many, from high external validity to the rigour of hypothesis testing. The main drawback, however, is that the measurement of the phenomenon of interest is usually highly imperfect. As discussed in the Appendix of Chapter 3, there is no obvious way to operationalize terrorism using the available information provided by the datasets in the field. We suggested using bombings as a proxy for underground armed activity, but, obviously, bombings can be employed for reasons other than the constraints of clandestinity. Despite its limitations, we were able to test several hypotheses that confirmed that our conceptualization of terrorism is not only internally consistent, but also that it has the capacity to generate hypotheses of various kinds that are interesting in themselves for the study of armed violence.

Case studies do not have as much external validity as quantitative comparisons, but, in compensation, they give us a broader lens to carefully trace the dynamics of asymmetry, control, and tactic choice—or, in other words, the causal mechanisms at work. Thanks to a detailed analysis of the cases, we can examine the strategic thinking of the armed groups and how they cope with the constraints of the underground and the possibilities opened by territorial control. As the quotations reproduced in Chapter 2 show, rebel leaders think carefully about the implications of (the lack of) territorial control for their own goals and tactics. In this chapter and the following, we describe their ruminations about the impact of clandestinity. The case studies, in sum, are an important complement to the previous quantitative analysis because they highlight the rebels' decision-making process as well as the connected sequencing of asymmetry, control, and tactics.

Underground Violence. Luis De la Calle and Ignacio Sánchez-Cuenca, Oxford University Press.
© Luis De la Calle and Ignacio Sánchez-Cuenca (2024). DOI: 10.1093/oso/9780198904816.003.0005

In this chapter we exploit variation across armed groups with regard to territorial control. Through case studies, we show not only the importance of territory for the choice of tactics, but also the way in which armed groups think and argue about gaining territory versus going underground. We compare three groups that offer variation on their level of territorial control: a fully underground organization (Tupamaros); an underground group that enjoyed a safe haven or sanctuary (ETA); and an insurgency which, despite seizing territory, often used terrorist tactics (Shining Path).

We start with the Tupamaros of Uruguay. Although there are more well-known cases of fully clandestine groups, such as the Red Brigades in Italy and the Red Army Faction in Germany, groups that otherwise fit our theoretical argument very well, we prefer instead to recount the story of the Tupamaros because they were the first rebel group to openly think about the implications of facing structural conditions that did not favour a territory-bound armed strategy. In fact, many other revolutionary groups acting in developed countries drew largely on Tupamaros' strategic thinking to justify their underground status.

Our second case is ETA in Spain, a group aiming for secession of the Basque territories from Spain and France to form a new country. Created during the last decade of the Franco dictatorship in Spain, the group toyed with the idea of controlling territory, but quickly came to the conclusion that an underground strategy would be more effective for its survival as well as for the fulfilment of its goals. The interesting twist of this case is that ETA, although fully underground in Spanish territory, had the ability to operate a sanctuary in French territory thanks to the permissiveness of the French state. France was not openly in favour of Basque demands but was disappointed with the pace of the Spanish transition, and so its government looked the other way as long as militants did not carry out attacks on French soil. Short of territorial control in France, ETA members nonetheless enjoyed a freedom of movement that facilitated the logistical consolidation of the organization, by offering a safe haven for both leadership and 'cell shooters', and a focal point to coordinate its financial strategy (ETA, for example, dragged Basque entrepreneurs to the French side of the border to force them to pay protection money in exchange for not being targeted). The sanctuary advantage, in this specific case, strengthened the underground group and increased its odds of survival, but had little influence on ETA's repertoire of violence because the group refused to carry out border operations, fearing spillover effects on French soil.

Our final illustration is *Sendero Luminoso* (Shining Path; SP) of Peru. Operating in a country with poor state capabilities, this Maoist group was

116 Underground Violence

able to seize and rule large areas of its mountainous hinterland and became involved in a dirty war with the military and the self-defence groups that emerged locally to contain the rebels' advances. But, at the same time, the Shining Path was always drawn towards a crush on the capital city, Lima, a place where state strength was at its highest. To operate there, SP cells had to abide by the rules of clandestinity, which evolved into a very different history of violence.

Taken together, these three illustrations show that for most rebel groups, the decision to pick a particular 'warfare toolkit' was made relatively early in the conflict and was largely conditional on the balance of power between the contenders, and—absent big shifts in that asymmetry of power—rebels stuck to it until the end. In Chapter 5 we will investigate how rebel groups adapt to power-balance changes by tracing the ebb-and-flows of the Palestinian insurgency and ISIS.

4.1. Tupamaros

The MLN-T (*Movimiento de Liberación Nacional-Tupamaros*, Tupamaros National Liberation Movement) was a revolutionary armed group created in Uruguay in 1966. Uruguay was the least likely country in Latin America for the emergence of a leftist insurgency; in fact, it was popularly known as the 'Switzerland of South America'. Uruguay was in 1966 the second-richest country in Latin America in terms of GDP per capita (after Argentina). Unlike Argentina, however, the country enjoyed at the time a consolidated democracy with a stable two-party system. Moreover, Uruguay possessed an inauspicious geography for a guerrilla: it is a flat and highly urbanized country, with no mountains or jungle in which the insurgents might hide.

The only favourable condition was the bad shape of the economy in the 1960s. There were clear signs of stagnation, plus high inflation, which led to growing social tensions and labour unrest that resulted in increasingly repressive governmental measures. However, this is probably insufficient to account for the emergence of the Tupamaros. Many countries have undergone economic crises that did not bring armed groups into existence. The origins of the MLN-T have to be found elsewhere, in the wave of insurgent movements that emerged after the success of the Cuban revolution in 1959 (Wickham-Crowley, 1992: 30–31). In the Marxist interpretation of the Cuban experience, the lack of objective conditions for revolution was not an unsurmountable obstacle if the insurgents were able to create them through their own armed campaign. In the words of 'Che' Guevara, 'it is not necessary to wait for the moment when all the conditions for revolution hold, the insurrectional foco may create them' (Guevara, 2002 [1960]: 13, our translation). According to the 'foco' theory, a small bunch of guerrillas acting in the countryside may gain local support and set in motion a sort of snowball effect that will eventually bring about a revolutionary uprising.

The Tupamaros shared the standard revolutionary view that the violence of a committed group might trigger a revolutionary insurrection by the masses; violence would reveal the state's vulnerability, raise class consciousness, and polarize the social conflict (Porzecanski, 1973: 14). This justification of violence falls under the label of 'armed propaganda'. As was explained in the brief document '30 preguntas a un Tupamaro' (Thirty Questions for a Tupamaro), written in 1968, 'revolutionary action in itself, the very fact of obtaining weapons, of getting the equipment, of carrying out deeds that break the bourgeois legality, generates revolutionary consciousness, organization, and revolutionary conditions'.[1] In the same document, violence is justified as follows: 'the people want change and they have to choose between the unlikely and remote possibility offered by some through proclamations, manifestos, and parliamentary action and the direct path embodied by the armed group and its revolutionary action' (our translation). This is almost identical to what Bakunin wrote in his 'Letters to a Frenchman on the Present Crisis' (1870) about the 'propaganda by the deed' doctrine (Bakunin, 1971: 195–6).

Despite sharing with 'Che' Guevara a similar philosophy of the revolution, the Tupamaros thought that establishing a revolutionary foco in the countryside was a non-starter in Uruguay due to the unfavourable geographic conditions and the high population concentration in urban areas. Thus, from the very beginning the group opted for urban guerrilla as the most adequate strategy in the special context of Uruguay. That meant acting underground and, therefore, choosing violent tactics that were consistent with clandestinity. The Tupamaros was a fully underground organization and therefore constitutes a pure case of terrorism according to Table 2.1.

The MLN-T was one of the first armed groups that ruled out the possibility of a rural guerrilla in which the insurgents gain territorial control. Consequently, the Tupamaros created an underground organization, with no territorial base or safe haven in the countryside or in any other country. The adaptation of guerrilla methods to the urban milieu was to have enormous consequences. The Tupamaros provided an example that was emulated by many other revolutionary groups in affluent countries (Torres,

---

[1] The document is reproduced in *Punto Final*, no. 58, 2 July 1968, pp. 5–8 (our translation).

118 Underground Violence

2002: 230). In the Federal Republic of Germany, an anarchist group called itself 'Tupamaros-West Berlin' in 1969 (it was the embryo of the group 2nd June Movement, see Baumann, 1977: 59–60; Smith and Moncourt, 2009: 46). More generally, the Tupamaros' influence can be traced in a number of European and North-American groups, including the Red Brigades in Italy (Ginsborg, 2003: 362), the Spanish First of October Anti-Fascist Resistance Groups, GRAPO (Moa, 2002: 233), and the Weather Underground Organization in the USA (Burrough, 2015: 124; Jacobs, 1997: 60). Moreover, the organizational innovations of the Tupamaros (the so-called 'compartmentalization' of the organization; see below) were widely adopted by other underground groups.

The Tupamaros, certainly, were not the first urban guerrilla in history. They were aware of precedents, including the urban campaign of the National Liberation Front in Algiers, the Irgun in British Palestine or the urban Resistance during World War II. Having said this, the MLN-T was the first revolutionary group that fully theorized and employed urban guerrilla.

In what follows we reconstruct the discussion that led to the adoption of the urban guerrilla strategy, the adaptation of tactics to the underground structure, and the anomalies that emerged when they deviated from the urban approach and tried to also act in rural areas.

Urban Guerrilla

Ironically, the origins of the Tupamaros' urban guerrilla go back to the sugar cane workers in Bella Unión, in the department of Artigas, in the rural north of the country. In 1961 Raul Sendic created the Artigas Sugar Cane Workers' Union, which carried out strikes, land occupations, and protest marches in Montevideo. The workers gained new rights and better work conditions. The peasants' actions resonated in the capital city, and Sendic became a leader for the Left. In the early 1960s, he still believed, under the influence of the Cuban model, that revolutionary potential was greater among rural workers than among urbanites. The peasants' struggle radicalized Sendic, who increasingly favoured the adoption of violent forms of protest. In 1963, after he was arrested, he said that a 'loaded gun is a better guarantee than both the Constitution of the Republic and the laws that establish rights' (Blixen, 2005: 98; our translation). Not much later, he went underground.

The MLN-T was the outcome of the confluence between Sendic's Union and an urban network formed in 1962 by several Leftist groups (ranging from Anarchists to Socialists), called *el coordinador* (the coordinator).

El coordinador was also in favour of radical politics and armed struggle. However, their members did not share Sendic's ideas about a rural revolutionary movement; they thought that the prevailing conditions in Uruguay suggested an alternative approach, based on actions in the urban centres. Sendic was eventually persuaded that this unorthodox strategy was more promising. The two groups merged formally in the new MLN-T in January 1966, during the Tupamaros Convention, attended by a few dozen activists (Brum, 2016: 58–9).

The formation of a guerrilla group was met with scepticism on the Left. In his memoirs, Eleuterio Fernández Huidobro, a member of *el coordinador* and one of the founders of the MLN-T, refers to an interview with Fidel Castro in 1967 in the Uruguayan Leftist periodical *Marcha* in which the Cuban leader was asked about the prospects of a guerrilla movement in Uruguay; his answer was categorical: 'Your country lacks the geographical conditions for armed struggle. There are no mountains. There are no jungles. No guerrilla can develop there' (Fernández Huidobro, 2005: 356; our translation). His words reflected the standard Guevarist line about the pre-eminence of the rural front. According to this argument, armed struggle was doomed if a rural guerrilla was not feasible. The Tupamaros broke with this assumption, which was paralysing in the context of Uruguay; they created a successful urban guerrilla.

The theoretical foundations of the urban guerrilla had been laid out by Abraham Guillén, a Spanish exile who participated in the defence of Madrid against Francoist troops during the Civil War. After spending time in prison, Guillén left Spain in 1948 and settled in Argentina. There, he became involved in the formation of the first Peronist guerrilla in 1959, known as *los Uturuncos*, still following the Cuban model (Carretero, 2020: 108–34). Its utter failure led him to reconsider his initial beliefs about the guerrilla. In the 1960s he developed a theory about the urban guerrilla, arguing that in highly urbanized countries (such as Argentina and Uruguay), the guerrillas were more effective acting in the cities, 'the jungles of cement', to use his own metaphor, being closer to the revolutionary subject, the working class. His main point was that the urban guerrilla is not aimed at militarily destroying the enemy's army; rather, violence was the instrument to gain the support of the population in the context of a long war. Once the people side with the urban guerrilla, the revolution would succeed. In Guillén's words:

> A revolutionary commander should not be subject to the myths of the classic strategy, in which all else is secondary to the conquest of space. In the case of the revolutionary, the fundamental strategic objective is not space. The positive force is the will of the people. (Guillén, 1973: 242; orig. Spanish: Guillén, 1966: 69)

120 Underground Violence

Guillén had moved to Uruguay in 1962, establishing close links with many of the radicals (Sendic included) who would found the FLN-T. In 1966 he published *Estrategia de la guerrilla urbana*, a brief essay on the urban guerrilla (part of which is reproduced in Guillén, 1973). Its influence on the strategic orientation of the Tupamaros was obvious, though there has been some controversy about the true authorship of the ideas on the urban guerrilla.[2]

In June 1967, the Tupamaros made public *Documento 1*, in which they provided a full presentation of their goals and strategy.[3] The geographical constraints are explicitly recognized: 'There are no places that are impenetrable or that make the establishment of an enduring rural foco possible.' Hence, 'armed struggle in Uruguay will be mainly urban. The struggle in the country-side will be auxiliary.'

The document lists some advantages of acting in big cities. Firstly, urban areas with little police presence can be safe for the militants. Secondly, cities make communication and interactions faster. Thirdly, logistical issues are easier to handle in the city. Fourthly, militants can maintain their normal life during the day and act during the night, except those who go fully underground. Fifthly, combatants do not have to adapt to the new conditions of the rural world—they act in areas they are already familiar with. Although a rural foco is not possible, the rural area works as a rearguard in which the militants can find refuge, or in which the guerrillas can carry out small-scale operations to divert security forces serving in the city. Lastly, the combatants who act in the city are closer to both the masses and the targets of violence.

The decision to go underground was more literal than in any other armed group: the Tupamaros used the sewer system to move rapidly and safely under the city. Sendic thought that the sewer was the counterpart to the mountains in the hinterland; that is, areas in which the army does not enter (Blixen, 2005: 301). Efrain Martínez Platero was in charge of the sewer territory and became known in the organization as 'the lord of the sewer' (Brum, 2016: 292–3).[4] The sewer was the most effective means to move secretly and swiftly within the enemy's territory.

---

[2] See, for instance, Blixen (2005: 155) and Marchesi (2019: 64). Carretero (2020: 174), in his biography of Guillén, makes clear Guillén's paternity of these ideas.

[3] The document can be found at http://www.archivochile.com/America_latina/JCR/MLN_T/tupa_de/tupade0001.pdf. Torres (2002) provides a full analysis of the document. Jorge Torres was a Tupamaro who was involved in the preparation of *Documento 1*. All the quotations from the document are in our translation.

[4] Regarding the experience of moving through the city sewer, see Fernández Huidobro (2005: 240–41).

Targets and Popular Support

Documento 1 clearly states that the constraints of clandestine violence influence the type of attacks that the organization can carry out: the number of combatants involved in an operation has to be small. This does not necessarily mean that the organization is small. Although the size of underground groups is rather uncertain due to its secret condition, it has been estimated that at the peak there were 400 armed Tupamaros, plus a wide network of militants who provided logistical assistance formed by several thousand people (between 2,000 and 4,000) (Waldmann, 2011). Brum (2016: 328) states that in the last months of the organization, between April and November 1972, when it was on the verge of collapse, 2,873 members of the FLN-T were arrested.[5]

Particularly during the early years, most activists were 'legal', leading a normal life and ready to act when the organization requested it. To maintain such a large organization, the Tupamaros implemented a policy of 'compartmentalization', so that the members of cells lacked information about what other cells did; this avoided breaches of security, but when things went wrong, it prevented any form of mutual help between cells (Porzecanski, 1973: 33–6).

The growth of violence was gradual. There were very few attacks in 1966 and in 1967, but a tenfold increase was observed in 1968 (Holmes, 2001: 81). In general, the levels of violence were always well below the Tupamaros' capacity. The peak (around 300 attacks) was reached in 1972, the year in which the organization was decimated and neutralized by the army. Clearly, the Tupamaros were not interested in maximizing violence or fatalities. For the FLN-T, the goal was not the destruction of the army, or a war of attrition that exhausts the enemy's capacity to resist; rather, violence was supposed to gain the support of the masses. That is, terror was not aimed at terrorizing the population, but at raising the popularity of the guerrilla campaign (Brum, 2016: 104). This required not only a selective use of violence, but also attacks that might be received with a sympathetic attitude by the population (the Tupamaros talked about *formas simpáticas*). Indiscriminate attacks were carefully avoided (consequently, few bombings were employed to minimize the risk of collateral victims). The propagandistic dimension of the attacks was crucial. For instance, some attacks had a 'Robin Hood' component, including robbing banks, the burning of a General Motors' factory coinciding with the visit of Nelson Rockefeller to Uruguay, or the kidnapping of a businessman who had declared himself to be a fascist. The 'populist'

---

[5] Blixen (2005: 239), a Tupamaro himself, reports considerably higher figures.

122 Underground Violence

precedent was an action by *el coordinador* in December 1963, when they assaulted a truck with special Christmas food and distributed it in a poor neighbourhood (Brum, 2016: 53–4). Some of these attacks even had a comical side, with the explicit goal of ridiculing or humiliating the state's security forces.

It took some time for the Tupamaros to move into planned killings. The first non-intended fatality was the policeman Juan F. Garay on 8 July 1969: a Tupamaro commando was trying to take guns from a police patrol; Garay resisted and was killed. The first planned killing happened on 13 April 1970, four years after the FLN-T was created: the target was Héctor Morán Charquero, a police officer who was accused of having tortured many arrested Tupamaros.[6]

According to our own calculations, the FLN-T killed in total 52 people over the period 1969–72. This figure is substantially lower than the death toll of most rural guerrilla groups, which are often counted in thousands. Only one person was killed with an explosive device; all others were shot dead. In terms of the target identity, 79 per cent of all fatalities were members of the security forces. Were we to conceptualize terrorism as violence against civilians, we would have to conclude that the Tupamaros were not terrorists. The low percentage of non-combatant fatalities is partly a consequence of the high selectivity of the attacks: collateral victims were few in number.

The self-restraint shown by the FLN-T was dictated by the need to maintain popularity among the masses. In 1971, two surveys estimated at least partial support for the Tupamaros in the 36–41 per cent interval; in July 1972, another poll revealed support of 20 per cent (Holmes, 2001: 151). In the presidential elections of November 1971, the candidate of the *Frente Amplio* (Broad Front), the Leftist coalition in which the FLN-T participated, gained 18.3 per cent of the vote, which is roughly consistent with the figures provided by the surveys. There was, therefore, a substantial reservoir of support for the armed campaign of the Tupamaros.

As is typically the case in many underground groups, state repression weakened the organization and produced the first fatalities among the Tupamaros, which led to a process of greater radicalization and violent escalation in which self-restraint had to be partially sacrificed. The FLN-T became a more remorseless organization, as the kidnapping and assassination of Dan Mitrione (on 10 March 1970) made clear. Mitrione was an FBI officer who was

---

[6] This is not unique to the Tupamaros. In the case of the Red Brigades in Italy, the group was created in 1970, the first non-planned killing happened in 1974, and the first planned killing was in 1976 (Sánchez-Cuenca, 2019: 69–70).

assisting the government of Uruguay in matters of counter-terrorism, including the use of torture to extract information. The decision to kill Mitrione in cold blood provoked a wave of repulsion, even among the Left. The Tupamaros were universally portrayed as assassins; Guillén himself was critical of the decision made by the underground group (1973: 270).

In the last months of its existence, the Tupamaros engaged in a bilateral struggle against the Uruguayan armed forces and police. By then, they had lost the original innocence of their early operations. In this combat between the state and the armed group, the Tupamaros forgot about the masses' mobilization. This evolution towards greater isolation from the population is observed in many other revolutionary groups; the longer the conflict goes on, the more self-referential and aloof these groups become (Della Porta, 1995).

The Allure of the Rural Guerrilla

Although the Tupamaros theorized in greater depth than any other group about the advantages of urban guerrilla warfare, they did not completely abandon the model of the rural guerrilla. In fact, as pointed out above, the origin of the FLN-T was a peasant union. The possibility of a rural guerrilla exerted strong feelings in the imagination of the Tupamaros, who conceived armed urban struggle as a second-best or lesser evil—that is, a necessary adaption to the specific conditions of Uruguay given the impossibility of launching a Guevarist campaign in the countryside.

The tension between the ideal of a rural guerrilla and the reality of the urban struggle is revealed in the capture of Pando in 1969, an operation that well fits the description we offered in Chapter 2 of a proto-guerrilla (the kind of actions that underground groups carry out to gain territorial control). This was a multi-member operation (a facility attack, in the terminology of Chapter 3), involving around 50 Tupamaros, who entered the municipality of Pando (14,000 inhabitants), and occupied six strategic buildings, including the police station. Given Pando's proximity with the capital city (separated by less than thirty kilometres), the occupation was indeed brief: after one hour, the occupiers left town. However, during the escape, the Tupamaros were intercepted by security forces; three activists were shot dead and many more were arrested. In the fighting, the Tupamaros killed a civilian and a police officer. The whole operation sought to replicate a traditional guerrilla act aimed at gaining control of public space. The imitation was so complete that the perpetrators carried white armbands (Brum, 2016: 117). In fully underground operations, the activists cannot wear any identifying clothing;

their operations largely succeed or not depending on the extent to which they blend into the population (see Chapter 2).

The most interesting aspect of Pando's occupation lies in its propagandistic intent. The Tupamaros were not really interested in controlling the municipality. Rather, the occupation was an act of propaganda that consisted in showing that they had the capacity to act as a guerrilla searching for territorial control. In a way, the Pando operation was a representation of a rural guerrilla action. It had an unmistakably symbolic dimension, since the Tupamaros decided to carry it out on the second anniversary of 'Che' Guevara's death. German Cabrera, a member of the FLN-T, commented retrospectively on Pando: 'From that moment on, it was possible to speak of guerrillas and guerrilla warfare, since this baptism in blood placed the FLN on a par with any other insurrectional movement in the media' (Cabrera, 2015: 68; our translation). In a similar vein, a Tupamaro interviewed in 1970, who maintained anonymity, said regarding Pando: 'It was intended to impress the public, the enemy, and us too. [...] By making the whole exploit into a homage to Che Guevara we intended—through the inevitable repercussion it was bound to have throughout the South American continent—that the affair should carry an explicitly Latin American message' (Gilio, 1972: 126). Thus, the Tupamaros considered that, despite their urban scope, the most efficacious form of propaganda was to put into practice an attack that corresponded to a rural guerrilla in search of territorial control.

Sendic never abandoned the possibility of creating a secondary rural front that would complement the urban. At the end of 1971 he launched the so-called Plan Tatú, contradicting the official FLN-T's doctrine as presented in *Documento 1*. The *tatú* is an armadillo of South America that hides by excavating tunnels under the ground. Sendic thought that it was possible to apply hit-and-run tactics against villages in the north of Uruguay by escaping from security forces thanks to the construction of a series of so-called *tatuceras*— hideouts dug underground in the countryside. The fact that the plan relied on the *tatuceras* reveals that the organization was not considering the possibility of gaining territorial control in rural areas. In fact, the whole idea of a network of *tatuceras* has to be interpreted as an attempt to reproduce a clandestine structure in the countryside. In a curious inversion, the rural foco attempted by Sendic was ultimately inspired by the urban model.

The Plan Tatú came late, when the repression of the army against the FLN-T was at its maximum. The first actions occurred during the first months of 1972 and were an utter failure (Brum, 2016: 315). In a sense, the Plan Tatú was final confirmation that the Tupamaros were correct when they ruled out the employment of Guevarist tactics in Uruguay.

Both the Pando operation and the Plan Tatú were incongruent choices: the nature of these actions did not fit the clandestine nature of the organization. Whereas the occupation of Pando was mainly a propagandistic deed, a sort of a fake representation of a traditional guerrilla, the Plan Tatú was a more ambitious (but ultimately defective) attempt to escape from the cell of pure terrorism in Table 2.1; in this regard, they both should be understood as proto-guerrilla operations. As was explained in Chapter 2, proto-guerrilla is an unstable or transition category: if it succeeds, the organization gains territorial control; if it fails, the group goes back to its original underground condition. The Tupamaros are an instance of the latter.

Conclusions

The Tupamaros were a pure underground group. Consequently, its actions were typically terrorist. Except for some minor deviations, the tactics employed were consistent with clandestinity. The FLN-T, therefore, constitutes a perfect instance for the analysis of the consequences of being underground (actor-sense) and acting underground (action-sense). The group behaved with a high level of self-restraint, carrying out mostly selective attacks against security forces. The death toll was quite low (only 52 fatalities in five years), but the actions had a major impact on Uruguay's political system and precipitated the military coup of 1973.

At the time, the most frequent label used to describe the Tupamaros was 'urban guerrilla'. Guerrillas proliferated in Latin America after the Cuban revolution. Given the geographical and social peculiarities of Uruguay, the Tupamaros' choice of the urban strategy made full sense. When similar 'urban guerrillas' of the revolutionary persuasion started to act on Western European soil in the 1970s, very much inspired by the Tupamaros, they were referred to as terrorist groups. Of course, 'terrorism' was also used (for instance, by the Uruguayan army with regard to the Tupamaros), but the 'urban guerrilla' label was more frequently employed. As we have seen in this section, urban guerrilla is associated with terrorism because urban groups have to act underground, hiding in the 'jungles of cement'.

4.2. ETA

The Basque separatist group operated in Spain from the late 1960s to 2011 (see De la Calle, 2015a, Ch. 4, for a detailed account of the roots of this organization; and Sánchez-Cuenca, 2001, for its strategic approach to

126 Underground Violence

violence). ETA illustrates very vividly how leaders sometimes envision strategies that are far detached from the actual conditions of the places in which they plan to attack, and, even more, how quickly they update and downgrade their strategic warfare.

Thinking about Armed Violence

Euskadi Ta Askatasuna (ETA, Basque Homeland and Liberty, in Basque) had been created in the late 1950s, as several young nationalist dissidents were unhappy with the inaction of the dominant, but outlawed, Basque Nationalist Party, whose policy of appeasement with the Francoist dictatorship they openly rejected. The justification for the use of violence against the dictatorship came from a Basque philologist, Federico Krutwig. He was the first to openly advocate armed struggle to achieve independence for the Basque people. In his book *Vasconia*, published in 1963 under a pen name of Fernando Sarrailh, Krutwig theorized that the best strategy was urban warfare, predating the Tupamaros' turn towards terrorism (Sarrailh, 1963: 401):

> Given that the Basque Country is mainly industrial, especially in the Basque area where one finds the best conditions for the beginning of the conflict, we must start with an urban campaign, even if this is usually secondary in revolutionary wars. (our translation)

For Krutwig, the urban guerrilla was a precondition of the rural guerrilla, without which a revolution would never be realized. Actually, in a very prescient way, he claimed that 'both mountain and urban guerrillas will never be able to militarily defeat the enemy, but the sheer fact that the occupation forces do not beat the guerrillas will be victory in itself' (Sarrailh, 1963: 403). Krutwig backed an action–repression–action strategy whose ultimate goal was insurrection by the Basque people—although he did not specify how this uprising was supposed to take place. Terrorist tactics for him were rightly sanctioned as long as they targeted security forces and state personnel.

After endless debates about the correct ideological orientation that the organization should adopt—more class-oriented (bringing in working-class migrants but leaving aside the native upper class) or more language-oriented (the opposite)—it would take around a decade for the group to systematically develop its armed struggle. It put its so-called military front in the hands of Xavier Zumalde, aka *El Cabra* (the Goat), a local cadre with little appetite for ideology but much for action against the dictatorship. Feeling almost total liberty to implement whatever organizational design he wished, Zumalde agreed with Krutwig that insurrection was the ultimate goal, but disliked Krutwig's urban-first approach. For Zumalde, influenced apparently by 'Che' Guevara, the armed militants had to be strong enough to survive in harsh rural conditions. Zumalde forced recruits to spend long hours walking around mountainous areas in the interior of the Basque Country just for the pleasure of training for mobile guerrilla warfare. These long 'survival drills' took some laughable turns such as when a small group of militants decided to occupy for three hours a hamlet near industrial Durango, but Zumalde's attempts to connect with the local inhabitants failed miserably because the latter fled from the militants who walked around in military fatigues, and with black-painted faces. In his own words:

> Right after starting the military training and urban and rural activities, I was obsessed with the idea of establishing links with the local population (in rural or urban settings). I dreamt of speaking with local people, assembling them in town squares or just simply establishing a road control with around 10 people and giving them a political speech full of patriotic zeal. Things seemed really easy from a tactical side. We felt ready to do these kinds of things everywhere in the Basque Country, without leaving a fingerprint behind. Our problem was that Basques in the 1970s were completely apolitical; they felt threatened or did not trust each other; less so an armed group. (Zumalde, 2004: 199–200; our translation)

Zumalde found it easy to organize drills but was unable to connect with locals. The Basque Country of the 1970s was a well-developed region (its GDP per capita was 60 per cent of the USA's GDP per capita in 1975), as well as densely populated (300 people per square km, roughly similar to that of Connecticut in the USA), where an open attempt by guerrillas to occupy territory would have been rapidly wiped out by the dictatorship. The territorial presence of the security forces and Francoist institutions was so evident that one of Zumalde's main concerns was always to target local collaborators of the security forces in mid-size industrial towns.

This confusion between rural drills and urban tactics was testament to Zumalde's incapacity to realize that a ground strategy was out of fashion given the structural conditions ETA was facing. As late as 1975, Zumalde—after being expelled from the group leadership due to his incapacity to carry out attacks, and writing from the comfort of exile—still defended a combination of urban and rural tactics; he did however concede that no traditional guerrilla warfare was possible in the Basque Country:

> We concluded that Euskadi, in fact, is a small land area in extension and not suitable for the development of mountain guerrillas. But here I have to clarify: for 'classic' mountain guerrillas; that is, the creation of armed nuclei, the development and growth of these, the liberation of zones, the politicization of the masses and creation of provisional governments in these zones, the grouping of sections, in companies, battalions, regiments, divisions, etc. Instead of this traditional model, we propose the development of a special guerrilla for Euskadi, based on perfect adaptation to its environment, climate, Basque temperament, economy, communication channels, etc., and we focus in principle on very small groups with great capacity for movement and concealment, and on this basis we turn the natural difficulty of 'small Euskadi' into a radical advantage: that is, we will take advantage of its smallness and the great development of its areas to move quickly and operate in any place that interests us. Thus, a guerrilla, normally, from his refuge, will have perhaps two or three hours of marching, a maximum of one night, to operate and retreat back to his refuge. (Zumalde, 2004: 179; our translation)

Zumalde remained a minor figure in ETA; he was not able to formulate a coherent strategy for the group, either through armed practice or theoretically. It was not entirely his fault. The debate within ETA about the correct strategic course of action took a long time and was highly divisive. In fact, by 1975, ETA had split into two factions, ETA politico-militar (pm) and ETA militar (m). The rift was precipitated by a bomb in Madrid in September 1974 that killed 13 people (12 civilians and one police officer). In terms of public image, it was a disaster for ETA; the majority within the leadership argued against claiming responsibility for the attack, while the minority thought they had to admit the truth. The disagreement, however, had deeper roots. The main schism was about the role of armed struggle in the context of regime change and transition to democracy. For ETApm, the end of the Francoist dictatorship would generate the conditions for a revolutionary uprising of the Basque people. In this scenario, ETA should have two branches, a political section oriented to mobilizing popular support for independence, and a military branch willing to carry out attacks, but subordinated to the political leadership. The approach was not that different from that adopted by other revolutionary groups in Europe. As Eduardo Bergaretxe, also known as Pertur, the mastermind of this approach, put it in 1976:

> The armed activity of the revolutionary group acts as a radical trigger in this process; repressive state attacks that seek to abort and punish the armed focus have a revolutionary impact on the masses that tend to react in a totally opposite way to that expected by the system: they are sensitized. [...] Armed activity has thus

contributed effectively to highlighting and sharpening the contradictions of the system and its oppressive nature, complementing the vindictive and conscientious agitation efforts of revolutionaries at mass level. [...]

The revolutionary process is thus acquiring maturity. The work of political agitation and propaganda, effectively supported by military activity, results in a quantitative and qualitative increase in the awareness and radicalization of the exploited and oppressed masses; this translates into an expansion of the area of influence and incidence of the revolutionary group, in the increasing implantation and insertion of this among those who must become the main protagonists of the Revolution: the working and popular classes. [...]

The dialectical pairing of military activities with all the group's work and mass actions advances the general revolutionary process quantitatively and qualitatively towards the phases prior to the armed insurrection; towards the violent and revolutionary seizure of power. (Amigo, 1978: 190–91; our translation)

Thus, for ETApm, the grand strategy was insurrection as it involved the subordination of military units to the demands and preferences of the political leadership of the time. Notice that here there is no longer any dream about guerrilla-making. Pertur suggests an armed structure based on territorial columns, pretty much like the one that the PIRA was by then abandoning in Northern Ireland, plus specialized units in charge of specific tasks (such as information, logistics, etc.), but always dependent on the central leadership led by the 'politicians'.

ETAm, in contrast, thought that the political transition in Spain would make little difference with regard to the independence of the Basque Country. The only grand strategy that might force the state to make territorial concessions was one of attrition. This required piling more violent pressure onto the state to the point where it would prefer to negotiate a way out instead of keeping on accruing losses. To sustain the pressure of violence, ETA's political branch would have to win local elections to rule in municipalities—and proselytizing and gaining recruits would be absolutely essential. This strategic design made ETAm more powerful and resilient than ETApm, which was disbanded in 1983.

José Miguel Beñarán, also known as Argala, was the main thinker behind this strategy. For him, the movement would be more successful if its political branch operated within the institutions and took advantage of their loopholes—whereas the military branch, without renouncing their leadership, remained clandestine and broadened its hit list to further damage the state. For instance, it was only after this split that ETAm started to kill military officers. After a decade in which violence had played a defensive, almost symbolic role, ETAm began to move on the offensive by broadening its target field and increasing the number of attacks (Casanova and Asensio, 1999).

This strategic turn went full circle when ETAm hosted a number of ETApm militants who walked away from the latter group, infuriated by its lack of armed activity. These militants had already come to terms with the fact that the insurrectional path was already closed and that the best that Basque militants could achieve was to extract a political negotiation with the Spanish state whose final outcome would be determined by the balance of power between them.

Figure 4.1 displays the evolution of lethal attacks for the whole period of ETA's activity. Before Franco's death in 1975, ETA targeted a few members of the security forces, collaborators, and regime officials. During the transition years, 1976–8, there was an explosion of protest and mobilization in Spain, consistent with what O'Donnell and Schmitter (1986: 7) called 'the revival of civil society', a typical phenomenon after a long authoritarian, repressive spell. The intensity of the protest was highest in the Basque Country. In this regard, the escalation of ETA's violence coincided with the decline of street protest and labour strikes after the first democratic elections in June 1977. ETAm tried to compensate for the decline in protests with a dramatic increase in the levels of lethal violence (Sánchez-Cuenca and Aguilar, 2009). In large part, the armed group's capacity to proceed with the military campaign was initially upped by France's reluctance to legally prosecute ETA militants hiding and proselytizing on its soil.

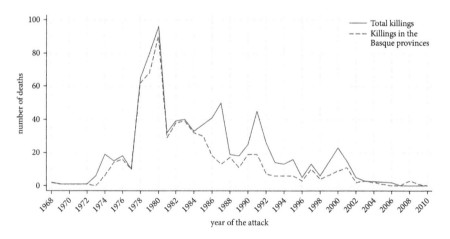

Figure 4.1 The evolution of ETA's killings

Source: Victims of ETA dataset (https://ic3jm.es/investigacion/proyectos/explaining-terrorist-and-insurgent-behavior/).

The French Sanctuary

Together with recruitment and public support for violence, the most relevant factor boosting ETA's military strength was the role played by France. Unlike the Tupamaros in Uruguay or the Red Brigades in Italy—groups that were forced to fully operate under the rules of clandestinity—ETA benefited enormously from an almost friendly attitude of the French authorities (officials and courts likewise) to its militants living in French territory—mainly in the bordering French Basque Country (Iparralde, in Basque nationalist-speak). France granted in practice a safe haven for the ETA leadership to build French-sponsored international prestige, recruit people fleeing Spain, train militants in the Landes forest, hide them in secure houses while inactive, and collect extortion fees from Basque businessmen to maintain the armed organization.

In the beginning, many members of ETA who were prosecuted in Spain during the dictatorship crossed the border and requested the official status of refugee.[7] From 1960 to 1972, around 30 refugees were deported from southern France by the authorities under allegations of not complying with the requirements of their statute—mainly by getting involved in political activities on French soil. ETA was also outlawed in France. In 1972, in reaction to the escalation of ETA members deported from southern France to other *departàments* or abroad (but never to Spain), several Basque refugees occupied the cathedral in Bayonne and called for a hunger strike. French authorities backed down and started to delay deportations and even issued a new permit of residence that offered more legal certainty to their holders.

One illustration, as reported by Morán (1996: 112–15), makes the point. After carrying out the killing of the then prime minister Admiral Carrero Blanco on 20 December 1973, the ETA cell that planted the bomb crossed the border and sought shelter in France. Some days after the attack, four unmasked self-defined ETA members gave a press conference in which they claimed responsibility for the action. No police showed up to prevent the terrorists' exchange with journalists. The Spanish government repeatedly requested its French counterpart to extradite the participants in the attack, but French judicial authorities rejected the request by arguing that the bilateral treaty between the two countries prohibited the extradition of subjects

---

[7] Our main source in this section is Consuelo Morán's extremely well-documented study on Spanish-French relations during the Basque conflict (Morán, 1996).

132   Underground Violence

whose crimes were political. Pierre Joxe, later to be French interior minister during the 1980s, even recalled that 'the action [the killing of Carrero Blanco] provoked a very primitive feeling of joy in France' (Morán, 1996: 115).

By 1976, there were around 600 refugees in French Basque Country. In 1979, the Spanish Minister of the Interior brought to a bilateral meeting a list of 127 members of ETA who were supposedly living in French territory with refugee permits. His French counterpart committed to end these permits, although the number of ETA members delivered to Spanish courts to be tried was still very limited. From then on, ETA members quickly adopted the rules of clandestinity to avoid being deported from southern France (Morán, 1996: 201).

The growing concern in France about the presence of ETA members was also prompted by the increase of para-state terrorist attacks on French soil against Basque militants (Woodworth, 2001: Ch. 6). Members of the Spanish security forces decided to bring pressure on the French state by carrying out covert operations against ETA militants in French Basque Country. This is a clear illustration of what we called in Chapter 2 'state terrorism', as security forces operating in a neighbouring country took advantage of secrecy to carry out attacks in a typical terrorist fashion—with car bombs and machine-gun shootings. By targeting some of the most relevant ETA figures, such as Argala, Peixoto, Antxon, and Txomin, the old days of dealing openly with organizational issues in southern France were gone forever for the terrorist group.

The failure of the 1981 *coup d'état* marked the consolidation of the Spanish transition. This was to no avail: the French Minister of the Interior in July 1981 compared Basque refugees to members of the French Resistance against Nazism (Morán, 1996: 225). The arrival of the Socialist Party (PSOE) to the Spanish presidency with an electoral landslide in late 1982 may have triggered some measure of counter-terrorist collaboration, as the socialists were also in power in Paris. But fast advances on many policies, such as economic integration, were not matched in the treatment of Basque refugees in French soil—as extradition requests were repeatedly struck down by courts and publicly disavowed by French authorities.

The rarefied climate in the French Basque Country took another turn when ETA's French counterpart, Iparretarrak (IK), upscaled its armed campaign by killing security officers in 1984. A small cadre of ETA-loving militants, IK thrived under the shadow of its older partner. In exchange, it had to comply with ETA's orders about not carrying out major actions in the French Basque Country that would increase police presence and makes ETA militants' moves in the region more difficult. However, IK's own process of radicalization pushed its members to increase the violence (Bidegain, 2007). These various elements made French officials infuriated about levels of local violence in southern France, and they started to deport ETA militants to third countries—usually in Latin America or in Africa. In September 1984, the French government authorized for the first time the extradition of three ETA militants to Spain, having accused them of committing blood crimes on Spanish soil. Faced with uproar among the French Left, the then president Francois Mitterrand declared: 'France cannot be a base for terrorists [...] the three Spanish Basques who are being extradited to Spain cannot invoke the right to exile while using our soil as a military base, from where they organized their killings' (Morán, 1996: 293).

Extraditions were, however, halted until 1986, when the French Socialists lost their majority and a new right-wing government was formed. A loose campaign of international and domestic terrorist attacks in France that year brought to the fore the importance of counter-terrorist cooperation. Spanish authorities still complained that ETA leaders lived comfortably on French soil, without much pressure from French security forces. In July 1986, the French government dusted off a 1945 decree that allowed it to unilaterally expel from the country any foreigner who was a 'threat to public order' (Morán, 1996: 346). Foreigners would be placed at the border, where Spanish security forces were free to arrest them. As most Basque militants did not have legal papers and were not French citizens, the government's decision spread panic. Several French newspapers interpreted this policy as the end of the ETA sanctuary in France. During the Chirac premiership 185 Basques were expulsed this way. In a famous bilateral meeting between Interior Ministers, the French minister, Robert Pandraud, outspokenly declared: 'I will give you every bit of information I have, and I'll proceed to expel and extradite [Basque militants], but everything will be halted if there are more terrorist attacks against Basque militants on French soil' (Morán, 1996: 354). Unsurprisingly, the GAL, the state-sponsored paramilitary group, became largely inactive afterwards.

ETA tried to bring pressure against the French state by carrying out a campaign against French companies, but it always stopped short of targeting French citizens and organizing attacks on French soil. Thus, its only remedy was to tighten the rules of clandestinity for its militants. Despite this, 1986 saw one of the biggest counter-terrorist operations against ETA, when a furniture-building plant was raided by the French police and they found a stockpile of weapons—including missiles—together with thousands of documents detailing the finances of the terrorist organization. The information was useful in achieving a deeper understanding of the inner workings of the terrorist group, and also facilitated the dismantling of several ETA commandos. In September 1987, the French police arrested one of the main leaders of ETA, Santi Potros, who was carrying a suitcase full of data about the composition of the commandos and the allocation of money to the different branches of the organization. With that information, 150 people were subsequently arrested and around 50 expelled from the country.

These two operations represented the end of ETA's French sanctuary. The increasing pace of police raids in southern France forced militants to move north, making it more difficult for the organization to operate and maintain links with its units in Spain. ETA's sanctuary in southern France until the late 1980s, although insufficient to prompt ETA to seize territory on either side of the border, helped it maintain the tit-for-tat relationship with Spain's increasingly successful counter-terrorist forces. The loss of its sanctuary implied a lower capacity to attract, train, and house potential militants. This was compensated for by carrying out more operations with remote-control car bombs, which put a premium on maximizing harm (because cars permitted hundreds of pounds of explosive) and minimizing the risks for the terrorists (who could detonate the device from a distance and had more time to run away).

The technology of the car bomb had been part of the repertoire of terrorist groups for some time. New-generation car bombs, with home-made explosives and electronic triggers, had systematically been used by the Provisional IRA since 'Bloody Friday' (21 July 1972), when the group created havoc in the business district of Belfast (Davis, 2007: 24). Despite including tech-skilled militants among its ranks, ETA did not carry out its first car bomb until October 1982 (one policeman died). As Figure 4.2 displays, ETA used this tactic sparsely during the next years (one attack in 1983 with one policeman dead; one attack in 1984, with two military men and one civilian dead; five attacks in 1985, with two dead). Not coincidentally, ETA's reliance on car bombs overlapped with the loss of its French sanctuary. In 1986, ETA detonated two massive bombs against the Civil Guard's vehicles in Madrid that claimed 17 lives; in 1987, it perpetrated infamous attacks against a supermarket in Barcelona (21 dead), and a Civil Guards' housing complex in Zaragoza (11 dead, five children among them).

The campaign gained full speed after the ill-fated negotiation between the Spanish government and ETA emissaries in Algiers in 1988–9. Returning to violence, ETA's leaders interpreted the process as a 'too little, too soon' negotiation, and believed that the government simply needed additional pressure to yield for good. Spain was scheduled to host the Olympics, the Universal Exhibition, and the European Capital of Culture in 1992. In ETA's mind, if they

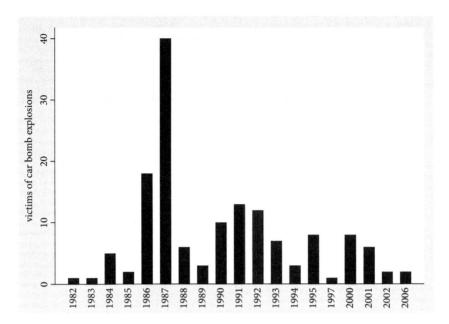

Figure 4.2 Victims of car bombs detonated by ETA
Source: Victims of ETA dataset.

showed their capacity to disrupt these events it would force the government back to the table in a weaker bargaining position.

Car bombs would play a critical part in the strategy. ETA blew up seven car bombs in 1990 (10 dead), twelve bombs in 1991 (13 dead), and seven bombs in 1992 (11 dead). But car bombs suddenly slowed down. ETA suffered a terrible strike when its long-lasting leadership, collectively called Artapalo, was arrested in Bidart (the French Basque Country) in March 1992, and with this, thousands of internal documents ended in security agencies' hands, which enabled the arrest of hundreds of ETA militants. This important counterterrorist operation brought to a halt ETA's attempts to derail the 1992 events and forced its leadership to rethink its strategy (Sánchez-Cuenca, 2009). Ultimately, the fall in violence observed in Figure 4.1 after the late 1980s can also be attributed to the effective suppression of ETA's sanctuary. In this sense, the ability for clandestine groups to maintain a sanctuary outside of their area of operations increases their chances of survival.

Without the French sanctuary, ETA's military capabilities shrank, so the group had to substitute its 'high visibility' targets for a larger number of attacks. The so-called 'socialization of suffering' strategy focused on killing non-nationalist politicians combined with growing pressure on nationalist moderates through the widespread employment of street violence (*kale borroka*, in Basque) against local officials and members of the Basque police force (De la Calle, 2007). Street violence (that included barricades, launching Molotov cocktails, defacing walls with death threats against public figures, etc.) became the 'entry-level training ground' for radicalized youngsters who routinely at weekends created havoc in urban centres to make sure everybody knew that the conflict was not yet over. Street violence was the breeding ground of the last cohort of ETA militants.

The 'socialization of suffering' strategy, although successful at keeping a steady flow of recruits, provoked a solid reaction from Basque civil society as well as from the Spanish government, who started to make illegal many associations organically connected to ETA. This concerted assault on ETA's legal façades brought its larger political front to a corner, and forced its leaders to accept, after several failed negotiation rounds, that the best endgame for the broader pro-secession movement would be to declare a unilateral and permanent truce.

Conclusions

ETA was one of the longer-lasting armed groups in Western developed countries. Despite its underground condition, its cycle of violence covers a long period, from 1968 to 2011. ETA's resilience was a consequence of, on the one hand, its degree of popular support, boosted by its network of associations and organizations that were built around the armed core, and, on the other, the sanctuary it enjoyed in southern France. Even after France opted to increase pressure on ETA, the leadership and 'illegal' members preferred to hide in France rather than in Spain. The sanctuary was not exactly equivalent to a liberated area in which the activists might move freely, but it ameliorated the conditions of clandestinity; when compared with the underground existence of the Tupamaros, ETA enjoyed greater spatial leeway. The more stringent conditions of ETA's life in France from the 1990s onwards account, to a great extent, for the loss of its capacity to attack.

Given the constraints of clandestinity and the nationalist goals pursued by the group, its terrorism adopted the form of a war of attrition with the Spanish state. This was a bilateral confrontation between a terrorist group and a state. When it became clear that ETA's violence, by itself, would not outlast the state, the group had to change its strategy, by trying to forge a political alliance of all nationalist groups; according to the plan, this political front would be able to pose a formidable challenge to the Spanish state. However, this strategy also failed. In March 2006, the state acceded to open negotiations, but a car bomb that killed two people in Terminal 4 of Madrid's airport on 30 December of that year forced the government to withdraw from the negotiating table. This deepened ETA's breach with its political branch, which thought that full institutional participation was the best alternative given the logistical weakness of the terrorist group (Whitfield, 2014). ETA announced a definitive ceasefire in October 2011 and moved slowly into a unilateral process of disarmament and disbandment, which was finally completed on 3 May 2018. The political party associated with ETA has been quite successful since then, securing over 20 per cent of Basque voters; thus, they have sufficient popular support to influence regional politics without recourse to violence.

4.3. Shining Path

We have analysed so far two cases of rebel groups that fully fit the intersection between the action- and the actor-senses of terrorism: both Tupamaros and ETA remained clandestine from the actor-sense, and their violence could be identified as largely terrorist—with bombings, shootings, and kidnappings accounting for most of it. There is nonetheless a 'non-overlapping' understanding of terrorism, which occurs when insurgencies complement their territory-seizing strategies with terrorist campaigns. In Chapter 3, we hypothesized that this will be the case when the group wants to operate in areas that remain under state control—usually the country's largest cities. If rebels want to have a base in those places, they will have to abide by the rules of clandestinity and resort to indirect forms of warfare.

We close this chapter with an analysis of the repertoire of violence carried out by Shining Path (*Sendero Luminoso*; SP) in Peru during the 1980s. Although SP is in some ways an obscure Maoist outlier in the concert of left-wing insurgencies in Latin America, its leaders correctly foresaw that in highly unequal societies, with a developing 'island core' (i.e., the capital city) surrounded by an ocean of poverty (the countryside), the fight to topple the regime had to take place simultaneously in the two arenas. Although ultimately a failure, this strategy has been inadvertently mimicked by fundamentalist groups such as the Taliban and ISIS.

The Communist Party of Peru–In the Shining Path of José Carlos Mariátegui, more popularly known as the Shining Path, was formed following a split from the Communist Party of Peru–Red Flag. It was created in 1969 and led by Abimael Guzmán until his death in 2021 in a high-security prison at the Callao naval base, where he had been imprisoned since 1992.

138 Underground Violence

In 1962, Guzmán had been hired as a philosophy professor at the then reopened National University of San Cristóbal de Huamanga, in Ayacucho, the heart of the historically marginalized and impoverished Andean region. There, Guzmán was radicalized in the ideological battles between Leninists, Trotskyists, and Maoists, and opted for the last of these philosophies. After being expelled from the Communist Party of Peru, Guzmán joined ranks with a communist splinter (Red Flag), but ended up creating his own political group, which managed to control a significant part of the university. He used the socio-economic centrality of the university in the Ayacucho region to train cadres and dispatch them to their home towns as teachers with the aim of proselytizing and preparing the youth for the forthcoming struggle (Degregori, 2011). Following Mao's lessons from the Chinese revolution, during the 1970s the organization built networks of rural cadres and combatants with the intention of moving the conflict as quickly as possible to the 'guerrilla' stage.

Curiously, SP's commitment to violence was adopted at the same time that the country was experiencing a quasi-revolutionary episode at the hands of the military government headed by Juan Velasco Alvarado. Velasco implemented a much-needed land reform together with a process of nationalization of private companies and price control schemes that sought to alleviate inequalities and empower the working classes. Yet, the long-term marginalization of the departments of Ayacucho, Apurímac, and Huancavelica (epicentres of the Senderista war), together with truncated political processes of working-class mobilization, became the roots of the rebellion. Power returned to right-wing military officers in 1975, with the overthrow of Velasco and the arrival of General Bermúdez. Unwilling to pay the political price for the fiscal austerity measures imposed since 1975 to address the economic crisis, the military called a constitutional assembly and laid the foundations of the democratic transition that returned Fernando Belaúnde back to the presidency in 1980, after 12 years of military interregnum. SP's armed struggle began on election day, as SP cadres burned the ballot boxes in Chuschi, a backwater district in Ayacucho. By showing its utter disrespect for the democratic process, the SP was signalling that its fight would not be easily deterred (McClintock, 1998).

Why Urban Warfare?

Peru in the 1980s was a deeply divided country, combining a moderately rich area in the Lima-Callao metropolitan conurbation with large pockets of poverty on the Andean Mountain range. While the state's capacity in the metropolitan area (plus in Arequipa and some coastal cities) might be considered similar to that of a medium-income country (like, say, Argentina or Uruguay), its capabilities in rural areas were minimal (i.e., similar to that of other impoverished Central American nations). Drawing on Mao's strategical thinking, the SP's aim was to liberate territory in the rural areas of the Andes and to consolidate a 'Peruvian Yunan' from where to defend itself against expected state reprisals.

However, the great theoretical contribution of Abimael Guzmán, who considered himself the so-called 'fourth sword of international communism' (after Marx, Lenin, and Mao), was to realize that in contemporary Peru, a Maoist armed strategy could not put all its eggs in the 'liberating territory' basket. Rural rebellion was doomed to fail if at the same time, synchronously, it did not also operate in urban areas that housed the main institutions and the country's economic and political elite (De la Calle, 2017). Thus, from the beginning of the war, the SP had commando cells that carried out actions in Lima. As has been argued in this chapter and throughout the book, the guerrillas, given that they could not aspire to controlling territory in the metropolitan area, had to operate clandestinely, which meant that they carried out fewer actions.

Interestingly, Guzmán's thoughts on the role of the cities evolved during the conflict. In the so-called 'interview of the century' published in 1988 (referred to in the Introduction),[8] Guzmán talked with journalists for the first time during the war; he acknowledged that the fight in the cities was subordinate to the fight in the countryside, but that they also complemented each other. Guzmán distorted Mao's thinking on insurrection in order to justify his simultaneous focus on the two theatres of war without breaking the mould of Mao's doctrine. For Mao, insurrection as a revolutionary action should only be employed in advanced capitalist countries, where the strategy was to first mobilize the working class in the cities and thereafter bring the struggle to the countryside. For poorer societies, the only solution was to build a grassroots, peasant-fed insurgency in the countryside and, once a rebel stronghold was consolidated, move on the offensive to encircle the cities and, under siege, force them to capitulate (see Mao's *Problems of War and Strategy*). Guzmán envisioned Peru as a poor, peasant society, so the rural strategy was the right one. However, as mentioned, he anticipated that having a bridgehead in the cities was also key to the fate of the revolution. Thus, Guzmán embodied the

---

[8] The full interview can be found here (accessed 23 January 2021): https://www.verdady reconciliacionperu.com/admin/files/libros/600_digitalizacion.pdf

Leninist thesis of insurrection as the ultimate stage for revolutionary success, but he limited its application to the cities. In his own words:

> The centre of operations has been in the countryside, but for the insurrectional stage the centre moves to the cities. At the beginning of the fight, recruits were transferred from the cities to the countryside; for the insurrectional stage, it will be the other way around. In this way, the epicentre of the struggle shifts to the cities. We have to create the best conditions to provoke convergence between the actions of the Popular Guerrilla Army and the insurrection in the cities. This is what we need just now. (our translation)

In a later interview with the Truth and Reconciliation Commission (CVR, in Spanish), Guzmán acknowledged that although Ayacucho was the epicentre of the struggle, the SP from the beginning had been organized in Lima, as his idea was to project the SP's presence and influence in the city. In Guzmán's own words, 'if Ayacucho was the cradle of Sendero, Lima was its catapult' (Zapata, 2017: 260; our translation). Lima offered safe and secure houses for the SP's leadership (which always hid in Lima), a loudspeaker for its propaganda, and a hotbed for recruiting ideologically committed cadres. And Guzmán did not shy away from endorsing terrorism. In his own words:

> Fortunately, the time when revolution was undertaken by isolated revolutionaries because of the lack of a revolutionary people is gone. Bombings are no longer the weapon of the dynamite man and have become a necessary component of the people's weaponry. (Valencia, 1992: 15; our translation)

Strategic Stages

We can identify four stages during the civil war. The first stage was called 'to raze' (*batir*), which was intended to expel authorities and security forces from the SP's so-called central area of operations (Ayacucho and Apurímac). Facing a very light state presence, the SP's rebel units were unexpectedly successful. Instead of settling on one liberated area in which to strengthen their organization and authority, they continued to move from one district to another, publicly court-martialling those identified by the *senderistas* as enemies of the people—authorities, cattle thieves, drunkards, sexual abusers, traders, and local landlords—and leaving behind unarmed committees in charge of overseeing local affairs (Zapata, 2017).

This early success had occurred because of the initial reluctance of president Belaúnde to pass responsibility for counterinsurgency to the military, as they had unseated him during his first stint in power (1963–8). Once Belaúnde decided to declare a state of emergency in some provinces in Ayacucho and dispatched the army and navy to regain power without any civilian oversight, the tables were turned. The military campaign, with countless indiscriminate massacres against the local population, also caught the SP off-guard, so its cadres retreated and left local sympathizers to their own devices. Short on weapons, SP squads were no match for the well-trained military units, which had little regard for human rights. Unlike many other rebel groups, the SP was never concerned about piling up more and better weaponry. During this initial stage of the conflict, they used dynamite cartridges stolen from mines, pistols taken from police officers, and more primitive tools such as axes and knifes. For Guzmán, militants had to be ready to give their lives for the broader cause, and these lives were a more powerful weapon than any firearm.

Thus, the deployment of the military resulted in the SP's strategic retreat. Unlike Mao, for whom the creation of liberated areas involved seizing and ruling territory, Guzmán understood that the SP's territorial control would be more about building the party than constructing parallel institutions. By playing cat-and-mouse, the incapacity of the security forces to decimate SP's units was considered a rebel success. But the spread of peasant self-defence groups (*rondas*) broke that belief because communities started to share information about local SP members with security forces. This is why it was so important for the party to increase the cost of defection by carrying out massacres as collective punishments against communities apparently switching sides (Granados, 1992: 32–6).

Figure 4.3 represents very well the dynamics of collective punishment in Ayacucho and its surrounding regions (for data sources, see De la Calle, 2017). The number of killings by the SP was relatively low during the first two years of the conflict but spiked during the following two, with more than 3,000 deaths in Ayacucho during 1983–4. The sheer physical exhaustion produced by the three-sided fight in Ayacucho (among the military, the SP, and the *rondas*) encouraged SP's leadership to broaden the conflict by transferring units to provinces where the military did not have a free hand because they were not yet under a 'state of emergency' declaration. In 1985 the SP established camp in the Alto Huallaga, one of the fastest-growing coca areas in the world. Access to the coca trade allowed SP units in the region to purchase better weaponry and carry out more audacious assaults (Weinstein, 2007: 81–95). The group also sought to accelerate its operations in Lima.

The arrival of a new president, Alan García (1985–90), gave precious time to the SP. Running on a social-democratic platform, García rejected the use

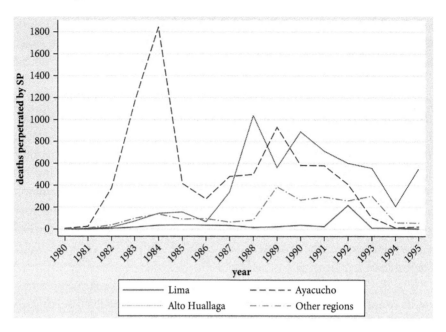

Figure 4.3 Time evolution of the SP's killings by region
Source: See De la Calle (2017).

of open repression against rebel groups, and enchanted them with calls for a negotiated end to the conflict. Obviously, the military was not happy with that stance and dragged its feet. This nonetheless changed when Guzmán decided to challenge García's bona fides through three prison uprisings led by SP inmates in 1986 in the middle of an international summit hosted by the Peruvian government in Lima. Infuriated by this provocation, García gave full powers to the military to deal with the riot, and the ensuing bloodbath killed hundreds of SP veterans in prison. From then on, the government brought an increasing number of provinces under emergency provisions, and transferred civilian power to the military to deal with the insurgency (Palmer, 1995).

Together with 'broadening the battlefield', the main contribution of the war's second stage was a greater focus on urban operations. In the beginning, Lima was a place to recruit cadres from the universities, industrial plants, and the so-called *pueblos nuevos* (unauthorized shanty towns), but armed actions there were mainly propaganda-driven spectacular attacks—such as the infamous hanging of dogs from streetlamps in December 1980 with signs that read 'Deng Xiaoping' (Gorriti, 1990: 188; McCormick, 1992: 25). When the military was deployed in Ayacucho in late 1982, the SP created the so-called

Metro committee (Comité Metropolitano), which was in charge of running armed operations in Lima and its surrounding areas. However, the Metro had a reputation of underperforming, for various reasons.

First, Lima militants complained that the dearth of weaponry jeopardized their operational plans. Unlike their rural counterparts, they were unwilling to carry out attacks without proper firepower, because in an urban environment they could easily be caught. At the same time, the leadership insisted that targets should be very carefully selected, mainly from those playing a role in the repression, which raised further obstacles to action (Jiménez, 2000: 222). Second, a number of Lima militants were not happy with *Sendero's* grand strategy that gave primacy to the countryside. They thought the rebellion had to focus on urban areas, where power resided. For the SP's Maoist leaders, that was simply ideological heresy that had to be punished, which inevitably delayed its plans of attacks in the city. Third, the initial Metro sought to mimic the organizational structure of rural battalions, where militants had ties across different sections. This format led to many police raids that decimated its ranks—also notably helped by allegations of infiltration, by both the police and rival far-left wing groups (such as the then-nascent *Movimiento Revolucionario Túpac Amaru*, MRTA). These setbacks forced the SP to implement a more close-knit, isolated system of communications between the different cells of the Metro (e.g. logistics, propaganda, death squads, etc.) to maximize survival and efficiency.

There was consensus within the SP on the idea that its units in Lima were not delivering. Table 4.1 reports the breakdown of operations by tactics from June 1984 to June 1986, as compiled by the SP itself (and reproduced by Mercado, 1987: 15–19). At the core of operations, comprising Ayacucho, Huancavelica, and Apurímac, the SP relied on guerrilla warfare attacks. In contrast, most attacks in Lima were propaganda-driven, with a much smaller

Table 4.1 The Shining Path's armed tactics, June 1984–June 1986

Tactics	Ayacucho, Huancavelica, and Apurímac	North, Centre, South, and Huallaga	Lima Metro	Other regions	Total
Guerrilla war	54.4	36.0	12.0	16.8	45.9
Sabotage	8.0	18.6	23.7	26.9	11.8
Selective killings	9.6	9.2	3.8	1.7	8.2
Propaganda and armed agitation	28.0	36.2	60.1	54.6	34.1

Source: The SP, as reproduced by Mercado, 1987. Unfortunately, we do not know how the SP themselves defined these tactics.

proportion of deadly attacks than in other core regions. Attacks in metropolitan Lima accounted for 8.4 per cent of all actions, but 17 per cent of sabotages and 15 per cent of all propaganda and armed agitation. The latter aimed to exploit the key role of the capital as a 'resonance box'. But failure to carry out selective killings in Lima became a burden. In the words of the SP: 'in the capital there is plenty of room for annihilating enemies, given the large concentration of central authorities' (Mercado, 1987: 18).

Given the inability of SP's Metro committee to keep pace with the violence in the countryside, SP's leadership made a bold decision in 1986, by militarizing one of its legal arms, Popular Aid (*Socorro Popular*, better known as *Sopo*), which was in charge of giving legal assistance to prisoners, helping them communicate with their relatives, and pressing authorities to investigate episodes of human rights' violations by security agencies (Jiménez, 2000). Popular Aid was a kind of public front for the SP, as this group had the triple advantage of offering a legal façade, a link between the leadership and the prisons, and a breeding ground for recruitment through the networks of relatives and supporters. Most Sopo leaders led double lives, complementing their public tasks in favour of prisoners with clandestine work in terrorist cells operating in Lima. This organizational switch was very successful, to the point that Lima became one of the main war theatres of the conflict in the early 1990s.

The SP was initially very selective in its recruiting process in Lima, and slowly promoted cadres from the 'starter-level cells'—dedicated to collecting information and spreading propaganda—to the more committed death-squad units in charge of carrying out assassinations and bombings. The party had a key presence in universities, youth associations, and the growing immigrant-fed shanty towns that surrounded the capital city (Burt, 1998; Degregori, 2011: Ch. 5). Given its clandestine network structure, it was important to avoid desertions in the cities. As one leading *senderologo* put it: 'Unlike the SP's rural cadres, who were peasants recruited locally from strong rebel groups, the urban cells largely comprised convinced militants, who blindly believed in the group's discourse' (Tapia, 1997: 137; our translation).

To not alienate the urban population, the SP was more careful about selecting targets in cities (De la Calle, 2017; Jiménez, 2000: 553–4). This cautious approach in the cities paid off, and polls show that the public were not overwhelmingly against the rebellion by the late 1980s. For instance, a public survey showed that 33 per cent of adolescents in urban low-class schools considered *senderistas* to be 'social fighters' rather than criminals or fanatics (Portocarrero, 1998: 205). Similarly, a countrywide study commissioned by the Peruvian Senate in 1989 found that 22 per cent of Peruvians did not identify SP members as 'terrorists' (Senado de la República, 1989).

This urban, clandestine armed network was given a major role during the third stage of the war. Starting from the early 1990s, Guzmán believed that the SP had reached the so-called 'strategic equilibrium' phase of the conflict: a highly unstable period in which the guerrilla war would give way to a manoeuvre war. In this stage, the principal fighting transfers from the countryside to the cities, with the goal, in this case, of forcing the collapse of the Peruvian government from within. *Senderologos* broadly agree that the 'offensive' was a final attempt to mask the SP's increasing weaknesses in the countryside, where many communities had set up government-backed self-defence squads (Degregori, 1998). The SP's leadership sees it otherwise, as stated by its number 2, Elena Yparraguirre:

> In the first plenary meeting of the new Central Committee, Abimael [Guzmán] laid out the thesis of the strategic equilibrium. He planned to liberate an area where we could set up a military and a political school; Yenan-like. The permanent committee was very aware of the need to educate new cadres. 800 new militants had flooded into the SP in Lima alone. Almost all were previously unknown to us. We were growing at an accelerating pace. (Zapata, 2017: 297; our translation)

Perhaps both sides were right: the SP's leaders misinterpreted the unprecedented entrance of new urban recruits as a signal of overall strength, and analysts wrongly inferred that the growing recourse to terrorism was a signal of rural weakness.

In any case, the SP leadership was willing to commit resources to bringing additional pressure on security forces and decision-makers in the capital city. If we go back to Figure 4.3, the number of killings by the SP reached its second peak of the decade in 1989 and did not go under the 400-threshold mark until 1993, in the aftermath of the arrest of its leadership. On the other hand, the number of deaths in Lima dramatically escalated in the early 1990s. Like ETA during the late 1980s, when the Basque organization thought it could force the Spanish government to concede by increasing its car bombs, the SP also expanded the number of bomb attacks in Lima to maximize its coercive leverage—as the Tarata example introduced in Chapter 1 illustrates. Bombs in Lima represented 37 per cent of total bombs in the country in 1988, with bombs themselves comprising 41 per cent of all attacks. By 1991, bombs represented 56 per cent of all attacks, and they were specially concentrated in Lima and Arequipa (68 per cent).

Regardless of the absolute numbers of attacks perpetrated in the different theatres of the conflict, Table 4.2 shows remarkable stability in the breakdown of tactics throughout the war. Following De la Calle (2015b), we

146 Underground Violence

Table 4.2 Control zones and share of tactics by presidency (all GTD1 attacks included)

	President Belaúnde (1980–85)			President García (1985–90)			President Fujimori (1990–2000)		
	control zones			control zones			control zones		
	state	contested	rebel	state	contested	rebel	state	contested	rebel
bombing	0.36	0.07	0.11	0.19	0.05	0.12	0.25	0.09	0.06
facility	0.51	0.69	0.66	0.46	0.58	0.54	0.41	0.43	0.55
assassination	0.13	0.23	0.22	0.34	0.36	0.33	0.33	0.55	0.38
N (towns)	250	56	54	309	90	87	87	32	43

distinguish between districts with rebel control (as measured by the SP's successful attempts to boycott elections), with contested control (rebels forced voters to cast many spoiled ballots, but the military was nonetheless able to run the election), and with state control (boycotts did not have an impact). Additionally, we use GTD1 data again to sort out three main tactics (see Chapter 3 on operationalization). Guerrilla-like (facility) attacks were dominant in rebel and contested areas—more so during the initial stage of the conflict, as the GTD database codes widespread rebels' sabotage operations as 'facility' attacks. In contrast, bombings were more common in safe state districts, with the sum of bombings and assassinations comprising over 50 per cent of attacks in state districts, both during the García and Fujimori presidencies.

Alberto Fujimori was elected President in July 1990 by running on a populist platform. He countered the SP's strategic equilibrium with the so-called *autogolpe* ('self-coup'). On 5 April 1992, he dissolved Congress and gave the military all the power and resources needed to smash the insurgency. Counterintuitively, the SP saw this as proof of a forthcoming US intervention, which would fuel the rebellion. It seems that Guzmán and the rest of the SP's central committee were making plans to relocate to somewhere in the countryside, but its units had been unable to secure a location (Zapata, 2017). In the middle of the most intense terrorist campaign in Lima, Guzmán and three leading *senderistas* were arrested in an upper-class neighbourhood of Lima. This gave Fujimori a tremendous boost and great popularity. By the end of 1993, only one year after the fall of Guzmán, *Sendero* was largely finished. His arrest had dramatic effects on the morale of the *Sendero* militants, and many gave up weapons and took advantage of the Repentance Law passed in 1992 (Bermúdez, 1995). Guzmán's later call for surrender simply copper-fastened the process.

Why did such a formidable insurgency come to an end so quickly? Part of the answer is offered by the SP's number 2 leader:

> Against the opinion of many analysts, I don't think that the peasant self-defence groups were so relevant for our defeat. Actually, their capacity to overcome our local structures was built after our arrest. I think the fall of our leadership was the turning point of the war. (Zapata, 2017: 306; our translation)

Other authors concur with this interpretation. The inevitability of the SP's victory ultimately relied on the strength of its invisible leadership—they had remained on the run for over two decades. Rather than from a quantitative assessment of military capabilities, *Sendero*'s energy was drawn from the qualitative capacity of its leadership to survive and rebuild networks of militants (Granados, 1992: 105–8). That was brought to a quick end when the leadership was finally captured in Lima in 1992.

Conclusions

The Peruvian civil war claimed more than 50,000 lives, between the SP, state repression, peasant *rondas* (self-defence groups), and the actions of other minor groups such as the MRTA and the far right Commandos Rodrigo Franco. Most of the violence was concentrated around the central Sierra region, where the SP fought for territorial control. Only Lima showed a different pattern, with many terrorist attacks, but no open control by the rebels. This dual nature of the conflict still resonates with the strikingly different testimonies about the conflict gathered from the rural areas and the capital city: whereas most people experienced the conflict as a low-intensity terrorist conflict, the Andean dwellers suffered an extremely damaging civil war.

A 2006 survey commissioned by the IDEHPUCP (Instituto de Democracia y Derechos Humanos; Institute of Democracy and Human Rights) about citizens' memories of the conflict clearly illustrates this remarkable pattern (see Sulmont, 2007). While 51 per cent of respondents from Lima overwhelmingly identified the 1980–90 decade with 'terrorism', respondents from Ayacucho split their answers between 'terrorism' (46 per cent) and 'massacres' (35 per cent)—a more ambiguous term that could also cover military behaviour (in Lima, a negligible 3 per cent gave this last answer). This radically different understanding of the conflict was also revealed when 60 per cent of Lima respondents argued that it is necessary to remember the past to make sure the violence never returns, compared to 61 per cent of Ayacucho respondents who preferred to forget it and not revive the past. It is no surprise that a

148   Underground Violence

majority of *limeños* (59 per cent) think that the SP's prisoners should have their political rights curtailed, whereas that opinion was held by 31 per cent of Ayacucho respondents, with a majority of 52 per cent in favour of granting full rights to those who had already completed their sentences. Clearly, for *limeños*, the SP was a terrorist gang whereas, for *ayacuchanos*, it was an extremely violent guerrilla insurgency.

4.4. Conclusions

The case studies in this chapter put flesh on the bones of the typology of violence presented in Chapter 2. Table 2.1 cross-tabulated two types of actors (those who are underground and those who have territorial control) and two types of actions (tactics that can be carried out clandestinely and tactics that require some degree of control over space). The resulting categories (pure terrorism, terrorism conducted by guerrillas, proto-guerrilla, and pure guerrilla) provide a useful conceptual framework to analyse the similarities and differences between types of rebel groups and types of violent tactics. This theoretical benchmark allows us to place actors and tactics in different cells according to the generative mechanism of violence. This mechanism, we claim, hinges upon territorial control.

The comparison between the Tupamaros, ETA, and the Shining Path is revealing. While the Tupamaros and ETA were underground groups, the Shining Path gained from the very beginning some degree of territorial control in several villages of the Andean range. According to the theory, we should find less tactical variation in the underground groups than in the group with territorial control. This has certainly proved to be the case. The Shining Path launched a dual strategy, by seeking to control vast areas in the hills and carrying out underground attacks in the capital. By contrast, both the Tupamaros and ETA had to limit themselves to underground tactics, which might be described as typically terrorist. The tactical heterogeneity of the Shining Path makes a single characterization of the group impossible. If we refer to it as a terrorist group, we miss its insurgent dimension; and if we say that it was a guerrilla, we do not take into account the SP's peculiarity of combining guerrilla and terrorist tactics (unlike the FARC in Colombia, which generally stuck to a purely guerrilla profile throughout its lengthy existence). We think that the description that best fits the Shining Path is that of being a guerrilla group that engaged in both guerrilla and terrorist attacks. Terrorism was concentrated in the capital, where the rebel group had to act in secrecy.

ETA did not have territorial control; it is a pure example of an underground group. However, ETA is different from the Tupamaros because, in the aftermath of Franco's death and during the first decade of democracy, it had a kind of 'safe haven' in the French Basque Country; and this might be considered as a surrogate of territorial control. In the case of ETA, at least initially, its members were able to move more or less freely and could store weapons and documents. The ensuing strength, which the Tupamaros never enjoyed, allowed ETA to launch a war of attrition with the Spanish state in the 1980s, which sought to overwhelm state resistance through a sustained campaign of violence against the security forces. Once the safe haven was gone, when France toughened its position on ETA, the organization proved unable to maintain pressure on the Spanish state. After the capture of the whole leadership in France in 1992, ETA never recovered and had to replace its war of attrition strategy with a more politically oriented approach aimed at inducing non-violent nationalist parties to participate in a wide coalition in favour of independence for the Basque Country.

The Tupamaros represents the purest form of terrorism. It developed a template, that of urban guerrilla, that was widely imitated by other underground groups thereafter. The Tupamaros argued that clandestinity in Uruguay was dictated by an unfavourable geography. As like many other revolutionary groups, they opted for shootings rather than bombings. Although the Tupamaros was fully aware of the physical constraints on their violent activity, this did not deter its leadership from employing guerrilla tactics in the beginning. To convey their strength and determination, they replicated a guerrilla assault on the municipality of Pando. But it was more a propagandistic tactic than an attempt to gain territorial control, and it did not end well. In a similar vein, the founder of the group, Raúl Sendic, engaged in a proto-guerrilla campaign in the countryside, the so-called Plan Tatú, to open a new battlefront. It was also an utter failure, illustrating the transitional nature of the proto-guerrilla category: had it succeeded, the Tupamaros would have had territorial control, moving the Tupamaros from the left column to the right in Table 2.1; but the failure of these attempts at seizing territory relocates the group back in the original cell, that of pure terrorism.

This brief summary of the three cases shows that our categories are able to capture the specificities of armed groups as well as to establish meaningful comparisons between them in terms of the relationship between rebels and territory. In the next chapter we show how our theoretical framework accounts for rebels' tactical shifts over time.

5
Within-Group Territorial Variation

Fine-grained comparisons of armed groups are useful to illustrate the range of variation we find in the relationship between rebels and territory. In Chapter 4 we examined: a fully underground group (the Tupamaros); an underground group with a sanctuary (ETA); and a group with territorial control that frequently employed terrorist tactics (the Shining Path). The analyses of the cases show, among other things, that the activists are aware of the constraints under which they act and the implications of organizing the struggle from the underground.

A more demanding test of our argument is to show that changes in the correlation of forces between the rebels and their rival states are closely matched by changes in rebels' repertoire of violence. If our conceptualization of terrorism identifies the 'joints' of political violence, we should observe updates in strategy and tactics when an armed group gains or loses territorial control. By looking at within-group variation, we keep the goals and organizational culture constant, while changing the constraints and opportunities that the rebels face. We proceed in this chapter to analyse two conflicts with such temporal variation, as well as visible international repercussions: the Israeli-Palestinian conflict and ISIS in Iraq and Syria.

The Israeli-Palestinian conflict requires little justification given its prominence in international politics and its protracted nature; it has been a source of political instability in the region for decades. Precisely because the duration is so long, we can trace the mutations of the Palestinian armed struggle, including the gaining and losses of sanctuaries out of Israel, the campaigns of international terrorism, the infiltrations into Israel, and its eventual territorial control in the occupied territories. The dynamics of the conflict was deeply affected by all these changes in the Palestinian movement's resources and constraints.

Regarding ISIS, its evolution is extraordinary: it started as an underground group in Iraq; it gained territory; alienated the local population; and then, when it was on the verge of defeat, it was 'resuscitated' thanks to the Syrian civil war. Eventually, it obtained large swathes of territory in Syria and

Underground Violence. Luis De la Calle and Ignacio Sánchez-Cuenca, Oxford University Press.
© Luis De la Calle and Ignacio Sánchez-Cuenca (2024). DOI: 10.1093/oso/9780198904816.003.0006

Iraq, and even claimed statehood over an area equivalent to the size of Great Britain. The new order, however, was fragile, and could not withstand their enemies' military pressure. The rise and fall of ISIS took place in a short span of time, comprising less than a decade. Thanks to this variation, we can analyse the effect of territorial gains and losses on their strategy and tactics.

5.1. The Israeli-Palestinian Conflict

Analysis of the Palestinian armed struggle is interesting on two grounds. Firstly, Palestinian armed groups acting in the late 1960s and 1970s were at the core of what Rapoport (2004) has dubbed the 'third wave of terrorism', which also featured European nationalist groups such as the PIRA and ETA (De la Calle, 2015a), and revolutionary organizations such as the Red Brigades and the Red Army Faction (Sánchez-Cuenca, 2019). The Palestinian organizations were not only a source of inspiration for activists elsewhere, but they also provided training to militants from several groups and organized joint operations with others—for example, with the Japanese Red Army (Farrell, 1990), or with the Red Army Faction (Aust, 2008; Smith and Moncourt, 2009). These forms of collaboration led to conspiracy theories arguing that an international terrorist network was in operation (Demaris, 1977).

Secondly, the Palestinian armed struggle shows wide internal variation. It displays an almost complete catalogue of violent conflict. Thus, we observe territorial and underground groups, hybrid groups, sanctuaries in foreign countries, international terrorism, guerrilla activity, and inter-state wars. There is also interesting variation across time, with different combinations of domestic, regional, and international activity. The Palestinian conflict, moreover, mutated in the early 1990s due to the Oslo Accords: on the one hand, the Palestinian Liberation Organization became the new Palestinian Authority, and established itself in the occupied territories; on the other, Hamas (which belongs to a different terrorist generation, that of Rapaport's 'fourth wave') emerged as the most formidable armed group in Gaza. Consequently, the bulk of armed violence moved to the occupied territories and to Israel itself, while Palestine-driven international terrorism disappeared altogether.

The Israeli-Palestinian conflict, therefore, puts our concepts to the test. As will be seen, the four categories described in Table 2.1 (pure terrorism, pure guerrilla, terrorism committed by guerrilla groups, and proto-guerrilla) can be found in the evolution of the conflict depending on the relationship between the armed groups and territory. This relationship also accounts

152 Underground Violence

for the adoption of international attacks. Our main goal is to persuade the reader that the conceptual apparatus of Chapter 2 can shed light on the modulations of violence among Palestinian armed groups.

A cautionary note: much has been written on the Israeli-Palestinian conflict, and so it would be pointless to provide another historical account. Although we cover quite a long period, from 1965 to 2008, we focus on a single aspect, the evolution of armed activity from the perspective of territorial control, paying little attention to the conflict's politics, except when necessary for historical context. We begin by offering a qualitative reconstruction of the Palestinian armed struggle, distinguishing two broad periods, before and after the first Intifada, and we complement this analysis with an examination of international terrorism, a form of terrorism that, until the creation of Al Qaeda, was indelibly associated with the Palestinians. At the end, we present some quantitative data that largely confirm the main findings of the qualitative analysis.

The First Cycle of Violence (1965–87)

After the 1948 military defeat of the Arab countries by Israel, Palestinians lacked a movement of their own. Arab countries, very much influenced by Pan-Arabism, did not foster the formation of a Palestinian nationhood. Palestinians, in turn, waited for an Egypt-led alliance of Arab powers to smash Israel (Rubin 1994: 9). In the 1960s President Nasser, the champion of pan-Arabism, became convinced that the existence of Israel was the main obstacle to Arab unification. Specifically, he came to believe that a Palestinian liberation movement could be useful to meet his own political goals. Once Israel were defeated under Egypt's leadership, the cause of Arab reunification would overcome the resistance of Syria and Jordan.

In this regard, the formation of the Palestinian Liberation Organization (PLO) was not a fully autonomous development by Palestinian leaders. In January 1964, the Arab League conference in Cairo authorized the Palestinian diplomat al-Shuqayri, under the strong influence of Nasser, to create a Palestinian political entity. On 28 May, 422 Palestinian delegates met in Jerusalem to establish the PLO and to draft the Palestine National Covenant. According to article 13, 'Arab unity and the liberation of Palestine are two complementary objectives, the attainment of either of which facilitates the attainment of the other. Thus, Arab unity leads to the liberation of Palestine, the liberation of Palestine leads to Arab unity.' In turn, article 9 declared, 'armed struggle is the only way to liberate Palestine'.

The PLO had a strong statist orientation from the very beginning (Sayigh, 1997: 98), with a constitution, a parliament (National Council), a government (Executive Committee), a treasury, and an army: the Palestine Liberation Army (the PLA) (Baracskay, 2011: 44). However, it was only a potential state, an institutional superstructure, lacking any territory of its own, as Jerusalem remained under Jordan's control at this time.

The PLA, generously funded by the Arab states, was a conventional army with tanks and artillery (O'Neill, 1978: 5). However, this type of military organization was ill-suited to the kind of irregular warfare that militants conducted in their fight against Israel. A Small band of fedayeen, grouped around Fatah, an organization created in the late 1950s, decided not to join the PLO (although it eventually did so in 1967). Its leader, Yasser Arafat, considered that a regular army, like the PLA, was not appropriate for the guerrilla activity necessary to hit Israel. Arafat, heavily impressed by the success of Algeria's National Liberation Front in 1962, believed that only irregular operations would work, given the strength of the Israel Defense Forces (IDF). Despite its small size (less than three hundred recruits), Fatah had the strategic support of Syria, whose aim was to counter Egypt's influence in the Arab world.

Fatah had bases in Syria and Lebanon. The initial attacks within Israel consisted of incursions from the Jordanian border, which aimed at destroying infrastructure. The first raid took place on 1 January 1965. To improve access to Israel, the fedayeen established new camps on the West Bank, close to the border separating Jordan from Israel, so that they could speed up their missions. Fatah avoided clashes with the Israeli army; their hit-and-run tactics were surgical-like operations with clear propagandistic intent. Their actions triggered the first Israeli reprisals against the Palestinian camps on the West Bank. Fatah's initial goal was to employ violence to mobilize the Palestinian population living in Israel, with the aim of provoking a strong reaction by Israel that would eventually push the Arab countries into intervening in an open war (Sayigh, 1997: 120). As in many other instances of nationalist armed struggle, the strategy was based on a spiralling process driven by the mechanism of repression backlash.

Fatah's violence was limited (10 killings in 1965, another 10 in 1966, and 16 in 1967)[1] and did not spark a revolution, though it had several important consequences. It radicalized the PLO, which had to adapt to the new situation by adopting irregular tactics. Moreover, it generated tensions among the Arab countries and between the Arab countries and Israel. A good illustration

---

[1] Official figures from the Israeli Ministry of Foreign Affairs (https://mfa.gov.il/MFA/MFA-Archive/2000/Pages/Terrorism%20deaths%20in%20Israel%20-%201920-1999.aspx, accessed December 2020).

may be the Samu incident in November 1966 (Shemesh and Tlamin, 2002), in which three Israeli soldiers were killed by a mine that had been planted by Palestinians who had crossed the Jordanian border. On the following day, the Israeli army entered the West Bank and carried out a retaliation operation in the village of Samu that included the demolition of Palestinian houses. Three civilians were killed. A battle with units of the Jordan army followed, with at least 15 Jordanian combatants killed. The operation triggered an unprecedented wave of protests and rioting among Palestinians on the West Bank. The Jordanian army tried to impose order, sometimes by killing protesters (three of them in Nablus on 21 November). These types of incidents generated growing tensions between the Arab countries and Israel. The king of Jordan could not withstand popular pressure at home after the Samu reprisal and moved closer to Egypt's position. Clashes between the Syrian army and the IDF were also frequent along the Israeli border. In June 1967, Egypt mobilized troops in the Sinai, and Israel responded by launching a devastating attack that initiated the Six Day War; Jordan and Syria joined the conflict, but they were also defeated. Israel was far superior in military terms and invaded the Sinai Peninsula and the Gaza Strip in Egypt, the Golan Heights in Syria, and the West Bank in Jordan.

The defeat of the Arab countries was a dramatic event that profoundly changed the geopolitical chessboard in the Middle East. Regarding the Palestinian conflict, there were several implications. Firstly, a significant number of Palestinians abandoned the occupied territories of the West Bank and the Gaza Strip; between 200,000 and 250,000 Palestinians went into exile, most of them relocating in Jordan. Simultaneously, after gaining control of Gaza and the West Bank (Jerusalem included), Israel found itself ruling over a million Palestinians, compared with the 300,000 living in Israel before the war (O'Neill, 1978: 7).

The Six-Day War transformed the Palestinian struggle from an inter-state conflict to an Israel-bound domestic one. In this vein, the Palestinian conflict was reframed: from 1967 onwards, the Palestinians would have to fight by themselves to liberate their people. This forced both the PLO and other armed groups to undergo a process of reflection on the most efficient tactics to employ in the post-war period. Of course, Palestinians had the protection of Jordan, Lebanon, and Syria, without which they would not have had camps outside Israel. The sanctuaries in these countries were certainly crucial for the survival of the armed groups. But now the guerrillas had to figure out how to fight for their people without relying on the Arab armies' direct intervention.

Fatah's immediate response to the Arabs' defeat in the war was to instigate an uprising in the occupied territories (Chailand, 1972: 62; Rubin, 1994:

16; Sayigh, 1997: 147). Armed attacks were intended to be the spark that would ignite the revolutionary flame. In September 1967, there was a call for a general strike on the West Bank, but it had an uneven following and the Israeli authorities repressed the protest. Punishment measures against armed resistance included curfews, house arrests, shutdowns of entire areas, and expulsions (Morris, 2001: 341). Israeli security forces effectively neutralized violence in the occupied territories. Throughout 1967, 1,000 Palestinian guerrillas were arrested in Israel and 200 killed (Morris, 2001: 366). Consequently, leaders and recruits had to leave the country and settle in sanctuaries outside Israel. There would not be much more insurgent activity in the occupied territories until the first Intifada in 1987 (Sayigh, 1997: 173).

The bulk of the rebels were in Jordan, on the East Bank. In terms of our theoretical framework, in 1968 the guerrillas gained territorial control in Jordan, but not in Israel. The PLO did not only have camps; it became a shadow state, with capacity to rule over Palestinians, which generated a dual power within Jordan. It provided health services and developed an administrative apparatus, with offices in Amman (Hudson, 1972: 67). Jordan, however, was not the theatre of armed operations. The goal was still to infiltrate Israel and attack there. But despite thousands of recruits trained in guerrilla tactics, Fatah had little capacity to do so. In this regard, the situation was not much unlike that of the African National Congress, with thousands of recruits out of South Africa and very little capacity to enter the country (see Chapter 2).

The PLO's operations in Israel were short-lived and limited, undertaken by roving groups of 10–15 fedayeen—with the violence resembling more that of an underground group acting in Israel than that usually associated with guerrilla warfare. The vast majority of the attacks were bomb explosions aimed at infrastructure and civilians, with almost no physical encounters between the fedayeen and the IDF, as is typically the case in terrorist violence. A significant event was the blowing up of an Israeli school bus in the Negev desert by a landmine on 18 March 1968, killing two teachers and wounding 28 children (Terrill, 2001: 95). The Palestinians claimed that the mine was situated in military terrain, but this response did not placate anger in Israel. In reprisal, the IDF announced that it would attack the Palestinian camp in Karameh. The battle that followed on 21 March displayed a type of violence very different from that involved in the raids into Israel. This was an open military clash between the IDF and the fedayeen, the latter being supported by the Jordanian army later on. Israeli soldiers entered Jordan as part of 'Operation Inferno'. The destruction of the PLO base took 15 hours of heavy fighting, in which the IDF found greater resistance than expected. The Palestinians, under the leadership of Arafat, fought vigorously, though the

156   Underground Violence

key factor was the intervention of Jordanian regulars. The estimates about fatalities diverge widely depending on the source: Israel accepts that 20 IDF soldiers were killed, but Jordan says the number was 75 (Terrill, 2001: 106); in his authoritative analysis, Morris (2001: 369) reports 33 Israeli military dead. The fact of the matter is that Israel achieved the goal of destroying the Karameh camp, but this did not prevent the formation of a nation-making legend around the Palestinian guerrilla and its leader, Yasser Arafat. The unexpected blow suffered by the IDF raised morale in Arab countries and the Palestinian community; the guerrillas were idealized and Karameh became a founding moment in the construction of Palestinian identity. In the following months, the number of recruits doubled or tripled. According to Sayigh (1997: 181), the growth rate was around 300 per cent; the number of full-time Fatah fighters increased to 2,000, plus 12,000 supporters in towns and camps. Given the prestige of Arafat after Karameh, he became the chairman of the PLO in February 1969 (Rubin, 1994: 19).

Thanks to de facto territorial control in Jordan, PLO guerrillas were able to participate in full military battles, like Karameh, with the IDF. But given the impossibility of holding control within Israel, or even to organize attacks from within the occupied territories, the Palestinian commandos had to limit themselves to covert, terrorist attacks within Israel. According to Table 2.1, the battle of Karameh would be a case of pure guerrilla violence (a group with territorial control employing guerrilla tactics), while the raids in Israel would rather fall in the cell of terrorist violence carried out by groups with a safe haven, acting out of their sanctuaries.

Despite the strength of the insurgency, Israel was able to contain the threat. Fatah intensified its attacks in 1969, but it failed to produce a security crisis or to liberate territory in the occupied zones. As an attrition strategy, the guerrillas were not able to impose a significant cost on its enemy. Israeli casualties did not increase substantially (55 people killed in 1968; and 33 in 1969). The only exception lay, perhaps, in the Gaza Strip, where incidents were numerous, particularly in 1969 and 1970, to the point that guerrillas gained control over some refugee camps (in many cases only during the night) and were able to settle local disputes and try informers (Sayigh, 1997: 209) This, however, was a rather short-lived achievement; after the death of two children caused by a grenade explosion in January 1971 in Gaza, the IDF carried out a cleansing operation that put an end to the presence of guerrillas in the Strip (Morris, 2001: 370).

During the period 1967–70, Palestinian operations against Israel were not able to take off, and the campaign was in deadlock at the beginning of 1970. The situation, however, changed abruptly in September. The PLO in

Jordan had become a serious threat to the legitimacy of King Hussein (camp-dwelling Palestinians made up around a third of the total population in the kingdom). The PLO acted as a state of its own and sought to gain the allegiance of the Palestinian community. The monopoly of violence was at stake, with dual structures of government. Jordan reacted by trying to limit the PLO's activities and influence. Already by June 1970 there were significant clashes between the Jordanian army and the fedayeen living in camps around Amman (with about 400 deaths; Morris, 2001: 373). There was a serious risk of a civil war erupting between the two sides. The fedayeen organized two assassination attempts against King Hussein in a couple of months. On 15 September, the PLO declared the creation of the first 'Arab Soviet' in the north of the country. Only two days later, after an international crisis caused by a multiple hijacking episode (see below), the Jordanian army began a full assault on the Palestinian guerrillas, with a death toll of between 3,000 and 5,000 (Sayigh, 1997: 267). This became known as 'Black September', and was a very heavy loss for the PLO. In a span of a year, Jordan was able to completely remove the guerrillas out of its territory.

The PLO had to leave Jordan. It found refuge and protection in Lebanon; its headquarters relocated to Beirut. Most militants settled in Lebanon too, to the south of the Litani river (the area became known as 'Fatahland'). The inflow of Palestinians in Lebanon altered the precarious political equilibrium of the country between the various religious groups, and precipitated the civil war that engulfed the country from 1975 to 1990. Reproducing a similar dynamic to that observed in Jordan, the PLO created again a state within a state. This led, inevitably, to clashes with Lebanese security forces. In terms of armed struggle, the PLO got involved in irregular guerrilla fighting against other parties in the civil war; it also launched operations infiltrating Israel from the north (Rubin, 1994: 56). In March 1978, for example, a Fatah commando crossed into Israel from the coast and seized a bus full of Israeli passengers. They drove the bus through the highway leading to Tel-Aviv and shot at cars (they killed a taxi driver). The bus then hit a roadblock; a shootout with IDFs followed and grenades were used, with a final toll of seven hostages and nine Fatah members being killed. Israel's response three days later was to invade South Lebanon and destroy PLO bases, killing several hundred Palestinians (Morris, 2001: 460).

In June 1982, Israel tried to crush the PLO by launching a full invasion of Lebanon. This time, the IDF went beyond the Litani river, moving north and reaching Beirut. The occupation of the capital culminated in the carnage of the Sabra and Shatila refugee camps carried out by the Phalangists, following the assassination of their leader Bashir Gemayel a few days before. The IDF was aware of what was about to happen and did nothing to prevent the hundreds of killings, which included women and children. The result was an utter disaster for the PLO. The guerrilla infrastructure was destroyed; Arafat had to leave the country and establish new offices in Tunis, far away from Israel and the occupied territories. It was a humiliating escape. For the PLO, it was the beginning of the end as a guerrilla group. Arafat, in a press conference after his speech to the UN in December 1988, renounced the armed struggle in favour of a comprehensive negotiation on the future of Palestine, based on the recognition of Israel. His words were this: 'We totally and categorically reject all forms of terrorism, including individual, group, and state terrorism' (Rubin, 1994: 110). The Intifada would force Fatah to reconsider this change.

International Terrorism

Since 1967, Fatah had had a serious competitor, the Popular Front for the Liberation of Palestine (PFLP), under the leadership of George Habash; it was also part of the PLO. Unlike Fatah's nationalist-only stance, the PFLP held pan-Arabic, secular, and Marxist ideas, and had a greater willingness to employ more extremist and spectacular tactics than Fatah. The PFLP criticized the guerrilla ambitions of Fatah. In the original PFLP platform, written in 1969, the border operations conducted by Fatah were described with contempt. The goal should be not to simply harass Israel, the PFLP argued, but to employ violence to create the conditions for a popular revolution. Violence, therefore, was overall aimed at mobilization. This understanding of violence as a mobilizing weapon is typical in revolutionary groups, as opposed to the attrition strategy that is usually found in those of national liberation (Sánchez-Cuenca and De la Calle, 2009). As the PFLP said, 'Amman can become an Arab Hanoi: a base for the revolutionaries fighting in Palestine' (Laqueur and Schueftan, 2016: 142).

The PFLP tried to carry out attacks in the occupied territories, but with limited success given the effective surveillance of Israeli security forces. The alternative was to carry out spectacular attacks against Israeli interests abroad. On the one hand, the attacks would attract international attention to the Palestinian cause; on the other, they would radicalize the Palestinian population both in Jordan and in Israel. As Habash himself said, 'these operations made the world aware of our people's suffering' (Habash and Soueid, 1998: 94).

The PFLP became infamous for hijackings. On 23 July 1968 three PFLP members hijacked a plane flying from Rome to Tel Aviv. The plane was diverted to Algiers. The terrorists only released the hostages after Israel liberated 15 Palestinian prisoners. This was just the first salvo of a long series of 29 hijackings between 1968 and 1977, 11 of which were carried out by the PFLP, and the other 18 by other Palestinian armed groups.[2]

The Palestinians did not invent hijacking. The first registered instances are in 1949–50, when defectors seeking asylum from the communist bloc diverted flights to Western airports (Koerner, 2013: 35). After the success of the Cuban revolution in 1959, four planes were hijacked and directed to Florida. During the 1960s, there were many more hijackings in the opposite direction (Americans who wanted to go to Cuba). According to Koerner (2013), hijackings became an epidemic. Many of these incidents were not politically motivated; strange as this may sound today, desperate people found hijacking an attractive escape option. Indeed, the Palestinians refined the art of hijacking, using the passengers as hostages and conditioning their liberation on concessions made by Israel (or other countries that held Palestinians in jail). The PFLP's hijacking of three planes on 6 September 1970, two of which were forced to land in Jordan, was the last straw in the tense relationship between the Jordanian government and the Palestinian armed groups (on 9 September a third hijacked plane landed in Jordan) (Rubin, 1994: 35). Black September occurred just a few days later.

A related and much harsher tactic was blowing up airplanes in mid-flight. The first case happened on 21 February 1970, when a Swissair plane flying from Zürich to Tel-Aviv exploded; the 38 passengers and nine crew died in the attack. This action was possibly in retaliation for the imprisonment of three Palestinians in Switzerland. The attack is attributed to a PFLP split, the Popular Front for the Liberation of Palestine-General Commando (PFLP-GC), led by Ahmed Jibril. The PFLP-GC tried the tactic twice again in 1971, but the attempts failed. In 1974, the Abu Nidal Organization (ANO; see below) exploded a TWA plane flying from Tel-Aviv to New York, killing 88 people (the attack was claimed by the Arab Nationalist Youth Organization, a name sometimes employed by ANO). In September 1983 it did it again, when a bomb exploded on a plane flying from Karachi to Dubai, killing 111 passengers and crew.

Before Black September, Fatah was not interested in international action; in fact, it did not commit a single international attack before 1971. The loss of Jordan, however, forced Fatah to reconsider the issue. Not having yet established a new infrastructure in Lebanon, and with very limited capacity

---

[2] The figures on Palestinian international terrorism in this section are from the Jaffee Center for Strategic Studies, as reported in Merari and Elad (1986).

160 Underground Violence

to attack Israel, Fatah decided to follow the PFLP's example, by launching a campaign of international terrorism (Merari and Elad, 1986: 23; Morris, 2001: 379; Rubin, 1994: 37). To avoid blurring the prestige of being a guerrilla, or the opprobrium of terrorism, international attacks were claimed by a new group, the Black September Organization (BSO), which allegedly was independent of Fatah. Revenge and the restitution of honour were key motivations. The first BSO attack was the assassination of the Jordanian prime minister in Cairo on 28 November 1971, which boosted the morale of many Palestinians (Sayigh, 1997: 309). On 11 March 1972, the BSO tried to kill King Hussein in London.

The most spectacular terrorist attack in the whole history of the Palestinian conflict was the BSO's seizing of the Israeli team residence during the Munich Olympics in September 1972 (Silke and Filippidou, 2020). Two athletes were killed and a further 11 were taken hostage. Their release was conditional on the liberation of 200 imprisoned Palestinians in Israel plus the two leaders of the Red Army Faction, Andreas Baader and Ulrike Meinhof, who were jailed in Germany. Israel refused to negotiate. Germany authorized the BSO commando (formed by eight Palestinians) and its hostages to leave the country. However, at the air base they were stormed by the German police in a poorly planned operation. In the following shootout, nine athletes, five terrorists, and one police officer were killed.[3] Because of the Olympics, there was widespread TV coverage, so the crisis unfolded on the TV sets of millions of homes. It was a live terrorist event that resonated across the whole world, catapulting the Palestinian movement to the forefront.

The cycle of the BSO's international terrorism was rather short. By the end of 1973 Fatah had decided to abandon international attacks. There were several reasons behind this strategic shift. Firstly, the goals in terms of propaganda had been achieved. After Munich, the Palestinian issue was well known and at the top of the international agenda. Further international attacks might have been redundant or even counterproductive to the PLO's claim of representing the Palestinian nation. Secondly, Fatah had reorganized its bases in Lebanon and was ready to launch attacks on the northern border of Israel. It again had a territorial base out of Israel. Thirdly, the mood of Arab countries changed after the Yom Kippur War of October 1973: although ultimately fruitless for Arab countries, this war was perceived as a kind of late compensation for the defeat of the Six Day War and was sold to the Arab public as

---

[3] The nine athletes died as a consequence of a grenade thrown by the terrorists into the helicopter that had brought them to the air base. Three terrorists survived and were imprisoned. However, on 29 October 1972, a flight going to Germany was hijacked. The hijackers threatened to blow up the plane if the three terrorists were not released. The German authorities acceded, and the terrorists found refuge in Libya.

a success. This opened a window of opportunity for a negotiation phase on the Palestinian question. The very fact of quitting the international campaign enhanced the political stature of Fatah. In this regard, the international campaign could be interpreted as a success (Merari and Elad, 1986: 90; Morris, 2001: 386). In the UN General Assembly of November 1974, the PLO was recognized as the legitimate representative of the Palestinian people by 90 countries, and Arafat was invited to talk (Baracskay, 2011: 113).

In the wake of the BSO's decision to quit, the PFLP also renounced hijacking. International terrorism, however, did not disappear altogether, as splinter groups took over. Habash's second in command, Wadi Haddad, decided to continue. One of his most spectacular deeds was a bold operation carried out in collaboration with the German RAF and commanded by the Venezuelan 'Carlos the Jackal' on 21 December 1975: they raided the meeting of the OPEC ministers in Vienna and took 20 hostages who were sent to Algiers.

The bloodiest and most enduring group was the Abu Nidal Organization (ANO), created in 1973, which was a splinter group from Fatah. The original name, in fact, was Fatah Revolutionary Council, although the group is better known by the name of its founder, Abu Nidal. Nidal opposed Fatah's decision to end the international campaign and the ensuing adoption of a diplomatic strategy of greater compromise. The first attack, which was typically terrorist, happened on 5 September 1973: the ANO seized the Saudi embassy in Paris, took 13 people hostage and asked for the liberation of Abu Wawud, a high-profile Fatah commander who was imprisoned in Jordan.

The ANO was never interested in attacking within Israel. It opted rather for international attacks from the very beginning. A very significant number of attacks were aimed at other Palestinian fighters. In 1978 the ANO started a systematic campaign against Fatah's (and other Palestinian groups') leaders, specifically against those who were regarded as 'doves'. The campaign culminated in 1991, with the assassination of Fatah's most senior figure after Arafat (and former companion of Nidal), Abu Iyad, and another Fatah high-rank leader, Abu Hol, in Tunis.

The ANO's attacks consistently sought to spoil any negotiation between Israel and Palestinian representatives. Since this favoured the stance of Israeli hawks, there has been endless speculation about the real motives of Abu Nidal and even whether he was a double agent working for Israeli secret services (Seale, 1992).

Although the ANO's attacks were covert in almost every case, it was never a fully underground group because it always benefited from the protection of a particular state. In return, Nidal mounted international operations that

162 Underground Violence

would play in favour of its protector's geostrategic interests. The first base of the ANO was in Iraq, where Nidal was the uncontested leader of the Palestinian community. When Iraq went to war with Iran, the ANO moved to Syria and carried out numerous operations against Jordan, gaining the favour of the Syrian authorities. In 1982 it tried to kill the Israeli ambassador in London. This contributed to triggering Israel's invasion of Lebanon (Baracskay, 2011: 149). A dispute within Fatah on whether to defend Beirut or flee the country led to an internal rebellion against Arafat. The ANO exploited this internecine quarrel, joining forces in the operation against Arafat, who eventually moved to Tunis. As a side effect, the Syrians allowed Nidal to expand his base in Lebanon. A significant number of Fatah's anti-Arafat recruits defected and joined ANO's camps in the Lebanese Beqaa Valley.

The most remarkable development in these years is that, for entirely unintended reasons, the ANO gained significant territorial control in Lebanon. The group was in the process of transforming itself into a guerrilla:

> Instead of the assassin armed with a bomb or a sniper's rifle, the organization now had men who could drive armored vehicles or could fire missiles, former Fatah officers with years of experience behind them and considerable military skills. [...] Instead of being a small, closed, clandestine outfit that Abu Nidal could direct by remote control, the organization was developing into a mass movement with its own strong leaders and cadres. (Seale, 1992: 143)

Here we can see the metamorphosis of an underground group into a territorial one with some degree of military power. What is unique is that Nidal rejected this possibility and preferred to return to international covert operations. Nidal's motivation for this kind of self-restraint is a matter of speculation, but it seems that he preferred to maintain absolute control over his organization.

After Syria, Abu Nidal moved to Libya, under the protection of Gadhafi. In the process of regaining control over the organization, Nidal set into motion an astonishing cleansing operation, killing around 600 of his own people between 1987 and 1988 (Seale, 1992: 288). The ANO's activity decreased substantially in the mid-1990s and disappeared altogether after Nidal's death in 2003.

The ANO was the purest group in terms of international armed activity. It specialized in spectacular and very often extremely cruel attacks all over the world. Because these attacks were covert, they perfectly fit the ideal type of terrorist violence, even if the ANO had successive sanctuaries in various countries.

The Second Cycle of Violence: The Two Intifadas

The PLO's expulsion from Lebanon in the early 1980s dealt a fatal blow to the Palestinian cause. After the Black September battle in Jordan, this represented the second time that the PLO had relinquished its base. Without a sanctuary close to the border, the PLO was unable to sustain a campaign of attacks in Israel. In any case, the infiltrations into Israel over the previous years had been fruitless in political terms: Israel had not made a single concession to the Palestinian people.

The early 1980s were years of lower armed activity compared with previous periods. The situation, however, changed quite dramatically with the start of a spontaneous popular uprising in the occupied territories at the end of 1987. The trigger event was an Israeli vehicle that crashed against a car of Palestinians, killing four of them. The rumour spread that this was intended, and people revolted against the occupation. The causes for the Intifada were complex and multifarious, including the fatigue of living under occupation for 20 years, a generalized feeling of humiliation and frustration, and the weakness of the PLO (Beitler, 2004: 90–96; Morris, 2001: 561–8; Shalev, 1991: 14–34). To the surprise of both the PLO and Israel, the protests did not wane; in fact, the rebellion lasted for several years. The protesters renounced the use of firearms from the very beginning. Demonstrations often had a violent side, such as throwing stones, using Molotov cocktails, burning tyres, forming barricades, and the like. In the most violent clashes with security forces, knives were sometimes used. This was accompanied by massive strikes and acts of civil disobedience, such as refusing to pay taxes. As on other occasions, Israel overreacted. In the first three weeks of the Intifada, 22 Palestinians were killed in the occupied territories; in 1988, 289 lost their lives, and in 1989 another 285; in 1990 the number was lower, at 195. In total, 989 Palestinians lost their lives because of Israeli repression in these years. Repression was indeed brutal; it included heavy tactics for crowd dispersal, curfews, arrests, deportations, and beatings. During the period December 1987–December 1990, 45 Israelis were killed by Palestinians in Israel or in the occupied territories.[4] The 989:45 ratio for the first three years of the Intifada speaks for itself: almost 22 Palestinians died for each Israeli killed.

The resilience of the Palestinians was possible thanks to the networks that had been established during the 1980s in the occupied territories. Islamist organizations played a key role through associations of all kinds (religious,

---

[4] Data about the two Intifadas come from B'tselem (The Israeli Information Center for Human Rights in the Occupied Territories). Regarding the first Intifada, see https://www.btselem.org/statistics/first_intifada_tables (accessed December 2020).

educational, sport, and charity, etc.). Under the heavy influence of the Iranian revolution and the successful mujahideen resistance to the Soviets in Afghanistan, the 1980s saw a dramatic expansion of political Islamism across many Muslim societies. The social capital produced by these networks was widely employed to coordinate and mobilize Palestinians in the occupied territories.

Although repression contained the scope of the protest, it did not eliminate it. The protest cycle was maintained until the Oslo accords of 1993 despite the high costs of participation, though with decreasing levels of mobilization. As popular participation diminished, levels of violence increased (Beitler, 2004: 125; Morris, 2001: 594), confirming the hypothesis of Della Porta and Tarrow (1986) that violence increases in the decaying phase of popular protest, being a substitute rather than a complement of mobilization.[5]

The creation of Hamas in December 1987 (an acronym for Harakat al-Muqawna al-Islamiyya, the Islamic Resistance Movement, meaning 'zeal') was part of the Islamist wave. It was a direct offshoot of the Palestinian Muslim brotherhood. Its short-term ambition was to lead a revolt by challenging the authority and leadership of the PLO. Although it shared a nationalist agenda with the PLO, Hamas questioned the negotiating stance of secular nationalists. Its founding charter was issued in August 1988, and leaves little room for ambiguity: article 13 reads 'There is no solution to the Palestinian problem except by Jihad. The initiatives, proposals, and international conferences are but a waste of time and sheer futility.'[6]

The stronghold of Hamas was the Gaza Strip. There, it capitalized on existing Islamic networks and institutions, including mosques, educational centres, charities, and civil associations (Levitt, 2006: 82). Hamas has a double structure, with its political and social chapter above ground, and the armed wing fully underground (Mannes, 2004: 125).[7] The overt branches developed strong ties with the community through religious activity and welfare provision (i.e., health and education) (Mishal and Sela, 2000: Ch. 1). Hamas' associational and service infrastructure was crucial for the maintenance of the underground branch: it was the source of safe houses, recruits, and weapon stores (explosives were once found in a Hamas kindergarten) (Levitt, 2006: 97). As in many other nationalist groups, Hamas' overt structure worked as a surrogate for the lack of any territory of its own. Thanks to it, the underground branch was able to host a few thousand recruits.

---

[5] De la Calle and Sánchez-Cuenca (2020) test (and confirm) this hypothesis through a large-n design.
[6] We follow the English version provided by Mishal and Sela (2000: Appendix 2).
[7] Hamas also had offices in Amman.

The contrast with the Palestinian Islamic Jihad (PIJ) is instructive. PIJ was founded in 1981 and was also under the heavy influence of the Iranian revolution. It shares with Hamas an Islamist orientation as well as its ideological radicalism. However, it is only an underground organization, lacking any above-the-ground structure (Mannes, 2004: 200). Because of this important difference, PIJ faces heavier logistical constraints than Hamas—hence its much more reduced size, with hundreds rather than thousands of recruits.

Hamas' adoption of armed struggle was gradual. The early attacks, carried out by small cells, took place during the first months of 1989. On 16 February, an Israeli soldier was kidnapped and killed, and a very similar operation was undertaken on 3 May. In response to these early attacks, Israel outlawed Hamas on 28 September 1989. During the initial years, attacks were punctual and scattered, falling short of a sustained campaign that might be regarded as a serious threat by Israel (Mishal and Sela, 2000: 57). In 1991, the organization considered the situation ripe for scaling up the offensive capacity of the underground branch. The context was characterized by a decline in the Intifada's popular mobilizations and greater hopes placed in the diplomatic approach, which would culminate in the Madrid conference of October. Under these conditions, Hamas centralized its armed cells and became a more institutionalized organization, called the Izz al-Din al-Qassam Brigades, after the name of the Palestinian fighter of the 1930s (Baconi, 2018: 27). The escalation of Hamas was driven by two factors: Israeli repression and intra-Palestinian competition between Islamist and secular armed groups.

At the end of 1992, Israel deported 415 militants of Hamas to South Lebanon, where they socialized with members of Hezbollah (with very similar grassroots, Hezbollah was starting to launch an ultimately successful campaign in South Lebanon against Israeli control). There, Hamas' militants learnt how to make car bombs and carry out suicide missions (Mishal and Sela, 2000: 65). Around half of them were allowed to go back to Israel one year later, in September 1993. The plan was to use these tactics in Israel and the occupied territories, with the explicit aim of breaking the Oslo Accord signed that very month. As Kydd and Walter (2002) showed, the peaks of Hamas' armed activity were significantly related to the milestones of the peace process.

Although it is often written that the first suicide attack was that of 6 April 1994—in reaction to the massacre on 25 February 1994 caused by Baruch Goldstein, an Israeli settler who opened fire in the Ibrahimi Mosque killing 29 Arabs (Baconi, 2018: 29; Schanzer, 2008: 41)—the truth of the matter is

166   Underground Violence

that there had been two earlier missions.[8] Suicide missions became Hamas' trademark. This is a quintessential terrorist tactic, as it is always done covertly and by surprise. Hamas, in fact, became the leading terrorist group within Israel in both the actor- and the action-sense. In the typology presented in Table 2.1, Hamas is a case of pure terrorism in the upper left cell, since it had to act clandestinely and specialized in terrorist tactics.

Hamas' terrorist activity peaked during the second Intifada. In this case, the triggering event was political provocation by Ariel Sharon, leader of Israel's Likud party (then in opposition): on 28 September 2000 he visited the al-Aqsa Mosque in Jerusalem, the third-holiest place in Islam. The second Intifada was different from the first, on two grounds. The first is that popular mobilizations were quickly replaced by terrorist tactics in general, and suicide missions in particular. The joint activity of the various Palestinian armed groups brought about the highest levels of internal violence ever experienced by Israel. During the 2000–2008 period (the Al-Aqsa Intifada and its aftermath), 728 Israeli civilians and 335 members of Israeli security forces were killed by Palestinian armed groups; in turn, 4,861 Palestinians were killed by the IDF (the ratio was 4,861:1,063, approximately 5:1). The Hamas offensive (the so-called '10-bomb campaign') unfolded between May and July 2001; this coincided with the decision to start firing Qassam rockets into Israel from the occupied territories (Baconi, 2018: 44–5). Under the premiership of Ariel Sharon, who had been elected in 2001, Israel launched in 2002 the operation 'Defensive Shield'; this was the largest military mobilization in the occupied territories since 1967, to destroy as much Palestinian infrastructure as possible, including the PA's headquarters in Ramallah. The operation succeeded in containing Palestinian attacks. The simultaneous construction of a fence effectively isolating the West Bank from Israeli soil made it much more difficult to infiltrate it for suicide missions. Rockets were not an adequate substitute for suicide bombings (Frisch, 2009).

By 2000 the peace process was going nowhere. Arafat had abandoned the negotiating table in Camp David in July 2000, a couple of months before the start of the Al-Aqsa Intifada. There were internal and external motives for the collapse of the peace process. Internal reasons included the fact that the offer made by Israel and supported by the USA did not solve the refugee

---

[8] The first one took place on 16 April 1993: a van with explosives was detonated by the driver in the West Bank, injuring several Israeli soldiers and killing one Palestinian. The attack was claimed by multiple groups, including Hamas and PIJ, although the criminal investigation attributed it to Hamas (Mannes, 2004: 135). According to a UN report released on 14 September 2013, just one day after the signing of the Oslo Accord, a 19-year old member of Hamas with an explosive belt blew himself up when he was about to enter a police station in Gaza; however, only the terrorist died (see https://www.un.org/unispal/document/auto-insert-180894/).

issue, did not end the illegal settlements, and required the PA to dismantle its armed groups (Pappe, 2017: 199–200). As for external motives, life in the occupied territories had not improved since the first Oslo Accord in 1993, with growing unrest in the Palestinian population; moreover, the PLO had to cope with the strong opposition of Hamas and other Islamist groups. At the beginning of the second Intifada, Fatah created its own underground group, the al-Aqsa Martyrs' Brigade, which carried out numerous suicide missions between 2002 and 2007. As Gupta and Mundra (2005) have shown through statistical analysis, attacks by Hamas and PIJ on the one hand and the PLO on the other are positively associated, which suggests a pattern of competition among the armed groups.

The tensions between Hamas and the PLO had been visible since the beginning of the first Intifada. The Islamist group contested the PLO's legitimacy as the only representative of the Palestinian people. To gain cultural and political hegemony in the occupied territories, Hamas not only engaged in activities oriented to community-building and terrorist attacks against Israel, but also set in motion a less visible, low-intensity campaign against Palestinian dissidents. Although precise figures are lacking, Hamas killed alleged informers routinely, as well as targeting Fatah's members (and vice versa).[9] The tensions with Fatah increased up until an all-out, final confrontation in 2007 (see below).

The context of the rivalry between Hamas and Fatah had long roots. Following the Cairo agreement signed on 4 May 1994, Fatah (the PLO) was in a position of superiority vis-à-vis Hamas, as Israeli's partial withdrawal from the occupied territories was replaced by the PLO taking over the new Palestinian Authority (PA). On 1 July 1994, Arafat returned to Palestine after years of exile. The PLO was in charge of maintaining security; however, this was a poisoned chalice. The PA lacked the means to enforce peace; and the more violence there was, the lower Israel's confidence about any solution based on coexistence between the two states. The relationship between the PA and Islamist groups became tenser after several Hamas and PIJ suicide missions in 1996 that were particularly traumatic for Israel. The PA arrested a number of Hamas' members and killed others in shootouts (Schanzer, 2008: 68). During the second Intifada, however, there were some joint operations between

---

[9] According to B'Teselem, 610 Palestinians were killed by other Palestinians during the period 2000–2008 (https://www.btselem.org/statistics/fatalities/before-cast-lead/by-date-of-event). During the first Intifada (1987–93), around 150 collaborators were killed by Hamas (Be'er and Abdel-Jawad, 1994: 206).

168   Underground Violence

the al-Aqsa and the al-Qassam Brigades, although they were undertaken out of opportunism rather than for strategic reasons. In general, Hamas tried to displace the PA, and the PA, in turn, sought to undermine Hamas' operational capacity.

Hamas emerged emboldened from the second Intifada. This is not because the group was victorious, but Fatah was clearly weakened, given the incongruence of its double dimension: institutional and insurgent. On the other hand, the Palestinian public seemed to lean towards Hamas. Consequently, the organization achieved some partial territorial control, mainly in Gaza. To a certain extent, it started acting like a proto-guerrilla (lower left cell in Table 2.1). In fact, thanks to the support of Iran and the Gulf countries, it was able to develop a militia with some significant degree of military capacity during the years 2004–5 (Aviad, 2009). Hamas used its military structure not to launch new attacks against Israel, but to consolidate its new, hegemonic position in Gaza. Of course, it continued firing rockets at Israel, but its main aim was to become the new rulers of the Strip.

After the brutal cycle of violence of the al-Aqsa Intifada, Sharon considered that Palestine was so shattered that the full transfer of power to the PA was a low-risk operation for Israel. The PA called for elections in the occupied territories in January 2006, and Hamas emerged as the dominant force in the new Parliament. This unexpected outcome led to increased fighting between the two factions (Frisch, 2009: 1058; Schanzer, 2008: 99). Fatah did not want to lose control over the Palestinian security forces, and so the situation continued to deteriorate. In June 2007, Hamas completed its transformation from an underground group into a full guerrilla outfit, with effective territorial control. Thanks to the accumulation of military power during the proto-guerrilla phase, Hamas carried out a quick military campaign to conquer Gaza. In a single week, from 7 June to 14 June, it succeeded. This was an open battle between Hamas and Fatah (Baconi, 2018: 131; Schanzer, 2008: 107). The result was the physical occupation of all centres of power and public institutions. Hamas was, de facto, the new ruler.

The Relevance of Territory for the Modulations of Armed Struggle

The Palestinian conflict has been in a state of permanent flux, and the armed actors have gone through huge transformations. The variation in terms of insurgency that we find in the conflict is probably unsurpassed. Table 5.1

Table 5.1 Varieties of Palestinian insurgent violence

	Territorial control in occupied territories	Safe havens	Guerrilla activity	Terrorist activity in Israel	Terrorist activity in the occupied territories	International terrorist attacks
Fatah (pre-1994), including the Black September Organization (BSO)	None	Jordan (up to 1970), Lebanon (up to 1982)	Clashes with the IDF in Jordan (1968–70), including the Battle of Karameh. Clashes with the IDF in Lebanon (1982)	Hit-and-run attacks, bombings, ambushes	Very little	BSO campaign of international attacks, 1971–3 (hijackings, hostage taking, assassinations)
Fatah (post-1994), including Al-Aqsa Brigades	Partial	None	Clashes with Hamas	Suicide bombings, assassinations	Suicide bombings, assassinations	None
Hamas (pre-2007)	Partial (Gaza, since mid-1990s)	None	Clashes with PA forces	Suicide bombings, assassinations, rocket attacks	Suicide bombings, assassinations, ambushes	None
Hamas (since 2007)	Complete (Gaza, since 2007)	None	2007 battle with Fatah for control of Gaza. 2008–9 battle with the IDF (Cast Lead Operation)	Rocket attacks		None
Abu Nidal Organization	None	Iraq, Syria, Lebanon, Libya	None	None	None	Hijackings, assassinations

summarizes this variation in a systematic way. Our main claim is that many of the differences highlighted in Table 5.1 were driven by territorial constraints. Fatah was, for several decades, a sort of 'displaced guerrilla': its base of operations was out of Israel. In fact, Fatah was involved in guerrilla battles both in Jordan and in Lebanon, but not in Israel. The group was never able to establish a base in the occupied territories, where there was limited violence until the first Intifada in 1987. Its attacks against Israel were few and narrow in scope: small commandos infiltrated Israel, planted a bomb or ambushed an Israeli patrol, and then returned to their sanctuary, in a typical terrorist or low-intensity guerrilla fashion. When Fatah lost territorial control in Jordan after Black September, it shifted into international terrorist attacks (under the 'Black September Organization' label), heavily influenced by the spectacular hijackings featured by the PFLP and its splits. Thanks to the peace process, the PLO became the Palestinian Authority (PA). Once the PA had partial control of the occupied territories, it created an underground group (the al-Aqsa Brigades) that committed suicide attacks on Israeli soil.

Hamas followed a quite different path. It was founded at the start of the first Intifada in the occupied territories, with a stronger presence in Gaza than in the West Bank. It had both an overt structure (a religious group involved in welfare provision, with a highly visible presence in the Palestinian community) and a covert one (the al-Qassam Brigades). Consistent with its underground nature, Hamas committed terrorist attacks both in the occupied territories and in Israel. Its peak of activity happened in the first three years of the second Intifada. Although the second Intifada was contained, thanks to the IDF's attacks on the occupied territories and the construction of the fence, Hamas emerged as the principal Palestinian group and was able to build a proto-guerrilla structure, with thousands of recruits. When Israel withdrew from the occupied territories, Hamas won the Palestinian elections and in June 2007 it used its guerrilla capacity to launch an operation to gain full territorial control in Gaza, occupying all public sites of power and becoming the new ruler in the area. That marked the transformation of Hamas into a truly guerrilla group with a significant degree of ruling capacity.

This stylized description can be confirmed by analysing the variation in the attacks carried out by the various Palestinian armed organizations. We rely on the RAND Database of Worldwide Terrorism Incidents (RDWTI), which was built upon the MPTI dataset and the RAND Terrorism Chronology. It covers the period 1968–2009. There are two reasons we prefer RDWTI to

GTD here: RDWTI collects a higher number of Palestinian incidents, and it starts in 1968 (whereas GTD begins in 1970).[10]

The main change in the Palestinian armed struggle has been the appearance of violence in the occupied territories after 1993. This year is important for two reasons: the signing of the Oslo Accord, which opened the way to the formation of the Palestinian Authority by the PLO, and the beginning of Hamas' campaign in the occupied territories and Israeli soil against the peace process. After 1993, international terrorism disappeared and violence in the occupied territories increases very substantially, reaching a peak during the second Intifada.

Figure 5.1 represents the evolution of the percentages of international attacks and of attacks in the occupied territories by all Palestinian armed groups (including Palestinian attacks without authorship). For the sake of the comparison, we exclude those attacks taking place in Israel, Jordan, Lebanon, and Syria (the three border countries in which the PLO held

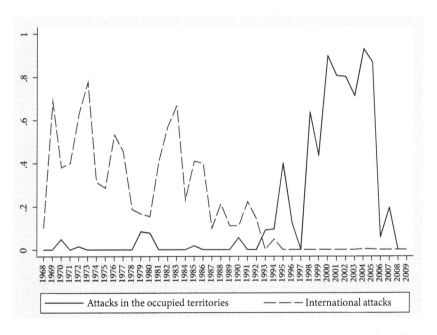

Figure 5.1 Evolution of the proportion of international actions and attacks in the occupied territories by all Palestinian organizations (RDWTI data)

---

[10] Despite these measurement differences, the two series are very similar (the Pearson's correlation is very high, 0.94). The only large discrepancy occurs in 1985 and it is due to the fact that the Israel Ministry of Foreign Affairs does not count the ANO's incident in the hijacking of Egypt Air Flight 648 on 23 November.

172   Underground Violence

bases). The data clearly show an inverse relationship between international actions and attacks in the occupied territories. When Hamas and Fatah were rooted in Gaza and the West Bank after 1993, international terrorism disappeared altogether.

If we break down Palestinian violence by the main groups—Fatah (including BSO, al-Aqsa Brigades, and generic PLO attacks), the PFLP, the ANO, Hamas, and the PIJ—and the location of the attacks—the occupied territories, Israel, border Arab countries (Lebanon, Jordan, Syria), and international—the various profiles of violence can be easily distinguished in Table 5.2. Fatah and the PFLP share similar percentages, with around one fifth of international attacks and another fifth in the occupied territories, while the majority of the attacks occur in Israel. By contrast, Hamas and the PIJ do not show any international or regional activity, concentrating their attacks in the occupied territories (Hamas) or in Israel (PIJ). Hamas emerges as the group that concentrates its attacks in the occupied territories, which is consistent with its social hegemony in the area. The most deviant case is the ANO: it only attacks out of Israel. The high percentage of attacks in border countries is due to the numerous attacks against Fatah's leaders living in the PLO's sanctuaries in Lebanon, Jordan, and Syria. Unlike the international attacks by Fatah and the PFLP, which were driven by their incapacity to act in Israel, the ANO chose, on ideological grounds, to act out of Israel, to the point that it had the opportunity to organize a guerrilla in Lebanon but, nonetheless, preferred to keep its international profile.

Both the profound change in 1993 (when armed activity in the occupied territories increased dramatically and international terrorism was

Table 5.2 Location of attacks by main Palestinian groups (horizontal percentages) (RDWTI data)

	Occupied territories	Israel	Regional (Lebanon, Jordan, Syria)	International	Total # of attacks
Fatah	19.92	56.7	5.75	17.62	522
PFLP	20.25	49.08	7.98	22.7	163
ANO	0	8.54	31.71	59.76	82
Hamas	67.01	32.84	0	0.15	676
PIJ	27.12	71.19	0.42	1.27	236
Total	38.95	46.04	4.17	10.84	1,679

Notes:
Fatah includes generic PLO attacks, BSO and the al-Aqsa Brigades.
Chi2=846.12 (significant at 0.001); Cramer's V=41.

abandoned) and the selection of geographical targets in each organization highlight the importance of territory. The Palestinian groups' strategies were, to a large extent, determined by their territorial bases and their capacity to attack Israel from either the inside or the outside.

5.2. The Islamic State

Whereas the ebbs and flows of the Palestinian insurgency slowly evolved over half a century, the spectacular rise and fall of the Islamic State has taken little more than a decade. It was initially founded as an Al Qaeda-minded clandestine group in the aftermath of the US invasion of Iraq; its sectarian bombs and audacious attacks gained the organization a following that became more powerful when in 2006 it took advantage of the first US withdrawal to capture large chunks of Anbar and Diyala governorates in deep Sunni territory. Its growing territorial dominance was halted by the US military surge, which added around 30,000 new troops on the ground (a 30 per cent increase) and forced the Islamic State to backtrack into clandestinity and underground violence. The change in the US administration, with the arrival of President Barack Obama, triggered a new withdrawal strategy that halved the number of US troops in a couple of years. This untimely departure happened to synchronize with the onset of the civil war in Syria, which offered a safe sanctuary to jihadist groups throughout the eastern region of the country. Both events fuelled the phoenix-like nature of ISIS by allowing the insurgency to capture large swathes of western Iraq, a process epitomized by the fall of Mosul in June 2014.

The swift transformation of ISIS from a clandestine group into a conventional army is really striking. After being toppled by the uneasy coalition of Kurdish ground forces, the Iraqi military, and US drone warfare, ISIS has, at the time of writing, inevitably gone back to clandestinity and scaled down its violence.

All these variations account for the confusion about how to identify the Islamic State. When we Googled 'Islamic state terrorism', the search engine yielded 30 million results. When we typed 'Islamic state territory', the number rose to 131 million. 'Islamic state guerrilla' gets 3 million and 'Islamic state insurgency' 3.6 million. As we discuss in the preface, all these concepts may be essentially right when thinking about the Islamic State (Byman, 2016). Our point here is that the different strategic stages of the organization were motivated by shifts in the balance of power between the jihadist insurgency and its enemies.

The Origins

It is not possible to write about the Islamic State without first portraying the life of its initiator and mastermind, Abu Musab al-Zarqawi (Warrick, 2015: Book 1). A Jordanian national, he combined jihadist stints in Jordan with tours of Afghanistan during the 1990s, before arriving in northern Iraq in early 2002. Five months into the US occupation of Iraq, the new Zarqawi group, named Jama'at al-Tawhid wa' al-Jihad (JTWJ), carried out three massive car bomb attacks against the Jordanian embassy and the UN headquarters in Baghdad (claiming 17 and 22 deaths respectively), and against the Shi'ite Imam Ali Mosque in Najaf (with 99 deaths, among them the then spiritual leader of the Supreme Council of the Islamic Revolution in Iraq). In a very prototypical terrorist fashion, these attacks went unclaimed, as the group wanted to exploit secrecy to build their internal strength before going public (Ingram, Whiteside, and Winter, 2020: 21, 44).

In the beginning, Zarqawi's fight had to be clandestine—both because of the asymmetric balance of power and the flat terrain (Brock, 2013: 35). Asked in 2006 about the difficulties of jihad in Iraq, Zarqawi plainly answered:

> There can be no comparison between our capabilities and the enemy's resources. Hundreds of our brothers are fighting hundreds of thousands of the enemy.... The land of jihad in Iraq is different from Afghanistan and Chechnya. The brothers in those two countries are helped either by forests or high mountains where they can hide from the enemy and prevent him from reaching them. Iraq is flat without mountains, wadis or forests. (Hashim, 2019: 24)

JTWJ's main strategic goal was to balance the initial asymmetry between the jihadists and the Iraqi government by triggering a civil war and prompting US troops to leave Iraqi soil (Brock, 2013: 39). Unlike Al Qaeda's classic emphasis on the far enemy (attacks against the US), Zarqawi thought the asymmetry had to be addressed at home through a threefold targeting strategy: (i) attacks against the occupation forces and their local allies in the new post-Saddam administration, to prevent its consolidation and increase the cost for the USA of staying in Iraq; (ii) attacks against the apostate Shia communities, as a way to polarize society and destroy any inter-sectarian bridges of cooperation; and (iii) attacks against Sunni groups collaborating with the new regime (Lahoud, 2014). JTWJ focused on targets that attracted not only media attention through very ghastly attacks—such as decapitations of kidnapped foreigners—but also some level of popularity to the organization

(Ingram, Whiteside, and Winter, 2020: 5). By draining the legitimacy of the new regime and weakening its military capabilities, Zarqawi anticipated a quick tactical shift from terrorism to more guerrilla-like warfare that would allow the organization to capture and rule territory (McCants, 2015).

It is worth quoting at length a letter that Zarqawi sent to Al Qaeda leaders in January 2004, as he clearly delineates his strategic thoughts on it. By that time, he still envisioned a fast track of territorial occupation leading to jihadist victory:

> We are striving urgently and racing against time to create companies of mujahidin that will repair to secure places and strive to reconnoiter the country, hunting the enemy—Americans, police, and soldiers—on the roads and lanes. We are continuing to train and multiply them. As for the Shi'a, we will hurt them, God willing, through martyrdom operations and car bombs.
>
> We have been striving for some time to observe the arena and sift those who work in it in search of those who are sincere and on the right path, so that we can cooperate with them for the good and coordinate some actions with them, so as to achieve solidarity and unity after testing and trying them. We hope that we have made good progress. Perhaps we will decide to go public soon, even if in a gradual way, so that we can come out into the open. We have been hiding for a long time. [...]
>
> It is our hope to accelerate the pace of work and that companies and battalions with expertise, experience, and endurance will be formed to await the zero hour when we will begin to appear in the open, gain control of the land at night, and extend it into daylight. We hope that this matter, the zero hour, will come four months or so before the promised government is formed. As you can see, we are racing against time.
>
> (Ingram, Whiteside, and Winter, 2020: 48)

JTWJ swore loyalty to Al Qaeda (AQ) in September 2004, rebranding itself as Al Qaeda in Iraq (AQI). In December 2004 the group made it into the US State Department's list of Foreign Terrorist Organizations (FTOs), and the next year Zarqawi became the most wanted man in Iraq, with a $25 million reward tag on his head.

Zarqawi clashed several times with AQ because of the communal violence that AQI was spearheading. For AQ leaders, its local branches had to be careful about picking targets, whereas Zarqawi thought that ultra-violent means would be beneficial for Sunni awareness and the expansion of the insurgency—even if very detrimental to broadening the appeal of the group. At its core, it was a controversy as much about means as about the right interpretation of those practising kufr—Muslims devoted to the wrong God (Maher, 2016). Zarqawi was ideologically aligned with Salafi theorists who sanctioned the slaughtering of infidels; for instance, he apparently endorsed the highly influential pamphlet 'Management of Savagery' written by AQ strategist Abu Bakr Naji (Ingram, Whiteside, and Winter, 2020: 5). AQI's characteristic impulse to punish infidels was transferred into ISIS, with the infamous slaughtering of Jazidi men, and the slavery of Jazidi women during the highest peak of the Islamic State's power in August 2014 (Al-Dayel, Mumford, and Bales, 2022).

The First Emirate

Encouraged by Al Qaeda's second in command al-Zawahiri to take steps to found Islamic emirates everywhere (Brock, 2013: 13), AQI merged in January 2006 with five other jihadist armed groups to create Majlis Shura al-Mujahideen (MSM), uniting all jihadist efforts to end US occupation and Shia rule in Iraq. Zarqawi was killed in Baqubah on 7 June 2006. But far from strangling the organization, his death pushed it to move forward and launch more ambitious attacks, with the creation four months later of the Islamic State in Iraq (ISI). Lack of a new pledge of allegiance to AQ highlighted the desire of the new group to 'walk alone', but it took years for security agencies to clearly grasp the implications of this split.

Data on Zarqawi's initial network, from April 2003 to April 2005, showed a heavy reliance on terrorist tactics, with 42 per cent being suicide bombs, plus an additional 10 per cent being other forms of IEDs. During this initial period, most attacks targeted security forces (49 per cent), with 36.2 per cent being loosely defined political targets and the rest civilians (al-Shishani, 2005). Zarqawi's death and the shift in the group's branding changed the repertoire of violence, with a lower reliance on suicide missions (Hashim, 2019).

After the fall of Fallujah in 2004, Ramadi became the capital of the nascent Islamic Emirate, and ground zero for the jihadist insurgency. The jihadists tried in April 2006 to take over the few outposts under US control in the city but they failed, clearing the way for the US counter-attack. Months of stalemate street fighting prompted the jihadists to start targeting local Sunni leaders who were complaining about the never-ending violence and calling for a compromise with the Iraqi government. This targeting spree prompted tribal leaders to trigger the so-called Anbar Awakening (*Sahwa*, in Iraqi), by which they turned their backs on the insurgency and started to collaborate with the occupation forces. In a well-known public statement, several tribal leaders denounced ISI in direct terms:

> We all say to the terrorists, leave because you do not have a place in Al-Anbar Governorate after now. We have discovered from where you get financed and who orders you to kill our Iraqi cousins. Leave now or you will be killed in an ugly way. We are determined to fight you face to face. God is great. (Fishman, 2009: 3–4)

The Sahwa therefore followed a counterinsurgency playbook we have seen elsewhere (self-defence groups in Peru, Christian militias in Lebanon). By draining resources from ISI's key constituencies, the balance of power between the insurgency and the new ruling coalition became more asymmetric, anticipating ISI's loss of territorial control.

Short of support from its key constituency, and also feeling weakened by the US military surge, ISI lost ground quickly in Ramadi, and by August 2007 the group had become fully clandestine again in the region. The failure to hold ground is epitomized by one desperate episode in which ISI attempted to smuggle into Ramadi a brigand of around 100 recruits with the goal of reclaiming the city (Whiteside, Rice, and Raineri, 2021: 7–9). Recruits were summoned to the vicinity of Ramadi, where they received military uniforms and weaponry. Despite being very well trained, they were spotted by a US military patrol before departing for Ramadi and heavy fighting ensued. The brigand was decimated and it never made it into Ramadi, blowing up in this way ISI's last chance to recover the city during that stage of the conflict.

Back to Clandestinity

The initial period of guerrilla insurgency ended prematurely due to several factors (Fishman, 2009: 21). From an organizational standpoint, the combination of territorial overreach, with operations all over the country, and logistical problems, such as blundered communications and the lack of adaptation of foreign fighters, hindered the growth of the insurgency. But there is little doubt that the two driving forces of ISI's decline were a US military surge that tipped the scales against the insurgents, and its draining of popular support led by Sunni tribes who rebuffed the jihadists' aggressive approach. Facing an increasingly sectarian war in which they had most to lose, the Sunni-led sahwa militias, backed by US strikes, were able to push ISI back to clandestinity and contain it successfully by mid-2008 (Ingram, Whiteside, and Winter, 2020: 86). As recounted by Hashim (2019), an ISI commander in Balad (Saladin province) acknowledged in his diary that by the end of 2007

178   Underground Violence

his unit was down to 20 members, from a high of 600 only months before. ISI would not recover previous organizational levels until 2012, with the US troop pullout and the onset of the Syrian civil war.

The ISI leadership recognized this failure in its own magazine by calling for a return to clandestinity and terrorism (Hashim, 2019). This clandestine period is illustrated by the increase in bomb strikes in Baghdad, with almost 400 victims in five months (August–December 2009). By becoming fully clandestine, the group was able to tighten its networks and recruit more from the security forces.

In the so-called Fallujah memorandum, anonymously written before the end of 2009, the organization acknowledged that the '[Islamic] State collapsed after its first establishment', but there were grounds to rebuild it (Ingram, Whiteside, and Winter, 2020: 107–45). The document fixes on two ideas: that the USA will leave sooner or later, offering a second chance of victory for the jihadist insurgency; and that it is necessary to gain the cooperation of Sunni tribes as a way to avoid in-group fighting and strategic manipulation from outside actors. To that end, it called to concentrate rebel attacks on Iraqi security forces and their collaborators, instead of targeting the occupying, but scheduled to leave, American troops. Facing a declining Sahwa campaign, it also laid out a new pact with the Sunni tribal communities by which ISI would gain territorial presence in exchange for compliance and protection.

In general, the memorandum highlights the realization that, in the presence of occupation forces and without counting on Sunni tribes, the best the insurgency can do is to wear down the new regime and derail its consolidation. More generally, the memorandum makes a considered plea for a strategic update:

> Military strategy should change according to the circumstances. The strategy of global war across Iraq that was previously practiced is no longer effective. The more effective strategy is to focus on specific targets and to break bones. (Ingram, Whiteside, and Winter, 2020: 145)

To the surprise of many, the strategy of 'specific targeting and breaking bones' very quickly yielded fruit. To begin with, the assassination campaign against Sunni tribal leaders participating in the Sahwa was a critical instrument for ISI to regain a foothold within western Iraq (Whiteside, 2016). Besides, the inability of the Iraqi government to keep Sunni tribes under the ruling coalition turbo-charged the new spread of ISI units. Secondly, ISI systematically carried out a campaign of prison breakouts that brought back to the organization a number of very well-trained, combat-experienced, militants, whose expertise was vital in feeding the middle ranks of the expanding rebel group (Lister, 2015: 45; Whiteside, Rice, and Raineri, 2021).

Thirdly, the renewed capacity of ISI to craft alliances with other insurgent groups and fill its leadership positions would have produced slower returns without the ill-fated withdrawal of the US troops (Carter, 2017). The Bush administration had signed an agreement with its Iraqi counterpart by which the US troops would be out of the main cities by 30 June 2009 and completely withdrawn by 31 December 2011. President Barack Obama, a few months into office, extended the first date to August 2010, but maintained the commitment to a full withdrawal by the end of 2011. The number of US troops in Iraq dramatically fell from a high of 170,000 in the third quarter of 2007 to a low of 50,000 in the second quarter of 2010. This publicly announced withdrawal had two perverse consequences. First, as mentioned, it allowed ISI to concentrate its firepower on collaborators and the Iraqi security forces instead of engaging the departing US troops. And second, it allowed ISI to capitalize on the predictable new weaknesses of the Iraqi regime by launching a very effective propaganda-driven media campaign that sought to convince audiences that the Islamic State was not a paper entity, but one headed by a leader with symbolic reminiscences—regarding Abu Omar al-Baghdadi's lineage to a tribe with 'predestined origins'. The fact that the Iraqi government and its US allies had several times claimed the death of al-Baghdadi during his four-year reign at the helm of ISI also added to his legend.[11]

Finally, the last nail in the coffin was the start of the civil war in Syria, which was a game changer for ISI, as it gave the organization the territorial presence it had lost in Iraq and, with it, the power to attract and train new recruits. This would signal the end of ISI's short crossing from its clandestine desert.

Expanding the Battlefield

ISI very soon took advantage of the breakdown of authority in Syria to move operatives there and grasp territory. The Islamic State insurgency had had a friendly relationship with the Syrian government for much of the 2000s, as it is believed that most foreign fighters joining ISI travelled to Iraq through Syria, with the latter looking the other way. After the start of the Syrian uprising, both AQ and ISI leaders foresaw the advantages of exploiting the collapse

---

[11] He was finally killed with a rocket attack on 10 April 2010. He was succeeded by another member of the same lineage, Abu Bakr al-Baghdadi, who became internationally famous in 2014 as the self-proclaimed Caliph of the Islamic State.

of the Syrian regime to establish an Islamic state in the country, a goal that had not been voiced by the rebel commanders up till that point. ISI senior operatives were dispatched to Syria, where they recruited jihadist prisoners amnestied by President Bashar Assad to found Jabhat al-Nusra (JaN) (Lister, 2015: 18). Its first attack was a massive suicide bombing in Damascus against a military compound that claimed 40 lives. Although this group was believed to be the Syrian offspring of Al Qaeda, JaN denied having links with ISI or AQ during the first half of 2012. By early 2013, JaN had amassed enough manpower and warfare skills to take over military facilities and seize territory in northern Syria.

Trying to take advantage of this wave, Abu Bakr al-Baghdadi claimed in April 2013 that JaN was part of an enlarged Islamic State of Iraq and Syria (ISIS), but this was resisted by some JaN members who decided to chart their own course—and were endorsed by the Al Qaeda leadership. With the group split into two, a jihadist civil war broke out, complemented by an ISIS feud with other armed opposition groups. ISIS was pushed out of northern Syria, but it was able to consolidate a territorial stronghold around Raqqa in November 2013. Attracted by the real territorial presence of the Islamic State, more than 40,000 foreign fighters travelled to join the Syrian civil war (Byman, 2019: 206), with most siding with ISI instead of JaN, given the former's more global calling.

After securing a territorial presence in Syria that brought them more recruits and more resources from smuggling and taxes, it was all but inevitable that the group spearheaded a powerful land-grab campaign in Anbar province in neighbouring Iraq. The combination of a safe haven in Syria and the US-driven military weakening of the Iraqi regime increased dramatically the level and audacity of ISIS operations in Iraq (Whiteside, Rice, and Raineri, 2021). Although we lack detailed data on ISIS' target profile, its own annual report points to three interesting metrics: (a) the absolute number of ISIS attacks skyrocketed from 2012 to 2013 as the group started to seize and hold territory in Syria; (b) the most violent provinces in Iraq were those where the group was fighting for control, with much lower levels of violence in Baghdad and Kirkuk—the safest state areas; and (c) car bombs hit the latter two cities disproportionately, showing a different tactical approach to that of state areas (Bilger, 2014).

Another illustration of the increasing level of audacity was the Abu Ghraib prison break in July 2013. This highly coordinated special operation carried out by ISIS involved the release of around 500 old-guard jihadist prisoners, contributing significantly to filling the upper echelons of the group for the 2014 uprising (Whiteside, Rice, and Raineri, 2021). More generally, ISIS masterminded a strategic combination of suicide attacks, insurgent tactics, and light-infantry, quasi-conventional assaults that overcame enemy lines defended by poorly trained soldiers (Lister, 2015: 388). In the usual way, ISIS suicide attacks aimed to wear out security forces' outposts on the outskirts of Sunni cities, to force them to retreat to safe barracks and leave ISIS cells as de facto rulers of the abandoned areas, paving the way for the final light-infantry assault. After arrival, foreign fighters were routinely trained in this combination of tactics. The first lessons were always about urban warfare, with themes such as planting mass-casualty bombs. For the group, these were critical skills, as militants should know how to handle attacks if the fate of its territorial control waned (Lister, 2015: 28).

This strategy was successfully exploited during the assault of Mosul in June 2014. Despite having a 15:1 disadvantage in troops, ISIS deployed a militarily savvy strategy that combined sleeper-cell bombings within the city with suicide attacks against city border outposts and concentrated assaults on essential facilities. Counting on Ba'thist security officers, with real military experience (Lister, 2015: 30), ISIS troops took advantage of an overstretched Iraqi military whose rank and file deserted en masse when faced with ISIS' reputation of cruel behaviour against its prisoners.

The capture of Mosul was the zenith of ISIS power. Operations in both countries had converged very quickly under the same leadership and strategy. At its peak, ISIS enjoyed territorial control over a large area of Syria and Iraq, comprising over 100,000 square kilometres and more than 11 million people (Jones et al., 2017: xi). Territorial control secured different means of tax extraction (e.g. oil, smuggling, fines, and dues), so that coercion was matched with a cunning use of the budget to buy loyalty and compliance (Revkin and Ahram, 2020). A carrot and stick policy was implemented, where efforts to better administer the provision of public services and price control went hand in hand with a very restrictive interpretation of Sharia law (and the persecution of non-Sunni populations like the Yazidi). As a corollary, ISIS troops surged and it became a conventional army of more than 31,000 soldiers, with thousands of foreign fighters.

An indisputable part of the rise of ISIS was its outstanding use of the media and new digital technologies (Farwell, 2014; Bloom, Tiflati, and Horgan, 2019). Abu Bakr al-Baghdadi, ISIS leader since 2010, was a master of secrecy and the strategic use of media appearances until his death in 2019. Few people will forget the image of al-Baghdadi proclaiming himself the Caliph of the Islamic State from the pulpit of the Great Mosque of al-Nuri in Mosul, and calling all Muslims to migrate to the new 'state' to fight for its survival and expansion (Ingram, Whiteside, and Winter, 2020: 178). A few months later, ISIS military leader al-Adnani elegantly praised the achievements of his troops:

> Oh, soldiers of the Islamic State, what a great thing you have achieved through Allah! [...] Who are you? Who are you, Oh soldiers of the Islamic State? From where have you come? What is your secret? Why is it that the hearts of the East and West are dislocated by their fear of you? Where are your warplanes? Where are your battleships? Why is it that the world has united against you? (Ingram, Whiteside, and Winter, 2020: 180)

A few days before the release of al-Adnani's audio, President Obama declared that 'We will degrade and ultimately destroy [the Islamic State]'. By the end of September 2014, the US air campaign against ISIS positions was in full motion.

The Downfall

Despite the widespread media splash about the Islamic State threat, its momentum passed away quickly. Perhaps the best illustration of the limits of the Islamic State is its siege of Kobani. Kobani is a Turkish-border town populated by the Kurdish minority, and ISIS became obsessed with taking it over, at the expense of losing hundreds of troops and proving the fallibility of its strategy. The siege employed suicide bombings, frontline battles, shelling, ambushes, and street-to-street fighting. Although ISIS came to control 50 per cent of the city after a month of siege, Kurdish militias in coordination with US drones ultimately repelled the invasion. This was a turning point for the USA too, as it found a credible partner on the ground that would allow it to fight against ISIS without redeploying thousands of troops again. For former US Secretary of Defense Ash Carter (2013–16), ISIS was no match for the US army, so it would have been relatively easy for US troops to crush the insurgency and regain territorial control. But the problem was what to do later, once in control. As Carter put it: 'Militarily, such a strategy would also cede our unique advantages in technology, firepower, and logistics to play on ISIS' turf—the streets of Iraqi and Syrian cities. Such an approach could well backfire and strengthen our enemy' (Carter, 2017). It took him over six months to figure out the right strategy, which involved partnering with the Kurds both in Syria and Iraq to supply them with weapons, logistics, and assistance, in exchange for their help on the ground.

Events took a turn for the worse when Turkey and Russia also became involved in the conflict. Turkey intervened in July 2015 to secure a buffer zone on its southern border and make sure that the PKK, a Turkish Kurdish armed group which seeks independence for Turkish Kurdistan, did not get help from its Syrian co-ethnics. Russia began its military participation in October 2015, with the goal of consolidating the regime and protecting its military assets in the country. Although this was for different reasons, both interventions strengthened the capabilities of ISIS' rivals, making the survival of the Islamic State more difficult.

ISIS started to lose ground in 2016. The Iraqi army retook Fallujah in June, and Kurdish forces made advances on both sides of the border. On 29 June 2017, Mosul was completely recaptured and the Iraqi government proclaimed the end of the Caliphate on Iraqi soil. On October 20 of the same year, Raqqa, the so-called capital of the Islamic State, also fell to Syrian Kurdish militias.

By mid-2017, the ISIS leadership had realized that there was no way they could successfully use conventional military means to contain their rivals' territorial inroads, if they had US air force backing. This is why, to the surprise of many commentators, they readily retreated from some of their liberated areas without much resistance (Hassan, 2018: 11). The increasing asymmetry in the balance of power between ISIS and the Iraqi and Syrian governments forced ISIS to go underground and resort once more to indirect tactics. ISIS may not be fully defeated as long as there are jihadists willing to fight; but the spread of any counterinsurgency will have to be recalibrated.

Dynamics

In this final section we explore some data that capture ISIS' shifts in warfare techniques. More specifically, we focus on temporal and geographic variation on attacks (Figure 5.2), tactics (Figure 5.3), and the use of ISIS' international attacks (Figure 5.4).

Figure 5.2 includes the number of monthly insurgent attacks in Iraq, from 2004 to 2017, as measured by the Iraqi Body Count project. The graph describes temporal as well as geographical variation, by distinguishing between the total number of insurgent attacks and those carried out in the Sunni provinces (al Anbar, Diyala, Nineveh, and Saladin) and Baghdad.

It represents strikingly well the dynamics of violence of the Iraqi war. The initial 'mission accomplished' call from the occupying forces was followed by a substantial reduction in the number of US troops, which clearly

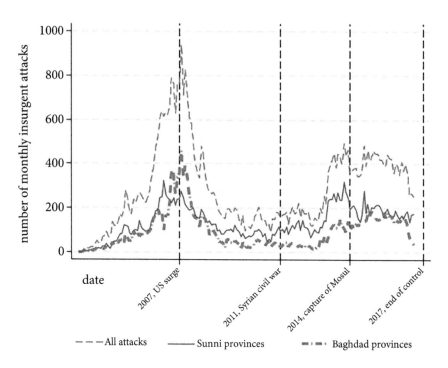

Figure 5.2 Number of monthly insurgent attacks in Iraq, 2004–17
Source: Iraqi Body Count Project.

threw a lifeline to the insurgency, as is visible from mid-2006. The insurgent spike was greatest in the Sunni triangle, where famous battlegrounds such as Ramadi and Fallujah lie. The US military surge of 2007 decimated insurgent ranks, and produced two interesting outcomes. First, most violence started to be heavily concentrated in the Sunni strongholds—with a lower role for Baghdad and the remaining Shia provinces. And second, the return to clandestinity took a heavy toll on the level of sustained violence the insurgents could manage.

In July 2011 the civil war broke out in neighbouring Syria, and the data also note a slow but steady spillover effect of jihadist violence into Iraq, visible in the run-up to the capture of Mosul and the declaration of the Caliphate. Although the series ends in 2017, it also hints at ISIS' decreasing levels of violence after most of its strongholds had been recaptured in Iraq by the end of 2017.

Instead of focusing on the absolute level of violent events, Figure 5.3 seeks to show how much the rebels rely on bombings compared to other tactics. Thus, it includes the percentage of monthly insurgent attacks with explosive devices since 2004, and again distinguishes between the Sunni provinces and

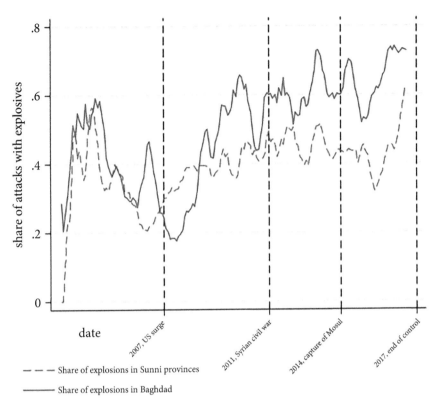

Figure 5.3 Share of monthly insurgent attacks with explosives in Iraq, 2004–17 (three-month moving averages)
Source: Iraqi Body Count Project.

Baghdad. The periods of clandestinity are nicely captured by percentages above the 40 per cent threshold—both during the 2004–6 initial occupation period, and in the aftermath of the US military surge and the Sunni Awakening (2007–11). The trend lines also illustrate the accelerated increase in the use of IEDs by mid-2017—a testament to the shrinking capacity of ISIS to hold territory, but also to its widespread dependence on explosive devices (Anfinson and Al-Dayel 2023). In line with our expectations, bombing devices are more common in Baghdad, a sprawling city where ISIS could not openly operate during the Caliphate, despite hosting a sizeable minority of Sunnis.

Both figures capture the final downfall of ISIS, with lower levels of violence and a higher reliance on bombings; they are both typical features of terrorist groups. An interesting discussion is the relationship between domestic attacks versus attacks abroad carried out by the Islamic State. ISIS leaders

186 Underground Violence

had seemingly contradictory preferences with regards to international terrorism. Once the Caliphate was proclaimed, ISIS leaders called Muslims all over the world to travel to Syria and Iraq to fight for consolidation of the State. But a few months later, with the start of anti-ISIS foreign intervention in the conflict, the leaders swung to promote an alternative route of striking those countries on their own soil. Al-Adnani's address on 21 May 2016 shows the organization's increasing desperation to attract more recruits as it calls for strikes in the West:

> If the tawaghit [idolatrous governments] have shut the door of hijrah [migration to the Caliphate] in your faces, then open the door of jihad in theirs. Make your deed a source of their regret. Truly, the smallest act you do in their lands is more beloved to us than the biggest act done here; it is more effective for us and more harmful to them [...] It has reached us that some of you do not act due to their incapacity to reach military targets, or their finding fault with targeting those who are called 'civilians', so they leave harming them, doubting the permissibility thereof. Know that inside the lands of the belligerent crusaders, there is no sanctity of blood and no existence of those called 'innocents'. Know that your targeting those who are called 'civilians' is more beloved to us and more effective, as it is more harmful, painful, and a greater deterrent to them. (Ingram, Whiteside, and Winter, 2020: 256)

To shed more light on this discussion, we have collected all attacks claimed by ISIS and its predecessors (AQI, ISI) as coded by GTD, from 2005 to 2020 (the last year with data publicly accessible). We break down the location of the attack into four categories: ISIS core (Iraq and Syria), ISIS regional (Middle East and North Africa), ISIS in the West, and ISIS abroad (without the West). Figure 5.4 reports the distributions. Notice that the left-hand Y axis corresponds to ISIS attacks in Iraq and Syria, whereas the right-hand Y axis represents attacks in the other three locations. As before, we include three lines identifying key moments in ISIS history: the onset of the Syrian civil war, the ISIS capture of Mosul, and the end of most ISIS control in 2017.

The results are noteworthy. Although with different metrics of intensity, attacks in the core area and in the Middle East and North Africa follow similar patterns of violence. Attacks in the West peak a little bit after the onset of the Caliphate and go quickly down without any further rise. Finally, attacks in other regions of the world (this includes most of Asia, and Russia) reach their highest mark when ISIS started to collapse, but also show a downtrend. Therefore, ISIS follows a different pattern than the PLO, because violence

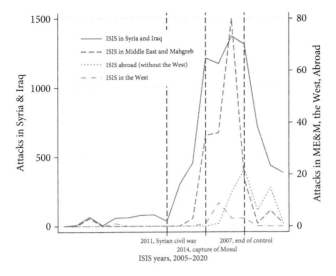

Figure 5.4 ISIS attacks at home and abroad, 2005–20
Source: Global Terrorism Database.

abroad gained more traction when ISIS had more territorial control. If we instead were going to use a broader definition of ISIS violence, encompassing all ISIS' regional branches, the trends remain similar.

5.3. Conclusions

Variations in the balance of power among contenders in a domestic conflict are usually closely mirrored by strategic shifts in the repertoire of violence of the actors involved. In this chapter, we have followed the ups and downs of the Palestinian insurgency and the most recent Islamic State in Syria and Iraq. Regardless of the different time frames and ideologies, rebel leaders in both conflicts likewise aimed at seizing and ruling territory, but sometimes they were forced to settle for an underground armed strategy and use indirect tactics to put pressure on their rival states and mobilize supporters. Both Arafat as well as al-Zarqawi acknowledged they were fighting against much stronger rivals, but they did not hesitate to take advantage of the opportunities they had to capture territory and upscale their insurgencies.

In addition to ideological differences, the two cases also show variation on other factors such as rebel competition, international terrorism, and the propensity to negotiate an end to the conflict. ISIS faced little competition in Iraq and even if there were thousands of rebel groups in Syria, it ran a monopoly of violence in Eastern Syria after defeating Al Nusra. Against this, heavy competition in the Palestinian rebel camp may have increased the number of attacks and encouraged the recourse to outbidding dynamics of terror (Bloom, 2005; Gupta and Mundra, 2005).

The role of international terrorism clearly requires more research. Whereas Palestinian insurgents largely resorted to attacks abroad when their fortunes in their homeland waned (and the other way around), ISIS was non-committal on this, issuing almost simultaneously a global call to attack Western targets everywhere and a call to migrate to its State. The data seem to support the hypothesis of a reinforcement between domestic and international violence for ISIS. Additionally, unlike Fatah's vertical decision-making procedures, ISIS is more comfortable with a decentralized, network-like cadre of perpetrators, sometimes teaming up with local groups to create its own outfits (like ISIS-Kurasan in Afghanistan), or by simply encouraging lone-actor militants to carry out attacks. The strategic innovations developed by Al Qaeda, plus the sensational global appeal that ISIS gathered during the short years of the Caliphate, can help us understand this varying attitude towards attacks on foreign soil.

Finally, it is worth mentioning that the Palestinian insurgency during the 1980s traded terrorism for a seat at the negotiation table. Thus, a weaker position was not directly translated into more attacks abroad. However, some highly ideological groups such as ISIS burn all their bridges to squeeze their bargaining range, which makes them more dependent on balance-of-power shifts. This may explain why the life cycle of ISIS has been relatively short, compared to other insurgencies capable of capturing and ruling territory.

Concluding Remarks

Terrorism: Back and Forth

The field of terrorism studies is peculiar. Since the scale of terrorist violence is limited compared with war, insurgency, or state repression, attacks and perpetrators can be analysed with an unparalleled degree of precision. Experts on terrorism have privileged access to the violent activity and the internal structure of underground groups compared with those who study insurgencies. Most terrorist attacks are recorded and can be studied in great detail; likewise, security forces usually obtain abundant information about the internal decision-making of terrorist groups and the individuals who form the leadership—hence the proliferation of fascinating monographs and small-n comparisons of these groups. This is not feasible in the case of insurgencies as they have many thousands of recruits and conduct thousands of attacks of all types. It is no surprise, therefore, that many experts on terrorism collaborate with governments, administrations, and think-tanks, playing a diffuse role midway between academia and the security sector.

Intimate knowledge about terrorist groups and their tactics is, however, a double-edged sword. The revolving doors of university campuses, government buildings, and consultancy firms put experts on terrorism in a distant corner within the wider community of experts on conflict and violence. The way in which they have approached the topic has been unabashedly descriptive and empiricist, lacking analytical and methodological ambition. For a long time, the main exception was those who applied game theory models to the interactions between terrorists and states. However, major questions about the determinants of terrorist groups, or the enormous variation in tactics and targets that is found among armed actors, remained unanswered. Unlike the study of civil war, empirical research on terrorism fell behind during the 1990s.

This status quo radically changed in the early 2000s. On the one hand, the attacks of 9/11 brought a lot of attention to the field; on the other, datasets such as GTD were made available. A wave of quantitative work followed,

Underground Violence. Luis De la Calle and Ignacio Sánchez-Cuenca, Oxford University Press.
© Luis De la Calle and Ignacio Sánchez-Cuenca (2024). DOI: 10.1093/oso/9780198904816.003.0007

opening the field to large-n comparisons and putting an end to what might be termed as the methodological exceptionalism of terrorism studies. The external validity of these quantitative contributions was indeed higher, but their internal validity was questionable due to the poor quality of the data, which often conflated very different types of violence.

In any case, this quantitative revolution has not addressed the ultimate problem, which goes deeper than the methodology employed (either small-n or large-n designs): the whole field has been marred by the absence of a satisfactory conceptualization. How can meaningful hypotheses be formulated if a minimum consensus on the nature of terrorist violence is missing? We are far from reaching an agreement on which groups (actor-sense) and tactics (action-sense) can be labelled terrorist.

Terrorism is a protean term and cannot be reduced to a dictionary-like definition. We talk about terrorism in irreducible ways. We have referred repeatedly to the actor- and action-sense of terrorism, but also to the various levels of aggregation that are involved when we discuss terrorism, from single attacks, to groups, to conflicts.

As this book seeks to make clear, we do not think that a conceptual morass is a necessary outcome. Our ambition has been to persuade the reader that beneath much of the academic debate, there is an underlying logic in the way in which we speak about terrorism. This logic stems from the feature that makes terrorist violence so unique: its underground condition. What distinguishes terrorism from other types of violence is that it does not require either occupation of space or long-lasting operations: it can be conceived as covert, ephemeral violence. We are not alone in holding this principle: many others have argued in this direction in the past. However, previous authors have not attempted to elaborate systematically on the implications of understanding terrorism as underground political violence.

In sum, we contend that our conceptual roadmap lays out a comprehensive view of terrorism. It is not only that there is an internal consistency, but, more importantly, our conceptualization possesses considerable unifying power. The concept of terrorism we propose accounts for several characteristics associated with the phenomenon. Thus, underground violence can be exported anywhere (hence the existence of international terrorism); it can be used by the state for covert operations as a form of underground repression (hence state terrorism); and it can even be carried out by a single individual (hence lone-actor terrorism). Our conceptualization of terrorism can account for these peculiarities of the phenomenon, which are absent in other types of violence.

On the other hand, we can easily derive meaningful hypotheses about the use of terrorism. As we have argued, the adoption of underground tactics is dictated in most cases by an asymmetry between armed groups and states. The absence of territorial control by an armed actor fighting the state is a strong indicator of a highly asymmetrical contest. We have leveraged this general proposition to formulate hypotheses in the actor- and action-sense. For instance, we have argued that, in the actor-sense, terrorism is more likely in countries that are neither too poor (the rebels become an insurgency) nor too rich (the state is able to either crush or buy off internal challengers). Underground violence is more likely in middle-income countries.

When it comes to the testing of propositions like this one, the empirical difficulties are considerable. The most pressing issue is perhaps how to collect data that is consistent with our conceptualization of terrorism. Ideally, we would like to have data collected and coded from scratch according to relevant theoretical categories, but this requires huge resources. It is more realistic to expect researchers to come up with more refined or sophisticated ideas on how to filter existing datasets, so that quantitative analyses can be interpreted meaningfully. Theory should be used to settle measurement issues.

We are sceptical about findings that have been obtained by uncritical use of the existing datasets on terrorism. These datasets contain amazingly rich information, but the coding rules are not based on a theory of violence. A related problem emerges when researchers impose certain conditions on the dataset that do not really capture terrorism. Thus, in the literature about the use of terrorism in civil wars, the dominant approach assumes that killing civilians is terrorism, whereas killing security forces is insurgent violence (see the Appendix in Chapter 3). We think that inquiring about the determinants of civilian victimization in civil wars is a fascinating research question, but it does not capture terrorism as such. As shown in Chapter 1, the view that terrorism consists of violence aimed at civilians is questionable on several grounds (terrorist groups also kill security forces, and non-terrorist groups kill civilians).

Problems are compounded when we seek to trace the evolution of violence within an armed group. Although, for large-n research, a classification of groups into clandestine and territorial is feasible, when it comes to a more detailed analysis, this typology is just too rough. There are complex cases in which an armed group goes through several stages regarding territorial control and tactical choice. The Palestinian-Israeli conflict and the rise and fall of ISIS (see Chapter 5) are excellent illustrations of the complications that emerge in the dynamic analysis of violence.

Because of its intrinsic complexity, terrorism cannot be analysed in the same way as civil wars, ethnic conflicts, or genocides. Terrorism cannot be reified as a conflict, as a tactic, or as a group; it can be any of these. What datasets on terrorism offer is a list of incidents or groups that are deemed terrorist. Building on these raw data, the researcher must aggregate the information depending on research interests and theoretical expectations. Terrorist incidents can be categorized by group, tactic, target, campaign, location, and so on; but no scholarly consensus yet exists on how this should be done. We think that the most sensible decision is to build categories and empirical indicators out of the underground nature of the violence. In the actor-sense, we have suggested that armed groups should be classified according to their degree of territorial control. In the action-sense, we cannot but rely on proxies. Thus, we have used bombings (that are typically, but not exclusively, employed by underground groups) as an indicator of terrorist activity. More indirect approximations can be conceived: for instance, we have also focused in on the location of the attack, by assuming that rebel actions taking place in the most populated cities are more likely to be underground.

Having made this basic point about the methodological problems that empirical researchers on terrorism face, we close the book with proposals for a future research agenda. These are all understudied or ill-studied issues, and deserve, we believe, further scrutiny.

Firstly, territorial control plays a huge part in our conceptualization, and we have tried to provide some operational rules in Chapter 2 to identify it on a systematic basis. However, we do not know much about the different shades of rebel control. Control is a very elusive concept and, in a changing environment such as a civil war, it defies any static approach. Rebels seek to displace authorities from the districts where they operate, but they show different patterns of settlement, and different ways to make inroads. Some rebel groups move rapidly towards the capital city without much consideration for the liberated areas that are left behind, whereas others put a premium on the management of space at the expense of speed and surprise. The growing literature on rebel governance is well-positioned to help launch this research agenda (Arjona, Kasfir, and Mampilly, 2015).

Secondly, the study of clandestinity is intriguingly underdeveloped. Despite the wealth of first-hand data on long-lived terrorist groups such as ETA, the PIRA, the Weathermen, or the Red Brigades, there have been few efforts to understand the effect of acting underground on internal organization, funding methods, and the links between clandestine militants and communities of support (an exception is Della Porta, 2013). Just as there are shades of territorial control, there are also shades of secrecy, but we lack a clear view on how they impact on the dynamics of terrorist violence.

Thirdly, we need to better understand how armed groups make the transition from being underground to being open; that is, how the transformation from a terrorist group into a guerrilla organization takes place. How do leaders come to realize that this leap forward is suddenly within their reach? What means do they think are necessary to achieve control? How does an organization transform itself to adapt to an above-the-ground existence? When do they combine an under- and above-the-ground structure? And, in a similar vein, there is interesting variation to be explained regarding the moment in which territorial control is gained. Thus, some armed groups gain territorial control almost from the very beginning (the Shining Path is a good case in point), while others spend long periods in the underground until they think they are ready to seize territorial control (an example is the Farabundo Martí National Liberation Front in El Salvador).

Fourthly, there is still much work to do to understand tactical choice. On the one hand, questions can be formulated about the employment of terrorist tactics among insurgencies with territorial control: why is it that some groups, such as the FARC in Colombia, employed low levels of terrorism compared with the Shining Path in Peru? Relatedly, why is it that some guerrillas deploy resources on international terrorist attacks, such as ISIS, whereas others avoid them, such as the Taliban? On the other hand, we also observe interesting variation in the choice of tactics among underground groups: some opt for bombs or selective shootings, while others mix these tactics. How to account for this tactical variation is a challenge for those who study political violence.

Fifthly, the study of targeting is surprisingly weak. This is curious, as part of the literature has rallied behind the idea that terrorism is defined by the nature of the target. Do the logics of attrition and mobilization call for attacks against different targets? Under what conditions do the constraints imposed by clandestinity limit the range of plausible target choices? Is the indiscriminate versus selective violence typology broadly used in civil war studies easily translatable into the field of terrorism? Clandestine groups produce violence of lower lethality and higher visibility, so empirical tests of targeting should be more widespread.

Sixthly, the issue of underground groups' recruitment has barely been explored. In his analysis of guerrillas, Weinstein (2007) distinguished between the economic and the social endowments of armed groups, arguing that groups that rely on economic incentives to attract recruits tend to engage in indiscriminate violence, whereas those that gain recruits through social incentives (e.g., ideology or social norms) tend to commit more selective attacks. Doubts can be raised about this theory when applied to jihadist movements. In the case of ISIS, for instance, the group committed many indiscriminate attacks but also operated on social incentives and coercion, shaping what Revkin and Ahram (2020) call an authoritarian social contract. Ideology was also crucial, as shown by the capacity of ISIS to attract more than 40,000 foreign fighters from more than 110 countries (Byman, 2019: 171). Some even participated in suicide missions, which implies a full, unconditional sacrifice for the cause that can only be explained in terms of ideological commitment and peer pressure. Although much more research is needed on this point, it seems reasonable to suppose that underground groups will use social incentives, rather than economic, to recruit new members. The consequences of this type of recruitment regarding willingness to negotiate with the state, type of violence, and other related issues remain to a large extent unexplored.

Seventhly, the terrorist groups that we have studied are those that adapted to their milieu and were able to survive for some years. However, there are many more that are extinguished quickly and leave little trace. This generates a significant selection problem. In a sense, most of the empirical illustrations we have used in this book correspond to rebel groups that were able to cope with the structural conditions they were facing and therefore chose the right armed strategy to survive. The rapidly extinguished groups, however, are so oblivious to strategic updating that they are easily wiped out or become irrelevant. The study of these short-lived experiences may be extremely useful for identifying the reasons why some groups survive and are able to challenge the state. An interesting case in point is that of the Mexican armed groups of the 1970s (Glockner, 2018), which were highly fragmented and an easy prey for the state. Their inability to coalesce and form a united front was largely a consequence of opposing views about the role of urban/rural struggle. The lack of a clear and common approach to armed struggle led to strategic mistakes. Consequently, these groups were not able to pose a serious threat to the Mexican state.

Lastly, we have argued that state terrorism exists, but in a limited sense: it is embodied in underground repression. It would be interesting to know under what conditions state terrorism is more likely vis-à-vis open repression. In some cases, states have considered that extra-legal means are not necessary to combat terrorism. But, on other occasions, states have organized or sponsored underground operations against terrorists (such as

Spain, which organized underground commandos to attack ETA members). The conditions that trigger state terrorism have to be investigated, as very little is known about this topic.

This is a long list of themes for future study. We would consider this book a success if others, inspired by our approach to terrorism, move forward with this research agenda.

References

Abrahms, Max. 2006. 'Why Terrorism Does Not Work'. *International Security*, 31(2): 42–78.

Abrahms, Max. 2012. 'The Political Effectiveness of Terrorism Revisited'. *Comparative Political Studies*, 45(3): 366–93.

Aguilera, Mario. 2013. 'Las FARC: Auge y quiebra del modelo de guerra'. *Análisis Político*, 77: 85–111.

Al-Dayel, Nadia, Andrew Mumford, and Kevin Bales. 2022. 'Not Yet Dead: The Establishment and Regulation of Slavery by the Islamic State'. *Studies in Conflict & Terrorism*, 45(11): 929–52.

Alperovitz, Gar. 1995. *The Decision to Use the Atomic Bomb and the Architecture of an American Myth*. New York: Alfred A. Knopf.

Al-Shishani, Murad B. 2005. 'Al-Zarqawi's Rise to Power: Analyzing Tactics and Targets'. *Terrorism Monitor*, 3(22). https://jamestown.org/program/al-zarqawis-rise-to-power-analyzing-tactics-and-targets/.

Amigo, Ángel. 1978. *Pertur: ETA 1971–76*. San Sebastián: Hórdago.

Anderton, Charles H., and Jurgen Brauer. 2021. 'Mass Atrocities and their Prevention'. *Journal of Economic Literature*, 59(4): 1240–92.

Anfinson, Aaron, and Nadia Al-Dayel. 2023. 'Landmines and Improvised Explosive Devices: The Lingering Terror of the Islamic State'. *Studies in Conflict & Terrorism*, 46(2): 162–82.

Anguita, Eduardo, and Martin Caparrós. 1998. *La voluntad. Una historia de la militancia revolucionaria en Argentina, 1973–1976*. Buenos Aires: Planeta.

Arjona, Ana. 2016. *Rebelocracy: Social Order in the Colombian Civil War*. Cambridge: Cambridge University Press.

Arjona, Ana, Nelson Kasfir, and Zachariah Mampilly (eds.). 2015. *Rebel Governance in Civil War*. Cambridge: Cambridge University Press.

Arreguín-Toft, Ivan. 2005. *How the Weak Win Wars: A Theory of Asymmetric Conflict*. Oxford: Oxford University Press.

Asal, Victor, H. Brinton Milward, and Eric W. Schoon. 2015. 'When Terrorists Go Bad: Analyzing Terrorist Organizations' Involvement in Drug Smuggling'. *International Studies Quarterly*, 59(1): 112–23.

Asal, Victor, Brian Phillips, and Karl Rethemeyer. 2022. *Insurgent Terrorism: Intergroup Relationships and the Killing of Civilians*. Oxford: Oxford University Press.

Asal, Victor, and R. Karl Rethemeyer. 2008. 'The Nature of the Beast: Organizational Structures and the Lethality of of Terrorist Attacks'. *Journal of Politics*, 70(2): 437–49.

Aust, Stefan. 2008. *Baader-Meinhof: The Inside Story of the R.A.F.* Oxford: Oxford University Press.

Aviad, Guy. 2009. 'Hamas' Military Wing in the Gaza Strip: Development, Patterns of Activity, and Forecast'. *Military and Strategic Affairs*, 1(1): 3–15.

Ayers, Bill. 2003. *Fugitive Days: A Memoir*. New York: Penguin.

Baconi, Tareq. 2018. *Hamas Contained: The Rise and Pacification of Palestinian Resistance*. Stanford, CA: Stanford University Press.

Bakunin, Mijhail. 1971. *Bakunin on Anarchy: Selected Works*, edited by Sam Goldoff. New York: Vintage Books.

Balcells, Laia. 2017. *Rivalry and Revenge: The Politics of Violence during Civil War*. Cambridge: Cambridge University Press.

Balcells, Laia, and Jessica Stanton. 2021. 'Violence against Civilians during Armed Conflict: Moving beyond the Macro- and Micro-level Divide'. *Annual Review of Political Science*, 24: 45–69.

Baracskay, Daniel. 2011. *The Palestine Liberation Organization: Terrorism and Prospects for Peace in the Holy Land*. Santa Barbara, CA: Praeger.

Barrell, Howard. 1992. 'The Turn to the Masses: The African National Congress' Strategic Review of 1978–79'. *Journal of Southern African Studies*, 18(1): 64–92.

Bar-Zohar, Michael, and Nissim Mishal. 2015. *Mossad: The Great Operations of Israel's Secret Service*. London: Biteback.

Baumann, Michael. 1977. *Terror or Love? Bommi Baumann's Own Story of his Life as a West German Urban Guerrilla*. New York: Grove Press.

Beccaro, Andrea. 2018. 'Modern Irregular Warfare: The ISIS Case Study'. *Small Wars & Insurgencies*, 29(2): 207–28.

Be'er, Yozhar, and Saleh 'Abdel-Jawad. 1994. *Collaborators in the Occupied Territories: Human Rights Abuses and Violations*. Jerusalem: B'Tselem. https://www.btselem.org/sites/default/files/publications/199401_collaboration_suspects_eng.pdf.

Begin, Menachem. 1972. *The Revolt*. 5th ed. Trans. by Samuel Katz. Jerusalem: Steimatzky's Agency Limited.

Beitler, Ruth Margolies. 2004. *The Path to Mass Rebellion: An Analysis of Two Intifadas*. Lanham, MD: Lexington Books.

Berger, Dan. 2006. *Outlaws of America: The Weather Underground and Politics of Solidarity*. Oakland, CA: AK Press.

Bergesen, Albert J., and Omar Lizardo. 2004. 'International Terrorism and the World-System'. *Sociological Theory*, 22(1): 38–52.

Bergman, Ronen. 2008. *The Secret War with Iran*. Oxford: Oneworld Publications.

Bergman, Ronen. 2018. *Rise and Kill First: The Secret History of Israel's Targeted Assassinations*, trans. by Ronnie Hope. London: John Murray.

Berkebile, Richard. 2017. 'What Is Domestic Terrorism? A Method for Classifying Events from the Global Terrorism Database'. *Terrorism and Political Violence*, 29(1): 1–26.

Bermúdez, Alejandro. 1995. 'Los "arrepentidos", una desbandada en Sendero'. Aceprensa, 1 February 1995.

Besley, Timothy, and Torsten Persson. 2011. *Pillars of Prosperity: The Political Economics of Development Clusters*. Princeton: Princeton University Press.

Biddle, Stephen. 2021. *Nonstate Warfare: The Military Methods of Guerrillas, Warlords, and Militias*. Princeton: Princeton University Press.

Bidegain, Eneko. 2007. *Iparretarrak. Historia de una organización política armada*. Tafalla: Txalaparta.

Bilger, Alex. 2014. *Backgrounder: ISIS Annual Reports Reveal a Metrics-driven Military Command*. Institute for the Study of War.

Bjørgo, Tore. 2005. 'Introduction'. In Tore Bjørgo (ed.), *Root Causes of Terrorism*, 2–15. London: Routledge.

Blakeley, Ruth. 2009. 'State Terrorism in the Social Sciences: Theories, Methods and Concepts'. In Richard Jackson, Eamon Murphy, and Scott Poynting (eds.), *Contemporary State Terrorism: Theory and Practice*, 12–27. Abingdon: Routledge.

Blixen, Samuel. 2005. *Sendic. Las vidas de un Tupamaro*. Barcelona: Virus.

Bloom, Mia. 2005. *Dying to Kill: The Allure of Suicide Terror*. New York: Columbia University Press.

Bloom, Mia, Hicham Tiflati, and John Horgan. 2019. 'Navigating ISIS's Preferred Platform: Telegram'. *Terrorism and Political Violence*, 31(6): 1242–54.

198 References

Boix, Carles, Michael Miller, and Sebastian Rosato. 2013. 'A Complete Data Set of Political Regimes, 1800–2007'. *Comparative Political Studies*, 46(12): 1523–54.

Boot, Max. 2013. *Invisible Armies: An Epic History of Guerrilla Warfare from Ancient Times to the Present*. New York: Liveright.

Boyle, Emma L. 2017. 'Was Idi Amin's Government a Terrorist Regime?', *Terrorism and Political Violence*, 29(4): 593–609.

Braithwaite, Alex. 2013. 'The Logic of Public Fear in Terrorism and Counter-Terrorism'. *Journal of Police and Criminal Psychology*, 28(2): 95–101.

Brock, Gary. 2013. *Zarqawi's sfumato: Operational art in irregular warfare*. Research monograph prepared for the United States Army Command and General Staff College, Fort Leavenworth.

Brum, Pablo. 2016. *Patria para nadie. La historia no contada de los Tupamaros de Uruguay*. Barcelona: Península.

Bueno de Mesquita, Ethan. 2005. 'The Quality of Terror'. *American Journal of Political Science*, 49(3): 515–30.

Burleigh, Michael. 2008. *Blood & Rage: A Cultural History of Terrorism*. London: Harper.

Burrough, Bryan. 2015. *Days of Rage: America's Radical Underground, the FBI, and the Forgotten Age of Revolutionary Violence*. New York: Penguin.

Burstein, Alon. 2018. 'Armies of God, Armies of Men: A Global Comparison of Secular and Religious Terror Organizations'. *Terrorism and Political Violence*, 30(1): 1–21.

Burt, Jo-Marie. 1998. 'Shining Path and the "Decisive Battle" in Lima's Barriadas: The Case of Villa El Salvador'. In Steve J. Stern (ed.), *Shining and Other Paths: War and Society in Peru, 1980–1995*, 267–306. Durham: Duke University Press.

Byman, Daniel. 2016. 'Understanding the Islamic State: A Review Essay'. *International Security*, 40(4): 127–65.

Byman, Daniel. 2019. *Road Warriors: Foreign Fighters in the Armies of Jihad*. Princeton: Princeton University Press.

Cabrera, Germán. 2015. *Un ex Tupamaro en el trópico. Memorias*. Montevideo: Penguin Random House.

Canetti-Nisim, Daphna, Gustavo Mesch, and Ami Pedahzur. 2006. 'Victimization from Terrorist Attacks: Randomness or Routine Activities?', *Terrorism & Political Violence*, 18(4): 485–501.

Carr, Caleb. 2002. *The Lessons of Terror: A History of Warfare against Civilians*. New York: Random House.

Carretero, José L. 2020. *Abraham Guillén. Guerrilla y auto-gestión*. Madrid: Confederación Sindical Obrera.

Carter, Ash. 2017. *A Lasting Defeat: The Campaign to Destroy ISIS*. Cambridge, MA: Belfer Center for Science and International Affairs, Harvard Kennedy School.

Casanova, Iker, and Paul Asensio. 1999. *Argala*. Tafalla: Txalaparta.

Castan Pinos, Jaume, and Steven M. Radil. 2020. 'The Territorial Contours of Terrorism: A Conceptual Model of Territory for Non-State Violence'. *Terrorism and Political Violence*, 32(5): 1027–46.

Chailand, Gerad. 1972. *The Palestinian Resistance*. Trans. by Michael Perl. Harmondsworth: Penguin.

Cheibub, José Antonio, Jennifer Gandhi, and James Raymond Vreeland. 2010. 'Democracy and Dictatorship Revisited'. *Public Choice*, 143(1–2): 67–101.

Clutterbuck, Richard. 1977. *Guerrillas and Terrorists*. London: Faber & Faber.

Coady, C. A. J. 2021. *The Meaning of Terrorism*. Oxford: Oxford University Press.

Cohen, Gerald. 2008. 'Casting the First Stone: Who Can, and Who Can't, Condemn the Terrorists?'. In Stephen Law (ed.), *Israel, Palestine and Terror*, 102–26. London: Continuum.

Collier, Paul, and Anke Hoeffler. 1998. 'On Economic Causes of Civil War'. *Oxford Economic Papers*, 50(4): 563–73.

Collier, Paul, and Anke Hoeffler. 2004. 'Greed and Grievance in Civil War'. *Oxford Economic Papers*, 56(4): 563–95.

Combs, Cynthia. 2018. *Terrorism in the Twenty-First Century*. London: Routledge.

Conquest, Robert. 1990. *The Great Terror: A Reassessment*. New York: Oxford University Press.

Cragin, R. Kim. 2008. 'Early History of Al-Qa'ida'. *Historical Journal*, 51(4): 1047–67.

Crelinsten, Ronald D. 1987. 'Terrorism as Political Communication: The Relationship between the Controller and the Controlled'. In Paul Wilkinson and Alasdair M. Stewart (eds.), *Contemporary Research on Terrorism*, 3–23. Aberdeen: Aberdeen University Press.

Crelinsten, Roland D. 2002. 'Analysing Terrorism and Counter-Terrorism: A Communication Model'. *Terrorism and Political Violence*, 14(2): 77–122.

Crenshaw, Martha. 1981. 'The Causes of Terrorism'. *Comparative Politics*, 13(1): 379–99.

Crenshaw, Martha. 1995. 'Thought on Relating Terrorism to Historical Contexts'. In Martha Crenshaw (ed.), *Terrorism in Context*, 3–24. University Park: The Pennsylvania State University Press.

Cronin, Audrey Kurth. 2009. *How Terrorism Ends: Understanding the Decline and Demise of Terrorist Campaigns*. Princeton: Princeton University Press.

Cronin, Audrey Kurth. 2015. 'ISIS Is Not a Terrorist Group: Why Counterterrorism Won't Stop the Latest Jihadist Threat'. *Foreign Affairs*, 94(2): 87–98.

Cunningham, David E., Kristian Skrede Gleditsch, and Idean Salehyan. 2013. 'Non-State Actors in Civil Wars: A New Dataset'. *Conflict Management and Peace Science*, 30(5): 516–31.

Dartnell, Michael Y. 1995. *Action Directe: Ultra-Left Terrorism in France, 1979–1987*. London: Frank Cass.

Davenport, Christian. 2007. 'State Repression and Political Order'. *Annual Review of Political Science*, 10: 1–23.

Davis, Mike. 2007. *Buda's Wagon: A Brief History of the Car Bomb*. London: Verso.

Degregori, Carlos I. 1998. 'Harvesting Storms: Peasants Rondas and the Defeat of Sendero Luminoso in Ayacucho'. In Steve J. Stern (ed.), *Shining and Other Paths: War and Society in Peru, 1980–1995*, 128–57. Durham: Duke University Press.

Degregori, Carlos I. 2011. *Qué difícil es ser Dios. El Partido Comunista del Perú———Sendero Luminoso y el conflicto armado interno en el Perú: 1980–1999*. Lima: IEP.

De Jonge Oudraat, Chantal, and Jean-Luc Marret. 2010. 'The Uses and Abuses of Terrorist Designation Lists'. In Martha Crenshaw (ed.), *The Consequences of Counterterrorism*, 94–129. New York: Russell Sage.

De la Calle, Luis. 2007. 'Fighting for Local Control: Street Violence in the Basque Country'. *International Studies Quarterly*, 51(2): 431–55.

De la Calle, Luis. 2015a. *Nationalist Violence in Post-War Europe*. Cambridge: Cambridge University Press.

De la Calle, Luis. 2015b. 'Fighting the War on Two Fronts: Shining Path and the Peruvian Civil War, 1980–95'. In Lorenzo Bosi, Niall Ó Dochartaigh, and Daniela Pisoiu (eds.), *Political Violence in Context*, 125–144. Colchester: European Consortium for Political Research.

De la Calle, Luis. 2017. 'Compliance vs. Constraints: A Theory of Rebel Targeting in Civil War'. *Journal of Peace Research*, 54(3): 427–41.

De la Calle, Luis, and Ignacio Sánchez-Cuenca. 2011a. 'What We Talk About When We Talk About Terrorism'. *Politics & Society*, 39(3): 451–72.

De la Calle, Luis, and Ignacio Sánchez-Cuenca. 2011b. 'The Quantity and Quality of Terrorism: The DTV Dataset'. *Journal of Peace Research*, 48(1): 49–58.

200 References

De la Calle, Luis, and Ignacio Sánchez-Cuenca. 2012. 'Rebels without a Territory: An Analysis of Nonterritorial Conflicts in the World, 1970–1997'. *Journal of Conflict Resolution*, 56(4): 580–603.

De la Calle, Luis, and Ignacio Sánchez-Cuenca. 2013. 'Killing and Voting in the Basque Country: An Exploration of the Electoral Link between ETA and its Political Branch'. *Terrorism and Political Violence*, 25: 94–112.

De la Calle, Luis, and Ignacio Sánchez-Cuenca. 2015. 'How Armed Groups Fight: Territorial Control and Violent Tactics'. *Studies in Conflict & Terrorism*, 38(10): 795–813.

De la Calle, Luis, and Ignacio Sánchez-Cuenca. 2020. 'Violence and Mobilization Probing the Inverted U-Shaped Link between Protest and Terrorism'. *Taiwan Journal of Democracy*, 16(1): 51–79.

Della Porta, Donatella. 1995. *Social Movements, Political Violence and the State*. Cambridge: Cambridge University Press.

Della Porta, Donatella. 2013. *Clandestine Political Violence*. Cambridge: Cambridge University Press.

Della Porta, Donatella, and Sidney Tarrow. 1986. 'Unwanted Children: Political Violence and the Cycle of Protest in Italy, 1966–1973'. *European Journal of Political Research*, 14(5–6): 607–32.

Demaris, Ovid. 1977. *Brothers in Blood: The International Terrorist Network*. New York: Charles Scribner's Sons.

DeNardo, James. 1985. *Power in Numbers: The Political Strategy of Protest and Rebellion*. Princeton: Princeton University Press.

Djankov, Simeon, and Marta Reynal-Querol. 2010. 'Poverty and Civil War: Revisiting the Evidence'. *Review of Economics and Statistics*, 92(4): 1035–41.

Downes, Alexander B. 2008. *Targeting Civilians in War*. Ithaca: Cornell University Press.

Drake, C. J. M. 1998. *Terrorists' Target Selection*. London: Macmillan.

Drakos, Konstantinos, and Andreas Gofas. 2006. 'The Devil You Know but Are Afraid to Face: Underreporting Bias and its Distorting Effects on the Study of Terrorism'. *Journal of Conflict Resolution*, 50(5): 714–35.

Dupré, John. 1993. *The Disorder of Things: Metaphysical Foundations of the Disunity of Science*. Cambridge, MA: Harvard University Press.

Echandía, Camilo. 2000. 'El conflicto armado colombiano en los años noventa: cambios en las estrategias y efectos económicos'. *Colombia Internacional*, 1(49–50): 117–34.

Enders, Walter, and Gary Hoover. 2012. 'The Nonlinear Relationship between Terrorism and Poverty'. *American Economic Review*, 102(3): 267–72.

Enders, Walter, and Todd Sandler. 2012. *The Political Economy of Terrorism*. 2nd ed. Cambridge: Cambridge University Press.

Enders, Walter, Todd Sandler, and Khusrav Gaibulloev. 2011. 'Domestic versus Transnational Terrorism: Data, Decomposition, and Dynamics'. *Journal of Peace Research*, 48(3): 319–37.

Falconí, Carola, Edilberto Jiménez, and Giovanni Alfaro. 2007. *Lucanamarca: memorias de nuestro pueblo*. Lima: COMISEDH.

Farrell, William R. 1990. *Blood and Rage: The Story of the Japanese Red Army*. Lexington, MA: Lexington Books.

Farwell, James P. 2014. 'The Media Strategy of ISIS'. *Survival*, 56(6): 49–55.

Fearon, James D., and David Laitin. 2003. 'Ethnicity Insurgency and Civil War'. *American Political Science Review*, 97(1): 75–90.

Fernández Huidobro, Eleuterio. 2005. *Historia de los Tupamaros*. Montevideo: Ediciones de la Banda Oriental.

Findley, Michael G., and Joseph K. Young. 2012. 'Terrorism and Civil War: A Spatial and Temporal Approach to a Conceptual Problem'. *Perspectives on Politics*, 10(2): 285–305.

Fishman, Brian. 2009. *Dysfunction and Decline: Lessons Learned from inside Al-Qa'ida in Iraq.* West Point: The Combating Terrorism Center at West Point.

Fortna, Virginia Page. 2015. 'Do Terrorists Win? Rebels' Use of Terrorism and Civil War Outcomes'. *International Organization*, 69(3): 519–56.

Fortna, Virginia Page. 2023. 'Is Terrorism Really a Weapon of the Weak? Debunking the Conventional Wisdom'. *Journal of Conflict Resolution*, 67(4): 642–71.

Fortna, Virginia Page, Nicholas Lotito, and Michael Rubin. 2020. 'Terrorism in Armed Conflict: New Data Attributing Terrorism to Rebel Organizations'. *Conflict Management and Peace Science*, 39(2): 214–36.

Foucault, Michel. 1966. *Les mots et les choses. Une archéologie des sciences humaines.* Paris: Gallimard.

Freeman, Michael. 2011. 'The Sources of Terrorist Financing: Theory and Typology'. *Studies in Conflict & Terrorism*, 34(6): 461–75.

Frey, Bruno. 2004. *Dealing with Terrorism: Stick or Carrot?* Cheltenham: Edward Elgar.

Frisch, Hillel. 2009. 'Strategic Change in Terrorist Movements: Lessons from Hamas'. *Studies in Conflict & Terrorism*, 32(12): 1049–1065.

Gage, Beverly. 2009. *The Day Wall Street Exploded: A Story of America in its First Age of Terror.* Oxford: Oxford University Press.

Gambetta, Diego. 2005. 'Can We Make Sense of Suicide Missions?'. In Diego Gambetta (ed.), *Making Sense of Suicide Missions*, 259–99. Oxford: Oxford University Press.

Gartenstein-Ross, Daveed, and Thomas Jocelyn. 2022. *Enemies Near & Far: How Jihadist Groups Strategize, Plot, and Learn.* New York: Columbia University Press.

Gerges, Fawaz A. 2009. *The Far Enemy: Why Jihad Went Global.* 2nd ed. Cambridge: Cambridge University Press.

Gilio, Maria E. 1972. *The Tupamaro Guerrillas: The Structure and Strategy of the Urban Guerrilla Movement.* New York: Saturday Review.

Gill, Paul. 2015. *Lone-Actor Terrorists: A Behavioural Analysis.* London: Routledge.

Gillespie, Richard. 1982. *Soldiers of Perón: Argentina's Montoneros.* Oxford: Clarendon Press.

Ginsborg, Paul. 2003. *A History of Contemporary Italy: Society and Politics, 1943–1988.* New York: Palgrave Macmillan.

Glockner, Fritz. 2018. *Los años heridos. Historia de la guerrilla en México, 1968–1985.* Planeta: Ciudad de México.

GMH. 2013. ¡*Basta ya! Colombia: memorias de guerra y dignidad.* Bogotá: Imprenta Nacional.

Golder, Ben, and George Williams. 2004. 'What is "Terrorism"? Problems of Legal Definition'. *UNSW Law Journal*, 27(2): 270–95.

Goodwin, Jeff. 2006. 'A Theory of Categorical Terrorism'. *Social Forces*, 84: 2027–46.

Gorriti, Gustavo. 1990. *Sendero. Historia de la guerra milenaria en el Perú.* Lima: Planeta.

Granados, Manuel Jesús. 1992. *El PCP Sendero Luminoso y su ideología.* Lima: Eapsa.

Guevara, Ernesto 'Che'. 2002 [1960]. *La Guerra de Guerrillas.* Tafalla: Txalaparta.

Guillén, Abraham. 1966. *Estrategia de la guerrilla urbana.* Montevideo: Manuales del Pueblo.

Guillén, Abraham. 1973. *Philosophy of the Urban Guerrilla. The Revolutionary Writings of Abraham Guillén*, trans. and edited by Donald C. Hodges. New York: William Morrow.

Gunaratna, Rohan. 2002. *Inside Al Qaeda: Global Network of Terror.* New York: Columbia University Press.

Gunaratna, Rohan, and Anders Nielsen. 2008. 'Al Qaeda in the Tribal Areas of Pakistan and Beyond'. *Studies in Conflict & Terrorism*, 31(9): 775–807.

Gupta, Dipak K., and Kusum Mundra. 2005. 'Suicide Bombing as a Strategic Weapon: An Empirical Investigation of Hamas and Islamic Jihad'. *Terrorism and Political Violence*, 17(4): 573–98.

Habash, George, and Mahmoud Soueid. 1998. 'Taking Stock: An Interview with George Habash'. *Journal of Palestine Studies*, 28(1): 86–101.

Hacking, Ian. 1999. *The Social Construction of What?* Cambridge, MA: Harvard University Press.

Hafez, Mohammed, and Quintan Wiktorowicz. 2004. 'Violence as Contention in the Egyptian Islamic Movement'. In Quintan Wiktorowicz (ed.), *Islamic Activism: A Social Movement Theory Approach*, 61–88. Bloomington: Indiana University Press.

Harnden, Toby. 1999. *Bandit Country: The IRA & South Armagh*. London: Hodder & Stoughton.

Hartwig, Jason. 2020. 'Composite Warfare and Civil War Outcome'. *Terrorism and Political Violence*, 32(6): 1268–90.

Hashim, Ahmed. 2018. *The Caliphate at War: Operational Realities and Innovations of the Islamic State*. Oxford: Oxford University Press.

Hashim, Ahmed. 2019. 'The Islamic State's Way of War in Iraq and Syria: From its Origins to the Post Caliphate Era'. *Perspectives on Terrorism*, 13(1): 23–32.

Hassan, Hassan. 2018. 'Out of the Desert: ISIS's Strategy for a Long War'. Policy paper 2018-8, Washington, DC: The Middle East Institute. https://www.mei.edu/publications/out-desert-isiss-strategy-long-war#:~:text=ISIS's%20post%2Dcaliphate%20strategy%20is,as%20its%20base%20desert%20areas.

Hastings, Justin V. 2010. *No Man's Land: Globalization, Territory, and Clandestine Groups in Southeast Asia*. Ithaca: Cornell University Press.

Heghammer, Thomas. 2010. *Jihad in Saudi Arabia: Violence and Pan-Islamism since 1979*. Cambridge: Cambridge University Press.

Heghammer, Thomas. 2020. *The Caravan: Abdallah Azzam and the Rise of Global Jihad*. Cambridge: Cambridge University Press.

Hempel, Carl G. 1965. *Aspects of Scientific Explanation and Other Essays in the Philosophy of Science*. New York: The Free Press.

Hendrix, Cullen. 2010. 'Measuring State Capacity: Theoretical and Empirical Implications for the Study of Civil Conflict'. *Journal of Peace Research*, 47(3): 273–85.

Hoffman, Bruce. 2006. *Inside Terrorism*. 2nd ed. New York: Columbia University Press.

Hoffman, Bruce, Jacob Ware, and Ezra Shapiro. 2020. 'Assessing the Threat of Incel Violence'. *Studies in Conflict & Terrorism*, 43(7): 565–87.

Hoffman, Frank G. 2007. *Conflict in the 21st Century: The Rise of Hybrid Wars*. Arlington, VA: Potomac Institute for Policy Studies.

Holmes, Jennifer. 2001. *Terrorism and Democratic Stability*. Manchester: Manchester University Press.

Holmes, Stephen. 2005. 'Al Qaeda, September 11, 2001'. In Diego Gambetta (ed.), *Making Sense of Suicide Missions*, 131–72. Oxford: Oxford University Press.

Honderich, Ted. 2008. 'Terrorisms in Palestine'. In Stephen Law (ed.), *Israel, Palestine, and Terror*, 3–16. London: Continuum.

Hopgood, Stephen. 2005. 'Tamil Tigers, 1987–2002'. In Diego Gambetta (ed.), *Making Sense of Suicide Missions*, 43–76. Oxford: Oxford University Press.

Horgan, John, and Max Taylor. 1999. 'Playing the "Green Card"—Financing the Provisional IRA: Part 1'. *Terrorism and Political Violence*, 11(2): 1–38.

Hudson, Michael C. 1972. 'Developments and Setbacks in the Palestinian Resistance Movement, 1967–1971'. *Journal of Palestinian Studies*, 1(3): 64–84.

Hultman, Lisa. 2009. 'The Power to Hurt in Civil War: The Strategic Aim of RENAMO Violence'. *Journal of Southern African Studies*, 35(4): 821–34.

Hussain, Syed Rifaat. 2010. 'Liberation Tigers of Tamil Eelam. Failed Quest for a "Homeland"'. In Kledja Mulaj (ed.), *Violent Nonstate Actors in World Politics*, 381–412. London: Hurst.

Ibrahim, Raymond. 2007. *The Al Qaeda Reader*. New York: Broadway Books.

Ingram, Haroro, Craig Whiteside, and Charlie Winter. 2020. *The ISIS Reader: Milestone Texts of the Islamic State Movement*. London: Hurst Publishers.

Jaber, Hala. 1997. *Hezbollah: Born with a Vengeance*. New York: Columbia University Press.

Jacobs, Ron. 1997. *The Way the Wind Blew: A History of the Weather Underground*. London: Verso.

Jalali, Ali A., and Lester W. Grau. 2001. *Afghan Guerrilla Warfare. In the Words of the Mujahideen Fighters*. St. Paul, Minnesota: MBI Publishing Company.

Jamieson, Alison. 2005. 'The Use of Terrorism by Organized Crime: An Italian Case Study'. In Tore Bjørgo (ed.), *Root Causes of Terrorism: Myths, Reality, and Ways Forward*, 182–95. Abingdon: Routledge.

Jiménez, Benedicto. 2000. *Inicio, desarrollo y ocaso del terrorismo en el Perú*. Lima: SANKI.

Jones, Benjamin F., and Benjamin A. Olken. 2009. 'Hit or Miss? The Effect of Assassinations on Institutions and War'. *American Economic Journal: Macroeconomics*, 1(2): 55–87.

Jones, Seth, and Martin Libicki. 2008. *How Terrorist Groups End: Lessons for Countering al Qa'ida*. Washington, DC: RAND.

Jones, Seth G., James Dobbins, Daniel Byman, Christopher Chivvis, Ben Connable, Jeffrey Martini, Eric Robinson, and Nathan Chandler. 2017. *Rolling Back the Islamic State*. Santa Monica: Rand Corporation.

Jones, Simon. 2010. *Underground Warfare 1914–1918*. Barnsey: Penn & Sword.

Joshi, Manoj. 1996. 'On the Razor's Edge: The Liberation Tigers of Tamil Eelam'. *Studies in Conflict & Terrorism*, 19(1): 19–42.

Kahler, Miles. 2009. 'Collective Action and Clandestine Networks: The Case of Al Qaeda'. In M. Kahler (ed.), *Networked Politics: Agency, Power, and Governance*, 103–24. Ithaca: Cornell University Press.

Kalyvas, Stathis. 1999. 'Wanton and Senseless: The Logic of Massacres in Algeria'. *Rationality & Society*, 11(3): 243–85.

Kalyvas, Stathis. 2006. *The Logic of Violence in Civil War*. Cambridge: Cambridge University Press.

Kalyvas, Stathis. 2019. 'The Landscape of Political Violence'. In Erica Chenoweth, Richard English, Andreas Gofas, and Stathis N. Kalyvas (eds.), *The Oxford Handbook of Terrorism*, 11–33. Oxford: Oxford University Press.

Kalyvas, Stathis, and Laia Balcells. 2010. 'International System and Technologies of Rebellion: How the End of the Cold War Shaped Internal Conflict'. *American Political Science Review*, 104(3): 415–29.

Kamm, F. M. 2008. 'Terrorism and Intending Evil'. *Philosophy & Public Affairs*, 36(2): 157–86.

Kassimeris, George. 2001. *Europe's Last Red Terrorists: The Revolutionary Organization 17 November*. London: Hurst.

Kepel, Gilles. 2003. *Jihad: The Trail of Political Islam*. Cambridge, MA: Harvard University Press.

Kilcullen, David. 2009. *The Accidental Guerrilla: Fighting Small Wars in the Midst of a Big One*. Oxford: Oxford University Press.

King, Anthony. 2021. *Urban Warfare in the Twenty-First Century*. Cambridge: Poility.

Klausen, Jytte. 2022. *Western Jihadism: A Thirty Year History*. Oxford: Oxford University Press.

Knoll, David W. 2017. *Al-Qaeda in the Arabian Peninsula (AQAP): An Al-Qaeda Affiliate Case Study*, Center for Naval Analysis. United States of America. https://policycommons.net/artifacts/2292557/u-al-qaeda-in-the-arabian-peninsula-aqap/3052776/.

Koerner, Brendan I. 2013. *The Skies Belong to Us: Love and Terror in the Golden Age of Hijacking*. New York: Crown.

Kreiman, Guillermo, and Mar C. Espadafor. 2022. 'Unexpected Allies: The Impact of Terrorism on Organised Crime in Sub-Saharan Africa and South-East Asia'. *Studies in Conflict & Terrorism*, 45(5–6): 348–67

Krueger, Alan B. 2007. *What Makes a Terrorist: Economics and the Roots of Terrorism*. Princeton: Princeton University Press.

Kurz, Anat, and Ariel Merari. 1985. *ASALA: Irrational Terror or Political Tool*. Boulder, CO: Westview Press.

Kydd, Andrew, and Barbara F. Walter. 2002. 'Sabotaging the Peace: The Politics of Extremist Violence'. *International Organization*, 56(2): 263–96.

Kydd, Andrew H., and Barbara F. Walter. 2006. 'The Strategies of Terrorism'. *International Security*, 31(1): 49–80.

Lacina, Bethany, and Nils Petter Gleditsch. 2005. 'Monitoring Trends in Global Combat: A New Dataset of Battle Deaths'. *European Journal of Population*, 21(2–3): 145–66.

LaFree, Gary. 2019. 'The Evolution of Terrorism Event Databases'. In Erica Chenoweth, Richard English, Andreas Gofas, and Stathis N. Kalyvas (eds.), *The Oxford Handbook of Terrorism*, 50–68. Oxford: Oxford University Press.

LaFree, Gary, and Laura Dugan. 2007. 'Introducing the Global Terrorism Database'. *Terrorism and Political Violence*, 19(2): 181–204.

Lahoud, Nelly. 2014. 'Metamorphosis: From al-Tawhid wa-al-Jihad to Dawlat al-Khilafa (2003–2014)'. In Muhammad al-'Ubaydi, Nelly Lahoud, Daniel Milton, and Bryce Price, *The Group that Calls Itself a State: Understanding the Evolution and Challenges of the Islamic State*, 8–26. West Point: The Combating Terrorism Center at West Point.

Lake, David A. 2002. 'Rational Extremism: Understanding Terrorism in the Twenty-First Century'. *Dialogue-International Organization*, 1(1): 15–28.

Laqueur, Walter. 1976. *Guerrilla: A Historical and Critical Study*. Boston: Little, Brown, and Company.

Laqueur, Walter, and Dan Schueftan (eds.). 2016. *The Israel-Arab Reader. A Documentary History of the Middle East Conflict*. 8th ed. London: Penguin.

Lee, Alexander. 2011. 'Who Becomes a Terrorist? Poverty, Education, and the Origins of Political Violence'. *World Politics*, 63(2): 203–45.

Legassick, Martin. 2003. 'Armed Struggle in South Africa: Consequences of a Strategy Debate'. *Journal of Contemporary African Studies*, 21(2): 285–302.

Levitsky, Steven, and Lucan A. Way. 2010. *Competitive Authoritarianism: Hybrid Regimes after the Cold War*. Cambridge: Cambridge University Press.

Levitt, Matthew. 2006. *Hamas: Politics, Charity, and Terrorism in the Service of Jihad*. New Haven: Yale University Press.

Lewis, Janet I. 2020. *How Insurgency Begins: Rebel Group Formation in Uganda and Beyond*. Cambridge: Cambridge University Press.

Lia, Brynjar. 2007. *Architect of Global Jihad: The Life of Al-Qaida Strategist Abu Mus'ab al-Suri*. London: Hurst.

Lifton, Robert Jay. 2000. *Destroying the World to Save It: Aum Shinrikyō, Apocalyptic Violence, and the New Global Terrorism*. New York: Henry Holt.

Linse, Ulrich. 1982. '"Propaganda by the Deed" and "Direct Action": Two Concepts of Anarchist Violence'. In Wolfgang J. Mommsen and Gerhard Hirschfeld (eds.), *Social Protest, Violence and Terror in Nineteenth- and Twentieth-Century Europe*, 201–29. Houndmills: Macmillan.

Lister, Charles. 2015. *The Syrian Jihad: Al Qaeda, the Islamic State and the Evolution of an Insurgency*. Oxford: Oxford University Press.

Lunstrum, Elizabeth. 2009. 'Terror, Territory, and Deterritorialization: Landscapes of Terror and the Unmaking of State Power in the Mozambican "Civil" War'. *Annals of the Association of American Geographers*, 99(5): 884–92.

Lutz, Brenda, and James Lutz. 2013. 'Terrorism in Sub-Saharan Africa: The Missing Data'. *Insight on Africa*, 5(2): 169–83.

McCann, Wesley S. 2023. 'Who Said We Were Terrorists? Issues with Terrorism Data and Inclusion Criteria'. *Studies in Conflict & Terrorism*, 46(6): 964–84.

McCants, William. 2015. *The ISIS Apocalypse: The History, Strategy and Doomsday Vision of the Islamic State*. New York: Palgrave MacMillan.

McCauley, Clark, and Sophia Moskalenko. 2014. 'Toward a Profile of Lone Wolf Terrorists: What Moves an Individual from Radical Opinion to Radical Action'. *Terrorism and Political Violence*, 26(1): 69–85.

McClintock, Cynthia. 1998. *Revolutionary Movements in Latin America: El Salvador's FMLN and Peru's Shining Path*. Washington, DC: United States Institute of Peace Press.

McCormick, Gordon. 1992. *From the Sierra to the Cities: The Urban Campaign of the Shining Path*. Santa Monica: RAND.

McCormick, Gordon H. 2003. 'Terrorist Decision Making'. *Annual Review of Political Science*, 6: 473–507.

Bolt, Jutta, Robert Inklaar, Herman de Jong, and Jan Luiten van Zanden. 2018. 'Rebasing "Maddison": New Income Comparisons and the Shape of Long-Run Economic Development'. Maddison Project Working paper 10.

Maher, Shiraz. 2016. *Salafi-Jihadism: The History of an Idea*. Oxford: Oxford University Press.

Mahoney, Charles. 2018. 'More Data, New Problems: Audiences, Ahistoricity, and Selection Bias in Terrorism and Insurgency Research'. *International Studies Review*, 20: 589–614.

Malkasian, Carter. 2021. *The American War in Afghanistan: A History*. Oxford: Oxford University Press.

Mangashe, Patrick. 2018. 'Operation Zikomo: The Armed Struggle, the Underground and Mass Mobilisation in South Africa's Border Region, 1986–1990, through the Experiences of MK Cadres'. *South African Historical Journal*, 70(1): 42–55.

Mann, Michael. 1993. *The Sources of Social Power. Vol. II: The Rise of Classes and Nation-States, 1760–1914*. Cambridge: Cambridge University Press.

Mannes, Aaron. 2004. *Profiles in Terror: The Guide to Middle East Terrorist Organizations*. Lanham, MD: Rowman & Littlefield.

Marchesi, Aldo. 2019. *Hacer la revolución. Guerrillas latinoamericanas de los años sesenta a la caída del muro*. Buenos Aires: Siglo XXI.

Melzer, Nils. 2014. 'The Principle of Distinction between Civilians and Combatants'. In Andrew Clapham and Paola Gaeta (eds.), *The Oxford Handbook of International Law in Armed Conflict*, 296–331. Oxford: Oxford University Press.

Merari, Ariel. 1993. 'Terrorism as a Strategy of Insurgency'. *Terrorism and Political Violence*, 5(4): 213–51.

Merari, Ariel, and Shlomi Elad. 1986. *Palestinian Terrorism Outside of Israel. 1968–84: Data and Trends*. London: Routledge.

Mercado, Rogger. 1987. *Algo más sobre Sendero*. Lima: Ediciones de Cultura Popular.

Merriman, John. 2009. *The Dynamite Club: How a Bombing in Fin-de-Siècle Paris Ignited the Age of Modern Terror*. New Haven: Yale University Press.

Metelits, Claire. 2010. *Inside Insurgency: Violence, Civilians, and Revolutionary Group Behavior*. New York: New York University Press.

Millington, Chris. 2018. 'Were We Terrorists? History, Terrorism, and the French Resistance'. *History Compass*, 16: e12440.

Mishal, Shaul, and Avraham Sela. 2000. *The Palestinian Hamas: Vision, Violence, and Coexistence*. New York: Columbia University Press.

Moa, Pío. 2002. *'De un tiempo y de un país'. La izquierda violenta (1968–1978)*. Madrid: Encuentro.

206 References

Moorcraft, Paul. 2018. *Total Onslaught: War and Revolution in Southern Africa since 1945.* Yorkshire: Pen & Sword.

Morán, Sagrario. 1996. 'La cooperación hispano-francesa en la lucha contra ETA'. PhD thesis, Universidad Complutense de Madrid.

Morris, Benny. 2001. *Righteous Victims: A History of the Zionist-Arab Conflict, 1881–2001.* New York: Vintage Books.

Mueller, John. 2006. *Overblown: How Politicians and the Terrorism Industry Inflate National Security Threats, and Why We Believe Them.* New York: Free Press.

Nacos, Brigitte. 2016. *Terrorism and Counterterrorism.* London: Routledge.

Núñez Florencio, Rafael. 1983. *El terrorismo anarquista, 1888–1909.* Madrid: Siglo XXI.

O'Leary, Brendan, and John Tirman. 2007. 'Introduction'. In Marianne Heiberg, Brendan O'Leary, and John Tirman (eds.), *Terror, Insurgency, and the State*, 1–17. Philadelphia: University of Pennsylvania Press.

O'Neill, Bard. 1978. *Armed Struggle in Palestine: A Political-Military Analysis.* Boulder, CO: Westview Press.

O'Neill, Bard E. 2005. *Insurgency & Terrorism: From Revolution to Apocalypse.* 2nd ed. Washington, DC: Potomac Books.

Palmer, David. 1995. 'The Revolutionary Terrorism of Peru's Shining Path'. In Martha Crenshaw (ed.), *Terrorism in Context*, 249–309. University Park: Pennsylvania State University Press.

Pappe, Ilan. 2017. *The Biggest Prison on Earth: A History of the Occupied Territories.* London: Oneworld.

Pécaut, Daniel. 2008. 'Las FARC: Fuentes de su longevidad y de la conservación de su cohesión'. *Análisis Político*, 63: 22–50.

Peli, Santo. 2014. *Storie di Gap. Terrorismo urbano e Resistenza.* Torino: Giulio Einaudi.

Phillips, Brian J. 2017. 'Deadlier in the US? On Lone Wolves, Terrorist Groups, and Attack Lethality'. *Terrorism and Political Violence*, 29(3): 533–49.

Popper, Karl. 1945. *The Open Society and its Enemies. Vol. I: The Spell of Plato.* London: Routledge.

Portocarrero, Gonzalo. 1998. *Razones de sangre.* Lima: PUCP.

Porzecanski, Arturo. 1973. *Uruguay's Tupamaros: The Urban Guerrilla.* New York: Praeger.

Powell, Alexander, Elizabeth Yang, Analeah Westerhaug, and Kaia Haney. 2021. *Maritime Sabotage: Lessons Learned and Implications for Strategic Competition.* Arlington, VA: Center for Naval Analysis.

Prette, Maria Rita (ed.). 1996. *Le parole scritte.* Progetto Memoria 3. Rome: Sensibili alle Foglie.

Primoratz, Igor. 1990. 'What Is Terrorism?', *Journal of Applied Philosophy*, 7(2): 129–38.

Rapoport, David C. 2004. 'The Four Waves of Modern Terrorism'. In Audrey Kurth Cronin and James M. Ludes (eds.), *Attacking Terrorism: Elements of a Grand Strategy*, 3–11. Washington, DC: Georgetown University Press.

Rawls, John. 1971. *A Theory of Justice.* New York: Belknap Press.

Reato, Ceferino. 2010. *Operación Primicia. El ataque de Montoneros que provocó el golpe de 1976.* Buenos Aires: Sudamericana.

Revkin, Mara, and Ariel Ahram. 2020. 'Perspectives on the Rebel Social Contract: Exit, Voice, and Loyalty in the Islamic State'. *World Development*, 132: 1–9.https://doi.org/10.1016/j.worlddev.2020.104981.

Richards, Anthony. 2015. *Conceptualizing Terrorism.* Oxford: Oxford University Press.

Richemond-Barak, Daphne. 2018. *Underground Warfare.* Oxford: Oxford University Press.

Rosendorff, B. Peter, and Todd Sandler. 2005. 'The Political Economy of Transnational Terrorism'. *Journal of Conflict Resolution*, 49(2): 171–82.

Ross, Jeffrey Ian, and Ted Robert Gurr. 1989. 'Why Terrorism Subsides: A Comparative Study of Canada and the United States'. *Comparative Politics*, 21(4): 405–26.

Rostica, Julieta. 2011. 'Apuntes "Triple A". Argentina, 1973–1976'. *Desafíos*, 23(2): 21–51.

Rubin, Barry. 1994. *Revolution until Victory? The Politics and History of the PLO*. Cambridge, MA: Harvard University Press.

Rubinstein, Richard E. 1987. *Alchemists of Revolution: Terrorism in the Modern World*. New York: Basic Books.

Russett, Bruce. 1993. *Grasping the Democratic Peace: Principles for a Post-Cold War World*. Princeton: Princeton University Press.

Ryan, Michael W. S. 2013. *Decoding Al-Qaeda's Strategy: The Deep Battle against America*. New York: Columbina University Press.

Sageman, Marc. 2008. *Leaderless Jihad: Terror Networks in the Twenty-First Century*. Philadelphia: University of Pennsylvania Press.

Sambanis, N. 2004. 'What Is Civil War? Conceptual and Empirical Complexities of an Operational Definition'. *Journal of Conflict Resolution*, 48(6): 814–58.

Sánchez-Cuenca, Ignacio. 2001. *ETA contra el Estado. Las estrategias del terrorismo*. Barcelona: Tusquets.

Sánchez-Cuenca, Ignacio. 2009. 'Explaining Temporal Variation in the Lethality of ETA'. *Revista Internacional de Sociología*, 67(3): 609–29.

Sánchez-Cuenca, Ignacio. 2019. *The Historical Roots of Political Violence: Revolutionary Terrorism in Affluent Countries*. Cambridge: Cambridge University Press.

Sánchez-Cuenca, Ignacio, and Aguilar, Paloma. 2009. 'Terrorist Violence and Popular Mobilization: The Case of the Spanish Transition to Democracy'. *Politics & Society*, 37(3): 428–53.

Sánchez-Cuenca, Ignacio, and Luis De la Calle. 2009. 'Domestic Terrorism: The Hidden Side of Political Violence'. *Annual Review of Political Science*, 12: 31–49.

Sarrailh, Fernando [Krutwig, Federico]. 1963. *Vasconia. Estudio dialéctico de una nacionalidad*. Buenos Aires: Ediciones Norbati.

Saul, Ben. 2019. 'Defining Terrorism: A Conceptual Minefield'. In Erica Chenoweth, Richard English, Andreas Gofas, and Stat his N. Kalyvas (eds.), *The Oxford Handbook of Terrorism*, 34–49. Oxford: Oxford University Press.

Sayigh, Yezid. 1997. *Armed Struggle and the Search for State: The Palestinian National Movement 1949–1993*. Oxford: Clarendon Press.

Schanzer, Jonathan. 2008. *Hamas vs. Fatah: The Struggle for Palestine*. New York: Palgrave Macmillan.

Schedler, Andreas. 2013. *The Politics of Uncertainty: Sustaining and Subverting Electoral Authoritarianism*. Oxford: Oxford University Press.

Schelling, Thomas C. 1966. *Arms and Influence*. New Haven: Yale University Press.

Schmid, Alex P., and Albert J. Jongman. 1988. *Political Terrorism*. New Brunswick: Transaction Publishers.

Schmitter, Philippe. 1986. 'An Introduction to Southern European Transitions from Authoritarian Rule: Italy, Greece, Portugal, Spain, and Turkey'. In Guillermo O'Donnell, Philippe Schmitter, and Laurence Whitehead (eds.), *Transitions from Authoritarian Rule: Southern Europe*, 3–10. Baltimore: Johns Hopkins University Press.

Schroefl, Josef, and Stuart J. Kaufman. 2014. 'Hybrid Actors, Tactical Variety: Rethinking Asymmetric and Hybrid War'. *Studies in Conflict & Terrorism*, 37(10): 862–80.

Seale, Patrick. 1992. *Abu Nidal: A Gun for Hire*. New York: Random House.

Segal, David. 1988. 'The Iran-Iraq War: A Military Analysis'. *Foreign Affairs*, 66(5): 946–63.

Sen, Amartya. 1999. *Development as Freedom*. New York: Alfred A. Knopf.

208 References

Senado de la República. 1989. *Encuesta de opinión: violencia y pacificación en el Perú*. Lima: Mimeo.

Serrano, Secundino. 2006. *Maquis. Historia de la guerrilla antifranquista*. Madrid: Temas de Hoy.

Shalev, Aryeh. 1991. *The Intifada: Causes and Effects*. Boulder, CO: Westview Press.

Shapiro, Jacob N. 2013. *The Terrorist's Dilemma: Managing Violent Covert Organizations*. Princeton: Princeton University Press.

Sheehan, Ivan Sascha. 2012. 'Assessing and Comparing Data Sources for Terrorism Research'. In Cynthia Lum and Les Kennedy (eds.), *Evidence-Based Counterterrorism Policy*, 13–40. New York: Springer.

Shemesh, Moshe, and Moshe Tlamim. 2002. 'The IDF Raid on Samu': The Turning-Point in Jordan's Relations with Israel and the West Bank Palestinians'. *Israel Studies*, 7(1): 139–67.

Silke, Andrew, and Anastasia Filippidou. 2020. 'What Drives Terrorist Innovation? Lessons from Black September and Munich 1972'. *Security Journal*, 33(2): 210–27.

Simpson, Thula. 2009. 'The Making (and Remaking) of a Revolutionary Plan: Strategic Dilemmas of the ANC's Armed Struggle, 1974–1978'. *Social Dynamics*, 35(2): 312–29.

Smelser, Neil J. 2007. *The Faces of Terrorism: Social and Psychological Dimensions*. Princeton: Princeton University Press.

Smith, J., and André Moncourt. 2009. *The Red Army Faction: A Documentary History. Vol. 1: Projectiles for the People*. Oakland, CA: PM Press.

Smith, M. L. R. 1995. *Fighting for Ireland: The Military Strategy of the Irish Republican Movement*. London: Routledge.

Spaaij, Ramón. 2010. 'The Enigma of Lone Wolf Terrorism: An Assessment'. *Studies in Conflict & Terrorism*, 33(9): 854–70.

Stampnitzky, Lisa. 2013. *Disciplining Terror: How Experts Invented 'Terrorism'*. Cambridge: Cambridge University Press.

Staniland, Paul. 2014. *Networks of Rebellion: Explaining Insurgent Cohesion and Collapse*. Ithaca: Cornell University Press.

Stanton, Jessica A. 2013. 'Terrorism in the Context of Civil War'. *The Journal of Politics*, 75(4): 1009–22.

START. 2019. Global Terrorism Database. Codebook: Inclusion Criteria and Variables. https://www.start.umd.edu/gtd/downloads/Codebook.pdf.

Steele, Abbey. 2017. *Democracy and Displacement in Colombian Civil War*. Ithaca: Cornell University Press.

Stepanova, Ekaterina A. 2008. *Terrorism in Asymmetrical Conflict: Ideological and Structural Aspects*. Oxford: Oxford University Press.

Stern, Jessica. 2003. *Terror in the Name of God: Why Religious Militants Kill*. New York: HarperCollins.

Stoddard, Edward. 2023. 'Maoist Hybridity? A Comparative Analysis of the Links between Insurgent Strategic Practice and Tactical Hybridity in Contemporary Non-State Armed Groups'. *Studies in Conflict & Terrorism*, 46(6): 913–37.

Stokke, Kristian. 2006. 'Building the Tamil Eelam State: Emerging State Institutions and Forms of Governance in LTTE-Controlled Areas in Sri Lanka'. *Third World Quarterly*, 27 (6): 1021–40.

Sullivan, Patricia L. 2007. 'War Aims and War Outcomes: Why Powerful States Lose Limited Wars'. *Journal of Conflict Resolution*, 51(3): 496–524.

Sulmont, David. 2007. 'Las distancias del recuerdo. Memoria y opinión pública sobre el conflicto armado interno en el Perú, 1980–2000'. *Memoria: Revista sobre cultura, democracia y derechos humanos*, 2(2): 9–28.

Tao, Ran, Daniel Strandow, Michael G. Findley, and Jean-Claude Thill. 2016. 'A Hybrid Approach to Modeling Territorial Control in Violent Armed Conflicts'. *Transactions in GIS*, 20(3): 413–25.

Tapia, Carlos. 1997. *Las Fuerzas Armadas y Sendero Luminoso*. Lima: Instituto de Estudios Peruanos.

Terrill, W. Andrew. 2001. 'The Political Mythology of the Battle of Karameh'. *Middle East Journal*, 55(1): 91–111.

Tilly, Charles. 2003. *The Politics of Collective Violence*. New York: Cambridge University Press.

Tonder, Gerry van. 2019. *Irgun: Revisionist Zionism, 1931–1948*. Barnsley: Penn & Sword Military.

Torres, Jorge. 2002. *Tupamaros. La derrota de las armas*. Montevideo: Fin de Siglo.

Valencia, Alberto. 1992. *Los crímenes de Sendero Luminoso en Ayacucho*. Lima: Impacto.

Valentino, Benjamin A. 2004. *Final Solutions: Mass Killing and Genocide in the 20th Century*. Ithaca: Cornell University Press.

Verwimp, Philip, Patricia Justino, and Tilman Brück. 2009. 'The Analysis of Conflict: A Micro-Level Perspective'. *Journal of Peace Research*, 46(3): 307–14.

Waldmann, Peter. 2011. 'How Terrorism Ceases: The Tupamaros in Uruguay'. *Studies in Conflict & Terrorism*, 34 (9): 717–31.

Walzer, Michael. 1977. *Just and Unjust Wars*. New York: Basic Books.

Walzer, Michael. 2004. *Arguing about War*. New Haven: Yale University Press.

Warrick, Joby. 2015. *Black Flags: The Rise of ISIS*. New York: Doubleday.

Weber, Max. 1946. *From Max Weber: Essays on Sociology*, edited and trans. by H. H. Herth and C. W. Mills. Oxford: Oxford University Press.

Weinberg, Leonard, Ami Pedahzur, and Sivan Hirsch-Hoefler. 2004. 'The Challenges of Conceptualizing Terrorism'. *Terrorism and Political Violence*, 16(4): 777–94.

Weinstein, Jeremy. 2007. *Inside Rebellion: The Politics of Insurgent Violence*. Cambridge: Cambridge University Press.

Whewell, William. 1847. *The Philosophy of Inductive Sciences*, vol. 2. 2nd ed. London: John W. Parker.

Whiteside, Craig. 2016. 'The Islamic State and the Return of Revolutionary Warfare'. *Small Wars & Insurgencies*, 27(5): 743–76.

Whiteside, Craig, Ian Rice, and Daniele Raineri. 2021. 'Black Ops: Islamic State and Innovation in Irregular Warfare'. *Studies in Conflict & Terrorism*, 44(12): 1190–217. https://doi.org/10.1080/1057610X.2019.1628623.

Whitfield, Teresa. 2014. *Endgame for ETA: Elusive Peace in the Basque Country*. London: Hurst.

Wickham-Crowley, Timothy P. 1992. *Guerrillas and Revolution in Latin America*. Princeton: Princeton University Press.

Wiktorowicz, Quintan. 2001. 'Centrifugal Tendencies in the Algerian Civil War'. *Arab Studies Quarterly*, 23(3): 65–82.

Wilkinson, Paul. 1985. 'Fighting the Hydra: Terrorism and the Rule of Law'. *Harvard International Review*, 7(6): 11–27.

Woodworth, Paddy. 2001. *Dirty War, Clean Hands: ETA, the GAL and Spanish Democracy*. Cork: Cork University Press.

Zapata, Antonio. 2017. *La guerra senderista: hablan los enemigos*. Lima: Taurus.

Zumalde, Xabier. 2004. *Mi lucha clandestina en ETA*. Arrigorriaga: Status.

Index

Tables, figures, and boxes are indicated by an italic t, f, and b following the page number.

Abu Nidal Organization (ANO), 159,
  161–162, 172
Afghanistan, 107
African National Congress (ANC), 40–41,
  84, 155
Al Qaeda, 6, 21–22, 31, 35, 39–40, 58–60
  sanctuaries, 58–59
Al Qaeda in Iraq (AQI), *see* Islamic State
al-Adnani, Abu, 182, 186–187
al-Baghdadi, Abu Omar, 179–182
al-Shabaab, 5, 105*t*
al-Suri, 21–22
al-Zarqawi, Abu Musab, 174–177
al-Zawahiri, Ayman, 55
Anarchist terrorism, 53–54
Antiterrorist Liberation Groups (GAL), 74
Arafat, Yasser, 153, 160–162
Argentine Anticommunist Alliance
  (Triple A), 74
Armed Islamic Group (GIA), 59, 63–64
armed propaganda, 34–35, 117
Armenian Secret Army for the Liberation of
  Armenia (ASALA), 57–58
asymmetry (of power), 8–9, 77–79, 100
  asymmetry and rebel tactics, 89, 194
  asymmetry and territorial control, 80
Aum Shinrikyo, 45
Ayers, Bill, 21–22

Baader, Andreas, 160
Bataclan terrorist attack, 43–44
Battle of Algiers, 7–8
Begin, Menachem, 54–55
Beñarán, José Miguel 'Argala', 129–130
Bergaretxe, Eduardo 'Pertur', 128
Bin Laden, Osama, 55, 59
Black September Organization (BS), *see*
  Palestinian Liberation Organization
bombs, *see* improvised explosive devices
Breivik, Andreas, 61

civilian victimization, 5–6, 23, 24–26, 48,
  193
  civilians as non-combatants, 30*t*,
    104–105, 111–112
  civilians as soft targets, 48, 56–57, 109
  distinction between combatants and
    non-combatants, 25, 28
  during civil war, 26–28
  as state repression, 25–26
civil war, 10, 27, 80–81, 105–108, 88*t*
clandestinity, *see* underground violence
classifications, 15
coercive violence, 31–32, 34, 36, 104–105
Cold war, 70, 87, 106–107
Colombian Revolutionary Armed Forces
  (FARC), 61–62
Correlates of war dataset (COW), 87, 88*t*
Criminal organizations, 45–48
Cuban revolution, 116–117

Domestic Terrorism Victims' dataset
  (DTV), 29, 29*t*, 30*t*, 103 n.11
Dupré, John, 17, 20–21

Escobar, Pablo, 45–46
Euskadi ta Askatasuna (ETA, Basque
  Homeland and Liberty), 54, 126
  and car bombs, 134–135
  French sanctuary, 131–135
  killings, 130, 130*f*
  rural guerrilla, 126–128
  and socialization of suffering, 135–136
  split, 128
  and street violence, 135–136
  and war of attrition, 129, 136–137
Extraditables, 45–46

Farabundo Martí Front for National
  Liberation, 67
Fatah, *see* Palestinian Liberation
  Organization

Flat terrain, 116, 174
Foco theory, 116–117
Foucault, Michel, 15
Fujimori, Alberto, 2–3, 146*t*, 146

Global Terrorism Database (GTD), 28–29, 83–84, 90, 94, 103–109, 170–171
Greek Revolutionary Organization 17 November, 21–22
Gross Domestic Product (GDP) per capita, 10
   Inverted-U link between GDP and terrorism, 11, 87, 89*f*
   GDP and territorial control, 82*t*, 85*f*, 86*t*
   GDP as a measure of state capacity, 10, 80
Gruppi di azione patriottica, 56
guerrilla, 4, 27–28, 33–34, 52
Guevara, Ernesto 'Che', 116–117
Guillén, Abraham, 119–120
Guzmán, Abigael ('Camarada Gonzalo'), 2, 137–140, 146

Habash, George, 158
Haddad, Wadi, 161
Hamas, 164–165, 168, 169*t*, 170, 172*t*
   al-Qassam Brigades, 165
   and peace process, 166–167
   and the PLO, 167
   and suicide missions, 165–166
   territorial control, 168
Hezbollah, 19–20, 40, 57, 64–65, 68, 70–71

improvised explosive devices, 11, 51–52, 54, 92–93, 95–96, 109
indirect tactics, 9, 76, 90, 100–101
indiscriminate violence, 24, 109
insurgency, *see* guerrilla
Intifada, First, 163–165
Intifada, Second (Al-Aqsa Intifada), 131, 166
Iparretarrak (IK), 132–133
Iran-Iraq war, 79
Irgun, 54–55
Irish Republican Army (IRA), 8–9, 29*t*, 54, 105*t*
Islamic Group (Egypt), 55–56
Islamic State (IS, ISIS, ISIL), 9, 12–13, 40, 47, 173–188
   Abu Ghraib prison break, 181
   Al Qaeda in Iraq (AQI), 176

Anbar Awakening (Sahwa), 177–178
attacks, 184–185, 184*f*, 185*f*
balance of power, 183
fall of Mosul, 173, 181–182, 184*f*
foreign fighters, 193–194
international terrorism, 186–188, 187*f*, 188
Jama'at al-Tawhid wa' al-Jihad (JTWJ), 4, 174–175
underground, 173–174
use of digital media, 182
tactics, 177, 179, 181–182, 184–185
territorial control, 177–178, 180, 181, 183
Israeli Defense Forces (IDF), 153, 155–158
Italian mafia, 45–46
ITERATE (International Terrorism: Attributes of Terrorist Events), 56–57 n.7, 103
Iyad, Abu, 161

Jabhat al-Nusra (JaN), 180–181
Jama'at al-Tawhid wa' al-Jihad (JTWJ), *see* Islamic State
Jemaa Islamiyah, 55–56
Jibril, Ahmed, 159

Kalyvas, Stathis, 19–21, 19*t*
Kidnappings, 43–44, 51–52, 76, 94, 95*f*, 96, 96*t*, 98*t*
Krutwig, Federico, 126

Liberation Tigers of Tamil Eelam (LTTE), 39–40, 65–66
Lucanamarca, 1

Maquis, 41, 56
McVeigh, Timothy, 61
Meinhof, Ulrike, 160
military power *vs.* power to hurt, 32, 51–52, 77, 109
military sabotage, 46–47
Montoneros, 69
Moro, Aldo, 19–20, 35
Mossad, 72–74
Mozambique Liberation Front (FRELIMO), 63
Mozambique National Resistance Movement (RENAMO), 63
Mussawi, Sayyed Abbas, 57

212   Index

Naji, Abu Bakr, 176
natural kinds, 15–16
New People's Army, 97–98, 105*t*
Nidal, Abu, 161–162
no-go areas, 40
Non-combatants: *see* civilian victimization

organized crime, 45–46, 104

Palestinian Authority (PA), 167–170
Palestinian Islamic Jihad, 165
Palestinian Liberation Organization
    (PLO), 152, 160–161, 163
  Black September, 156–157
  Black September Organization
    (BSO), 73–74, 159–161
  Fatah, 12, 153–154, 168–170, 172
  and Hamas, 167–168
  hijackings, 159
  internal organization, 153
  international attacks, 171–172
  Karameh battle, 155–156
  Oslo accords, 151, 164, 165, 171
  Palestine National Covenant, 152
  Popular Front for the Liberation of
    Palestine (PFLP), 158–159, 161, 172
  Popular Front for the Liberation of
    Palestine-General Commando
    (PFLP-GC), 159
  rejection of terrorism, 157–158
  and safe havens, 156, 169*t*
  territorial control, 156, 160–162
  varieties of insurgent violence, 169*t*
People's Revolutionary Army (Ejército
    Revolucionario del Pueblo), 69
People's Will, 19–20
power to hurt, *see* military power
principle of distinction, 25
propaganda by the deed, *see* armed
    propaganda

Qassem, Naaim, 68

rebel weakness, 109–110, 111*f*, 112, 113*f*
recruitment, 99, 193–194
Red Army Faction (RAF), 9, 151, 160–161
Red Brigades, 19–20, 34–35
repression, 26
the Resistance, 56
roving groups, *see* maquis

safe haven, *see* sanctuaries
sanctuary, 40–41, 97, 99, 99*f*, 100*t*
Schelling, Thomas, 32, 77
secrecy, 39, 43, 47, 57, 97, 192–193
Sendic, Raul, 118, 124
Shining Path (Sendero Luminoso), 1–3, 137
  attacks, 143–144
  killings, 141, 142*f*, 145, 147
  and Maoism, 139–140
  and peasants (rondas campesinas), 141
  and popular support, 144
  urban guerrilla, 142–145
  strategic stages, 140–141
  tactics, 145–146, 146*t*
  and territorial control, 141, 143*t*,
    145–146
Six Day War, 153–154, 160–161
suicide missions, 29

targets, direct and indirect, 5–6, 31–32, 90
taxonomy, *see* classifications
territorial control, 3–4, 8, 11, 39–42, 83–84,
    88–89, 192
  as liberated zone, 1, 38, 47, 54
  operationalization of territorial
    control, 41–42, 81, 84
  sanctuary as surrogate of territorial
    control, 9–10, 40–41, 149, 164
terrorism, 4–6
  actor-sense/action-sense, 9, 49–52, 53*t*,
    65, 102
  and asymmetry, 8, 76, 79, 191
  in civil war, 105–106, 109, 110
  as a communicative act, 31
  datasets, 103–104, 113, 191–192
  definitions, 4, 22–23, 30–31, 38, 47–50,
    103–104
  and economic development, 10–11, 80,
    86–87
  field of terrorism studies, 189
  international terrorism, 7, 56–57, 188
  in legal codes, 50
  legitimacy, 21–22
  lone actor, 7, 60–61
  and mobilization, 34
  operationalization, 102
  and random violence, 24
  state-sponsored terrorism, 72, 74
  state terrorism, 7–8, 33, 71–73, 194–195

transition from terrorism to guerrilla, 68, 123–124, 193
types, 30
as underground violence, 4, 38, 44, 52, 192–193
'weapon of the weak', 77, 109–110, 112
terrorism in armed conflict dataset (TAC), 110
Tilly, Charles, 17–18
Tupamaros National Liberation Movement (T-NLM), 55, 116
attacks, 121–122
and geographic conditions, 117
and influence on other groups, 117–118
plan Tatú, 124
popular support, 122
recruits, 121
and rural guerrilla, 117–118, 123–124

seizure of Pando, 123–124
selective violence, 122
and the underground, 123

Unabomber (Theodore J. Kaczynsky), 61
underground violence, 6, 38–45, 46
in capital cities, 5, 65, 67–68, 97–98, 100–101
USS Cole, 6

Walzer, Michael, 24
war of attrition, 32–33
Weather Underground Organization, 21–22
Whewell, William, 7

Yom Kippur War, 160–161

Zedong, Mao, 139–140
Zumalde, Xavier, 126–128